The Bible, the Bullet, and the Ballot

african christian studies series (africs)

This series will make available significant works in the field of African Christian studies, taking into account the many forms of Christianity across the whole continent of Africa. African Christian studies is defined here as any scholarship that relates to themes and issues on the history, nature, identity, character, and place of African Christianity in world Christianity. It also refers to topics that address the continuing search for abundant life for Africans through multiple appeals to African religions and African Christianity in a challenging social context. The books in this series are expected to make significant contributions in historicizing trends in African Christian studies, while shifting the contemporary discourse in these areas from narrow theological concerns to a broader inter-disciplinary engagement with African religio-cultural traditions and Africa's challenging social context.

The series will cater to scholarly and educational texts in the areas of religious studies, theology, mission studies, biblical studies, philosophy, social justice, and other diverse issues current in African Christianity. We define these studies broadly and specifically as primarily focused on new voices, fresh perspectives, new approaches, and historical and cultural analyses that are emerging because of the significant place of African Christianity and African religio-cultural traditions in world Christianity. The series intends to continually fill a gap in African scholarship, especially in the areas of social analysis in African Christian studies, African philosophies, new biblical and narrative hermeneutical approaches to African theologies, and the challenges facing African women in today's Africa and within African Christianity. Other diverse themes in African Traditional Religions; African ecology; African ecclesiology; inter-cultural, inter-ethnic, and inter-religious dialogue; ecumenism; creative inculturation; African theologies of development, reconciliation, globalization, and poverty reduction will also be covered in this series.

The Bible, the Bullet, and the Ballot

Zimbabwe: The Impact of Christian Protest in Sociopolitical Transformation, ca. 1900–ca. 2000

Fabulous Moyo

PICKWICK *Publications* • Eugene, Oregon

THE BIBLE, THE BULLET, AND THE BALLOT
Zimbabwe: The Impact of Christian Protest in Sociopolitical Transformation, ca. 1900—ca. 2000

African Christian Studies Series 8

Pickwick Publications
An Imprint of Wipf and Stock Publishers
199 W. 8th Ave., Suite 3
Eugene, OR 97401

www.wipfandstock.com

ISBN 13: 978-1-62032-723-4

Cataloguing-in-Publication data:

Moyo, Fabulous.

The Bible, the bullet, and the ballot : Zimbabwe: the impact of Christian protest in sociopolitical transformation, ca. 1900–ca. 2000 / Fabulous Moyo.

xvi + 254 pp. ; 23 cm. Includes bibliographical references.

African Christian Studies Series 8

ISBN 13: 978-1-62032-723-4

1. Bible—Study and teaching—Zimbabwe. I. Title. II. Series.

BR1447 .M69 2015

Manufactured in the U.S.A.

To my father
Jairos
And mother
Annah
For everything

Contents

Illustrations

Abbreviations

AIC	African Initiated/Independent Churches
ANC	African National Congress (South Africa)
ANC	African National Council (Zimbabwe)
ATR	African Traditional Religion/s
BCC	British Council of Churches
BSAC	British South Africa Company
BSAP	British South Africa Police
CAP	Central Africa Party
CCR	Christian Council of Rhodesia
CPP	Convention People's Party
DRC	Dutch Reformed Church
FRELIMO	Frente de Libertacao de Mocambique
FROLIZI	Front for the Liberation of Zimbabwe
LMS	London Missionary Society
LOMA	Law and Order Maintenance Act
LTA	Land Tenure Act
MDC	Movement for Democratic Change
NAZ	National Archives of Zimbabwe
NDP	National Democratic Party
NGK	Nederduits Gereformeerde Sending-Kerk

RATU	Rhodesia African Trade Union
RICU	Reformed Industrial and Commercial Workers Union
SACC	South African Council of Churches
SRANC	Southern Rhodesia African National Congress
SRCC	Southern Rhodesia Christian Council
TTL	Tribal Trust Lands
UANC	United African National Council
UCM	University Church Movement
UDI	Unilateral Declaration of Independence
WCC	World Council of Churches
ZANLA	Zimbabwe African National Liberation Army
ZANU	Zimbabwe African National Union
ZANU PF	Zimbabwe African National Union Patriotic Front
ZAPU	Zimbabwe African People's Union
ZIPA	Zimbabwe People's Army
ZIPRA	Zimbabwe Peoples' Revolutionary Army

1

Introduction

> Personally I believe the European has a god in whom he believes and whom he is representing in his churches all over Africa. He believes in the god whose name is spelt Deceit. He believes in a god whose law is "ye strong, you must 'civilise' the 'barbarous' Africans with machine guns. Ye Christian Europeans you must 'Christianize' the pagan Africans with bombs, poison gases, etc!"
>
> In the colonies the Europeans believe in the god that commands "Ye administrators, make Sedition Bill to keep the African gagged, make Deportation Ordinance to send the Africans to exile whenever they dare to question your authority make an ordinance to grab his money so that he cannot stand economically.[1]

Overall Field of Study

WRITTEN BY THE SIERRA Leonean journalist, activist and politician Isaac TA Wallace-Johnson (1895–1965) and published in Ghana's *African Morning Post* in 1936 by Nnamdi Azikiwe (1904–1996), who would later become Nigeria's first African President, the article led to the detention of both men by Ghana's colonial government. In the cradle of African nationalism, this expression of African sociopolitical grievances depicted Christianity as expressly part of the colonial machinery. The stance of Wallace-Johnson and Azikiwe's highlights the growing strength of African feeling in the

1. Azikiwe, "Has the African a God?," 22–23.

middle decades of the twentieth century about the relationship between Christianity and colonialism, which was shared by participants in movements for African independence, and was reflected in the work of later scholars.

This work explores the vexed relationship between Christianity and colonialism, especially in the last twenty years of white rule in what is now Zimbabwe.[2] The title, *The Bible, the Bullet and the Ballot*, captures the range of forces that were at work in the nationalist movement at the time. The book seeks to assess the justification of the negative evaluation of the influence of Christianity on Africans in the late colonial period in relation to Zimbabwe. In order to do this, a detailed exploration of the role of the Zimbabwean Christian community in the wider political engagement against colonialism between c. 1960 and 1980 is offered. The approach of the church[3], and institutions to which Christians belonged, to the questions of universal suffrage and the armed struggle will be of particular concern. Between these three fundamental issues, the "Bible" representing Christianity, the "Bullet" representing the armed struggle, and the "Ballot" universal suffrage or the struggle for democracy, there was a complex interplay.

Christianity, together with its institutions and adherents, were an important part of the wider sociopolitical narrative in Zimbabwe of the struggle for the restitution of Africans' political rights. The specific sociopolitical developments within the historical period under discussion will be explored, alongside the responses of representatives of the Christian community.

Colonialism has been identified as an aspect of imperialism, in which an imperial power imposes its control, and takes legal sovereignty, of a

2. Zimbabwe went through several name changes in the general period under the scope of this study. It was known as Rhodesia, then Southern Rhodesia, and the name was changed back to Rhodesia after the dissolution of the Federation in 1964. Briefly in 1979, after the Internal Settlement, its name became Zimbabwe-Rhodesia before Zimbabwe was adopted in 1980. In this work, it will generally be referred to by its current name but in exceptional cases where a point needs to be emphasised the old name will be used, but in inverted commas for example "Rhodesia." Similarly names of places, towns, or cities that have changed will be referred to by their current names, e.g., Gwelo will be Gweru. An institution or organization will be referred to by the name by which it was known at the time of the events being referred. In direct quotations these names will be written as they appear in the quoted documents.

3. The term church will be used in its broader sense, when referring to Christian denominations. In cases where a specific denomination is meant it will be referred to by its specific name such as the Roman Catholic Church or the Anglican Church.

territory without a process of widespread settlement.[4] Although colonization can be part of the process of colonialism, such as the extensive white settlement in Kenya or Zimbabwe, it is not always a feature. The level of white settlement in places like Botswana, Malawi and Zambia was significantly lower than that of Zimbabwe.[5]

The attitudes of scholars to the role of Christianity in colonialism are considerably varied. In 1967 the Kenyan academic Ali Mazrui asserted, "Just as Augustine had allied Christianity with a concept of *Pax Romana,* so did Christianity later come to be linked to the whole vision of *Pax Britannica.* In Africa Christianity came to be particularly associated with colonization."[6] In 1980, he went further, "The God of Love was mobilized behind the mask of 'imperial pacification.' The message of Christianity discouraged Africans not only from fighting each other but also from resisting the colonial presence."[7]

Others share this wholly negative perspective on the involvement of Christianity in colonialism. Frantz Fanon in *The Wretched of the Earth* declared, "[W]e should place DDT, which destroys parasites, carriers of diseases, on the same level as Christianity . . . The church in the colonies is a white man's church, a foreigners' church. It does not call the colonized to ways of God, but to the ways of the white man, to the ways of the master, the ways of the oppressor."[8]

Claire Robertson observes how agents of Christianity often preceded and encouraged colonial advance, "If they found their progress in making converts impeded on occasion, they sometimes promoted political control to put them in a better position to succeed. Thus the missionary played a critical role in perpetuating the idea of 'the white man's burden' as a justification for European conquest."[9]

Based on their researches of the interaction between colonialism and Christianity on the border of South Africa and Botswana John and Jean Comaroff have stressed the correspondence between Christian mission and secular colonialism, arguing that conversion and civilization were

4. Stanley, *The Bible and the Flag*, 34–35.

5. Fieldhouse, *Colonialism,* 4–6.

6. Mazrui, *Towards a Pax Africana*, 198.

7. Mazrui, *The African Condition*, 123–24.

8. Fanon, *Les Dames de la Terre*, 7; Fanon, *Nationalism*, 494.

9. Robertson, *Africa*, 314.

"two sides of the same coin."[10] Although not all missionaries held the same view, missions were representative of colonial values, "From early on, the colonial evangelists gave up in practice, if not always in their public pronouncements, on the fragile distinction between salvation and civilization, between the theological and the worldly sides of their mission."[11] So too Richard Gray in *The Colonial Moment* observes of missionaries in Southern Africa, "most missions with a few notable exceptions, welcomed the extension of colonial rule"[12] and "White supremacy . . . seemed to many missionaries working there almost to be part of God's establishing order."[13] On this construction, mission-founded churches, with vested interests in the colonial establishment, would be unlikely partners of movements for African independence. The Comaroffs' view stands in contrast to the more nuanced approach of Norman Etherington, who contends that the relationship between empire, or colonialism, and Christianity was a complex one. He argued, "In some areas colonial officials fiercely resisted the admission of missionaries into lands already under imperial control, in others, missionaries resisted colonial schemes such as those in New Zealand and Malawi."[14] Brian Stanley, in *The Bible and the Flag*, offers a similar conclusion about missions, "Their relationship to the diverse forces of British imperialism was complex and ambiguous. If it was fundamentally misguided, their error was not that they were indifferent to the cause of justice for the oppressed, but that their perceptions of the demands of justice were too easily molded to fit the contours of prevailing western ideologies."[15]

Many scholars recognize the significant role played by missionaries in offering education in most colonial territories, although the nature and purpose of the education offered by missions is also another subject of intense debate among academics. Some see that it was only intended to serve colonial interests.[16] Walter Rodney, the Guyanese historian and political activist, believed that "colonial schooling was education for subordina-

10. Comaroff, *Revelation and Revolution*, 8.

11. Ibid., 58

12. Gray, *The Colonial Moment*, 170.

13. Ibid., 174

14 Etherington, *Missions and Empire*, 2; see also B. Stanley, ed., *Missions, Nationalism, and the End of Empire*, 2003.

15 Stanley, *Bible and Flag*, 184.

16. Crowder, *West Africa*, 454–81; Stanley, *The World Missionary Conference*, 167–204.

tion and exploitation."[17] The influence of missionary education is amply evident in the biographies of many African nationalists. Kwame Nkrumah believed that the vice-principal, and the first African staff member, of the Methodist-founded Achimota College near Accra, Kwegyir Aggrey, was "the most remarkable man" he ever met. Aggrey stressed the promotion of co-operation and harmony between "black" and "white."[18] He expressed this philosophy illustratively, "You can play a tune of sorts on the white keys and you can play a tune of sorts on the black keys but for harmony you must use both black and the white."[19]

Also notable evidence of the pervasive influence of Christianity on African nationalists was their employment of Christian imagery in the liberation struggle, including messianic terminology. Nkrumah's Convention People's Party (CPP) challenged the colonial government in Ghana with imagery evoking the *Lord's Prayer* (Matthew 6:9–11), "O imperialism which art in Gold Coast, Disgrace is thy name."[20] Similarly, imagery from the beatitudes (Matthew 5:3–12) was drawn on, as CPP members encouraged their colleagues, "Blessed are they who are imprisoned for self- government's sake; for theirs is the freedom of this land."[21] In response to this use of imagery, CLR James commented, "The pious held up their hands in horror."[22]

In Kenya Jomo Kenyatta, a product of the Scottish Thogoto Mission,[23] took a critical view of Christianity which he viewed as cultural imperialism against Kenya's traditional religions.[24] Kenyatta famously depicted the mutual cooperation between Christianity and colonialism: "The white man came and asked us to shut our eyes and pray. When we opened our eyes it

17. Rodney, *How Europe Underdeveloped Africa*, 264.

18. Although this work employs the racial categories of "black and white" the author does not ascribe to artificial and non-scientific classification of the human race based on skin colour.

19. Nkrumah, *The Autobiography*, 4.

20. James, *Nkrumah*, 108.

21. Ibid.; Kedourie, *Nationalism*, 128.

22. James, *Nkrumah*, 108.

23. Murray-Brown, *Kenyatta*, 40ff.

24. Kenyatta, *Facing Mount Kenya*, 269ff. The term African Traditional Religions (ATR) will be used to refer to the religions of Africa whose beliefs and practices are distinct from other world religions and have been passed down from generation to generation from time immemorial.

was too late—our land was gone."[25] Julius Nyerere, who became the first African President of Tanzania and was supported and encouraged by the Catholic Maryknoll Fathers, took a different view of Christianity during the colonial period. Roman Catholic support in Tanzania, as with that offered to nationalist groups by other denominations, as will be seen in Zimbabwe, was not without self-interest. A Catholic leader would be likely to prove a help to the Catholic Church. Nyerere, guided by his strong Christian faith, distinguished colonialism from Christianity, believing only the former, and not the latter, was problematic. Philosophically he regarded "the democratic system" as the "application of Christian principles to politics," and Christianity as an aid to the African nationalist cause.[26]

In response to the caricature of Christianity advancing "with the sword, a case of gin or paper treaties in one hand and the Bible in the other," HS Meebelo wrote, "This does not seem to be the case in Zambia . . . there was hardly any occasion when they (missionaries) established a mission by use of force . . . Nor do they seem to have distributed spirituous liquors or to have waved paper treaties in face of African traditional rulers in order to establish themselves."[27]

Albert Luthuli, of the African National Congress (ANC), and also a devout Christian, commented on the general African perception of colonialists and agents of Christianity in South Africa, "The average African says the white man is the cause of all his troubles. He does not discriminate between white men and see that some come here for material gain and others come with the message of God."[28] His compatriot Bishop Desmond Tutu modified Kenyatta's illustrative imagery, but offered a positive twist, "When the missionaries came to Africa they had the Bible and we had the land. They said, 'let's pray.' We closed our eyes. When we opened them, we had the Bible and they had the land. In the long run perhaps we got the better end of the deal."[29] African non-Christians might not have agreed,

25. "Lancaster Conference," *The Guardian*, 30 January 1962. Kenyatta believed that Christianity as propagated by Europeans was calculated to vindicate the superiority of whiteness over blackness. He questioned why the forces of evil in Christianity were viewed as "black" and angels as "white." Kenyatta called for a reinterpretation of Christianity and a reversal of symbolism especially between the colors "black" and "white."

26. Listowel, *The Making of Tanganyika*, 168.

27. Meebelo, *Reaction to Colonialism*, 26–27.

28. Mazrui, *Pax Africana*, 198.

29. Massaquoi, Desmond Tutu, 168.

and maybe many Christians also, since now in the postcolonial era the call for land redistribution can be heard in several countries.

The debate on the role played by Christianity during the colonial era raises key questions relating to colonial Zimbabwe. Was it a conservative force, resisting African aspirations for political independence? Or was it a positive sociopolitical force towards Africans' ideological and practical initiatives to ending colonialism? Was the significant role of church leaders like Tutu and Allan Boesak in challenging white rule in South Africa preceded by earlier examples in other African contexts?

In studies of the struggle leading to independence in Zimbabwe, the role of churches and Christian individuals has received less attention. In *Our War of Liberation*, Robert Mugabe notes that Roman Catholic involvement in the liberation struggle was "a belated one."[30] Canaan Banana in *The Church and the Struggle for Zimbabwe*, argued that the Protestant voice was "silent" and Protestant efforts toward the end of war in fact served the colonialists' cause.[31]

This work will seek to examine the extent to which Christian involvement was a factor in helping decolonization in Zimbabwe. The central argument of this book is that the role of the Christian church, especially the Protestant church, was highly significant in the struggle against colonialism in Zimbabwe although it has been underestimated. This challenges a number of accounts of the events of the independence struggle.

In David Lan's significant study, *Guns and Rain*, he has remarkably little to say about the role of Christianity in the independence movement. He argues that it depended on a complex interplay of forces from the past (spirit mediums speaking the words of their ancestors), and the present (the guerrillas, with their political aims and socialist ideals). Lan builds, from the fruits of his local study, the case that African religion was highly significant in Zimbabwe African Nationalist Union Patriotic Front's (ZANU PF) part in the liberation struggle. This was true of "the majority of guerrillas [who] observed most if not all of these ritual prohibitions," and leaders who claim to have been helped by *mhondoro* (royal ancestor spirits), including Robert Mugabe.[32] Reference in Independence Day celebrations to the legendary anti-settlers spirit medium Ambuya Nehanda, leads to Lan's striking view, "With Nehanda established as the mhondoro, who

30. Mugabe, *Our War of Liberation*, 153ff.

31. Banana, *The Church and the Struggle*, 256–59.

32. Tekere, *Lifetime of Struggle*, 73.

protects the whole of the new nation state, it is almost as if Zimbabwe had become to be regarded as a single spirit province."[33] So too in Fay Chung's *Re-living the Second Chimurenga* "One of the most striking characteristics of the liberation struggle was the power of the traditional religious leaders, the *vana sekuru*." Chung argued, "They held a special position in the psyche of the freedom fighters."[34]

Chung also emphasizes the significant role of communism in the liberation struggle. Some young radical ZANU guerrillas sold out for a "socialist revolution" and were skeptical of both Zimbabwean "nationalism" and its older leadership that comprised of Ndabaningi Sithole, Joshua Nkomo and Mugabe. The pro-Communists, led by Wilfred Mhanda, were particularly opposed to Mugabe "whom they had judged as an old-style nationalist who would create in Zimbabwe a neo-colonial regime" and also "feared would become a fascist dictator."[35]

Whilst some sideline the role of Christianity in the movement for Zimbabwean independence, others see its contribution in a wholly negative light. J.A.C Mutambirwa in *Journal of Southern Africa Studies* follows the line of scholars who saw Christianity as detrimental to independence movements, "Christianity was cultural imperialism which sought to liquidate African culture . . . educational activities of the missionaries were the dosage that white settler and British South Africa Company imperialism required to produce the 'literate' industrial black army that was needed to exploit the mineral wealth of the country . . . Furthermore, Christianity will be exposed as an ideology that encouraged the African to accept his defeat and humiliation."[36]

Mutambirwa argues that mission education was tailored to an agenda of social control, to serve the labor needs of white settlers.[37] The credibility of such claims find support in the testimony of Ethel Tawse Jollie, the first woman in the Southern Rhodesian government of 1923 who wrote, "As a matter of fact, the education obtained in missions is only part of the training the native has been getting, for the railway, the mine, the house, the store."[38] Mutambirwa contended that the key issues which gave rise to

33. Lan, *Guns and Rain*, xvii and 218.

34. Chung, *Second Chimurenga*, 197ff.

35. Ibid., 174

36. Mutambirwa, "The Impact of Christianity," 69.

37 Thompson, *The Making of the English Working Class*, 54.

38. Jollie, *The Real Rhodesia*, 268.

African nationalism were the need for the franchise, land allocation, racial and economic discrimination, and African culture. On these issues the missionaries were on the side of settlers.[39] He also highlights the continuing invocation of Nehanda in the liberation struggle, even by those professing Christianity.[40] To Mutambirwa, "The answer is clear: The Bible had no influence on African nationalism."[41] Christianity did not play a significant role in the nationalist struggle for the restitution of Africans' political rights.

Lawrence Vambe, a Zimbabwean social historian, though not wholly negative about the role played by Christianity in colonialism, in *An Ill-Fated People* argued, "I think that every honest African will say that the Christian church has failed as a symbol of peace, understanding and brotherhood among men and needs to re-examine its position seriously."[42] A similar pattern of identifying Christianity with colonialism was continually expressed in postcolonial Zimbabwe. "*Varungu vakatigarira pasi vakatirongera*" (whites sat down and plotted against us) was the notable sentiment of Professor Claude Mararike of the University of Zimbabwe Sociology Department to his students in 2004.[43] If one is to take into cognizance the shenanigans of the Berlin Conference of 1884 Mararike's claim seem to have some credence. A similar view continues to be expressed by Zimbabwe's nationalist politicians, especially those of ZANU PF. In this "colonial chicanery" Christianity is identified as part of the "colonial machinery" that helped to perpetuate the subjugation of Africans and played no significant role in the Africans' struggle for independence.[44]

An early positive assessment of the contribution of Christianity to the struggle for independence was offered by an active participant. In *African Nationalism*,[45] Rev. Ndabaningi Sithole, a key player in the nationalist struggle, described "the role the Christian church has played in the forging of African nationalism on the anvil of history.," and argued that African nationalism in Zimbabwe rose as a result of the influence of Christianity.[46] Sit-

39. Ibid. 76

40. Ibid., 77

41. Ibid.

42. Vambe, *An Ill-fated People*, 234.

43. Professor Cl Mararike, to a University of Zimbabwe masters research student, the author was present at the time of the interview.

44. Ibid.; see also, Bulhan, *Frantz Fanon*, 40–43.

45. Sithole, *African Nationalism*, 51–74.

46. Ibid., 51.

hole contended that Christian ideas spurred African nationalism, though they were "unwittingly" transmitted by missionaries who themselves were supporters of colonial rule. He asserted, "Christian and non-Christian Africans have reaped, in varying degrees, the blessings of the Christian faith, and this is as it should be since God himself sends rain on the just and the unjust."[47]

Other studies by participant observers offer positive assessments of the role of the Zimbabwean churches in relation to ending colonialism. Sister Janice McLaughlin's *On the Frontline* focuses on the contributions of four rural Roman Catholic mission stations, Avilla, Mutero, St Albert's and St Paul's Musami to the efforts of ZANU PF in the armed struggle. She argued that the experiences and attitudes of these missions reflected the wider willingness of the rural Roman Catholic Church to identify with the nationalists and their openness to radical changes. The rural Roman Catholic Church offered substantial help to ZANU nationalists.[48]

Ian Linden's *The Catholic Church and the Struggle for Zimbabwe* gives Roman Catholic theology a prominent place in the struggle against colonialism.[49] He presents the Roman Catholic Church in Zimbabwe as divided in its support for African nationalism, with the rural church largely behind the nationalists and the urban church propagating a message that was not relevant to the aspirations of nationalists and Africans in general. Linden and McLaughlin's accounts, whilst at times critical of aspects of the Catholic tradition, have little to say of the political involvement of Protestant churches, a dimension this work seeks to highlight.

Ranger and Ncube's study of south-west Zimbabwe in *Religion in the Guerrilla War* highlights the need for an approach that demonstrates both chronological and geographical awareness. They note regional differences, from the "religious" northern Zimbabwe, where Lan's study was undertaken, to the "secular" southwest, where traditional religion played little part in the war. The approach of African religion also differed across the country: in Dande, spirit mediums tended to encourage war, but in the *Mwali/Mlimu* cult, peace and fertility was promoted. So too, Christianity was well rooted and "popular" in some areas, but less so in southwest Matebeleland. Ranger and Ncube also stress the need to recognize how the church contribution varied over time. In the 1950s protests against threats of eviction,

47. Ibid., 57.

48. McLaughlin, *On the Frontline.*

49. Linden, *The Catholic Church.*

destocking, agricultural rules, and forced labor were led by progressive African Christian leaders and a mission educated elite. In the 1970s some Christian leaders dismissed guerrillas as terrorists with a secular ideology. The backlash against mission stations and schools brought the closure of some missions and the killing of some missionaries.[50]

This research focuses on the role of Christians at national political level, unlike that of Lan and McLaughlin, which were local level studies. That Christians believed that they had a role to play across Africa in movements for independence is seen in the declaration of the All African Council of Churches—in 1963, "We identify ourselves with the aspirations of our people towards the development of dignity and mature personality in Christ and we exhort the churches in this nation to participate wholeheartedly in the building of the African nation."[51] The materials explored for this research suggest that there is evidence to support this perspective and challenge the strongly held viewpoint that Christianity was an entirely conservative force in Zimbabwe's colonial history, and to demonstrate that the significant influence of Christianity in the struggle of Africans to attain their political rights needs to be acknowledged. In doing this attention will be paid to the activities of the mainline churches in general and in particular those of the Protestant churches, who have been less studied than those of Roman Catholic Church.

Sources and Methodology

The principal sources for this research are materials held in the National Archives of Zimbabwe (NAZ) in Harare and at the Methodist Church in Zimbabwe archives in Harare (MCZA).[52] The documentary evidence tended to consist of public pronouncements by the church or political leaderships, which yield broad insights, but personal perspectives tend to be necessarily excluded. Alongside these, more than fifty letters, some personal and others official, by church leaders were also consulted.

The focus of this study is primarily the activities of mainstream denominations. Attempts were made by the author to access evidence from

50. Ncube and Ranger, "Religion," 35–37, 52–55.

51. All Africa Conference of Churches, *Drumbeats from Kampala*, 15–16; Koschorke et al., *A History of Christianity*, 246–47.

52. The author gratefully acknowledges the help of the staff of these libraries in the completion of this research.

African Independent or Initiated Churches (AICs), but these did not prove fruitful. Their theological tradition made them reluctant to offer pronouncements of a political nature at the time under primary investigation, c.1960–1980. Documents or manuscripts from the AICs during the period under study were not found, although in recent years some AICs have come out in support of the current Zimbabwean political establishment.

In the archival material relating to the early sixties, and before, the African voice from the leadership of the church is largely silent since the leadership was primarily white, as was African church historiography during the sixties.[53] Most documents on public record come from the church leadership who were viewed as representing the voice and interest of those they led. This explains why the section in this book covering the 1960s the missionary voice tends to predominate. The distance of time also means fewer interview sources are available for the earlier periods of this study. As the church leadership gradually Africanized by the mid to late sixties, the African voice became clearer, and by the seventies the African voice in the church's public pronouncements became the dominant one.

Although this work is primarily based on archival research it is supplemented by interviews. According to Oppenheim, interviews have the advantages of reproducing the words of the interviewed activists in a direct and striking manner as they are presented in excerpts and also help to highlight the factors and events that the participants believed to have been significant.[54] A range of thirty open-structure interviews were conducted in Zimbabwe from across ethnic regions and with individuals from different denominations and political affiliations.[55] Most of the interviewees were former or current political activists; and others were in church or political leadership during the sixties or seventies. Interviewees in Zimbabwe appeared to feel free to express their views, even though most did not come from within the political establishment. The political tensions prevailing in Zimbabwe during the time of the archival research from 2005 to 2008, created further difficulties in accessing sources from libraries, with a reluctance to release manuscripts that might be seen to be unfavorable to the political establishment of the time. Despite persistent attempts to overcome

53. Hastings, "African Church Studies."

54. Oppenheim, *Questionnaire Design*, 81–82; on advantages of interviews, see also McNiff, *You and Your Action*, 124; David & Sutton, *Social Research*, 160ff.

55. Interviews offer important details on events that the interviewee may not have revealed in public and provide richer information as a result of being able to probe further.

this difficulty, it may be that not all the relevant sources were disclosed. Certainly some materials listed in the catalogues were not available to the public. A range of secondary material was also accessed. Zimbabwean material tends to be written from a perspective favorable to the political establishment at the time of writing, creating significant challenges when trying to harmonize divergent perspectives.

The primary focus of this work is not to examine the wider issues of international colonialism,[56] but to examine the experience of Zimbabwe. However, the conclusions have implications for the wider debate. From the key question relating to the role of the mainline churches in ending colonialism, a series of others flow. Was independence in Zimbabwe a triumph of Nehanda and Africa Traditional Religion? Were other widespread religious forces at work? Was Christianity able to break free of its colonial past and connections? Were the efforts of churches in Zimbabwe genuinely African, or merely a local reflection of wider international trends and pressures? Were factors such as the willingness of Christian leaders to compromise, or equivocate over the resort to violence, a help or a hindrance to the cause of independence? Did Zimbabwean mainline churches, with different trajectories, play a significant, if not critical, role in the fight for Africans political rights especially in the critical years of c.1960 to 1980? Was it the Bible, or the Bullet, or secular political pressures, the Ballot, which were of greatest significance in ending colonial rule?

56. On Africa alone, without focusing on other colonized territories elsewhere, the scope of this subject can be observed in the following selection of works: Gifford & Roger-Louis, *Decolonization*; Mamdani, *Citizen and Subject*; Sartre, *Colonialism and Neo-colonialism*; Wilson, *African Decolonization*; Christopher, *Colonial Africa*; Howe, *Anticolonialism*.

2

The Early Colonial Period, ca. 1880–1959

THE IMPACT OF THE wider world has been felt on the Zambezi valley for thousands of years. Legends[1] suggest that the biblically mentioned kingdoms of Hiram and Ophir endowed by gold and ivory which enriched king Solomon and the queen of Sheba (1Kings 9:28; 10:11; 22:48) were located in this valley which is also shared by Zambia and Mozambique.[2] Professor Tudor Parfitt has promoted the theory that Zimbabwe was the last place where the biblical Old Testament Ark of the Covenant reached and disappeared.[3] Besides these theories that Judeo-Christian ties with this country may be longer than previously thought, Arab traders are generally regarded by most historians as the first known outsiders to contact this part of Africa followed by the Portuguese.

Archaeologists believe the San were the first occupants of both the southern African geographical territory and, specifically, the present day Zimbabwean territory. The various rock paintings by the San throughout Zimbabwe, as well as other parts of southern Africa, further substantiate archaeological claims that they were the first known people group to occupy the area.[4] On the other hand evidence of Bantu occupation, whose descendants now numerically dominate this vast landscape, can only be traced back to a later date ca. 200 AD in Zimbabwe.[5]

1. Mackenzie, *The Partition of Africa*, 22.
2. Yamauchi, *Africa and the Bible*, 86.
3. Parfitt and Semi, *Judaising Movements*, 14; Parfitt, *The Lost Ark*.
4. Douglas, *Zimbabwe Epic*, 18.
5. Beach, *Zimbabwe*, 6.

Fig. 1 Rock Painting Attributed to the San
Courtesy of the National Archives of Zimbabwe (NAZ)

Between ca.200 BC and ca.1000 AD, Bantu farming communities migrated south into the Zimbabwean landscape largely displacing the San who were, and to some extent still are, hunter-gatherers.[6] They pushed them further south into the south western areas of southern African territory. Most of them can still be found today in Botswana and Namibia and a few more in some parts of South Africa, Zambia and Zimbabwe.[7] There are various theories related to the nature of Bantu migration into Southern Africa and Zimbabwe.[8]

It is through the arrival of these Bantu pastoralists that the 10th century witnessed the first signs of an embryonic Bantu society developing on the central plateau region of modern Zimbabwe that expanded to the south east end of modern day South Africa by the end of that century, with variations of Bantu languages.[9] As the Bantu migrated and settled in the south-

6. Beach, *The Shona*, 6.

7. Samkange, *Origins*, 4.

8. For a detailed discussion on this matter, see Beach, *Zimbabwe*, 6ff; Hammond-Tooke, *The Bantu Speaking Peoples*; Stock, *Africa South of the Sahara*.

9. Samkange, *Origins*, 4.

ern parts of Africa, besides witnessing a growth in cattle ownership, there was an increase in iron production as a result of significant development in iron working skills among the Bantu.[10] Gold mining and ivory which later became part of their main traded commodities led to contact with Arab traders from the Mozambican Indian ocean coast. These developments steadily led to the increase of wealth in the Zambezi region.[11] This status possibly enabled cattle barons to establish a complex settlement between the mainland and the Mozambique Sofala coast,[12] at the crossroads of seasonal grazing areas, in the name of Great Zimbabwe, whose ruins today give evidence of a great pre-European Bantu past.[13]

Fig.2 Arial View of Great Zimbabwe as it Stands Today
Courtesy of NAZ

There are no written or oral records relating to the existence of Great Zimbabwe.[14] The principal source is archaeological evidence.[15] Although there have been historians in the past who tried to ascribe its creation to

10. Beach, *The Shona*, 9
11. Isichei, *A History of Christianity*, 68.
12. Beach, *Zimbabwe*, 30.
13. Beach, *The Shona*, 41ff.
14. Ibid., 44ff.
15. Ibid.

external sources, such as to Arabs[16]—archaeological evidence remains inconclusive—the consensus among scholars, at the time of conducting this research, is that its origins are local.[17] The minerals and other tradable goods within this Bantu territory, such as ivory and gold, for the Asian markets in relation to the local demands for Asian products, notably beads and cloth, mainly from India, may have led to the establishment of the Great Zimbabwe as a trade center between the Indian Ocean coast of Sofala and the inland communities.[18]

Fig.3 Great Zimbabwe's Conical Tower
Courtesy of NAZ

At its political and economic height, Great Zimbabwe is estimated to have been home to about 20,000 to 40,000 people. The site was occupied for around 300 years, and by 1450 the area had been abandoned, probably due to drought, overpopulation and exhausted supplies of firewood.[19] The real reasons for abandoning the site remain a subject of speculation.[20] From the time of the Great Zimbabwe state, ca.13th to 15th century, five more influential states developed within the Zimbabwe plateau: these were the Torwa state

16. Samkange, *Origins*, 2.
17. Beach, *The Shona*, 44.
18. Douglas, *Zimbabwe Epic*, 28.
19. Hastings, *The Church*, 49.
20. Beach, *Zimbabwe*, 44.

of the 15th to the 17th century located in the south-west of the plateau; the Mutapa state of the 15th to the 19th century in the north which overlapped with the Torwa state; the Changamire state of the 17th to the 19th century located in the south-west which overlapped with the Mutapa state;[21] and the two Nguni-speaking states of Gaza, in the south-east and the Ndebele state in the south-west which developed in the mid nineteenth century.[22]

Shona Origins and Their Traditional Socio-Political Organization

The Bantu of the Zimbabwean landscape later became known as Shona, a term whose origin is unclear,[23] ruled by paramount chiefs and powerful kings, and generally organized into autonomous multiple communities under the guidance of elders who worked under *Ishe* or *Mambo*, paramount chief or king.[24] Powerful kings over large populations of people of above 5 000 such as those under rulers like Munhumutapa or Changamire Dombo were an exception to the Shona's general sociopolitical organization.[25] Even in relation to these exceptions, they tended to be democratic in their practices rather than dictatorial. Dr. Stan Mudenge observed, "The Mutapa state throughout its history was never a militaristic one nor were the powers of the Mutapas excessively oppressive. The genius of the Mutapas was in the creation of resilient institutions which accorded with the environment and culture of the people."[26]

21. Douglas, *Zimbabwe Epic*, 9.

22. Beach, *Zimbabwe*, 24.

23. There is controversy surrounding how the various Bantu speaking groups of Zimbabwe came to be called Shona. Some scholars believe the name was first employed by the Ndebele in the late nineteenth century as derogatory until they themselves began calling themselves Shona. Before then they used to identify themselves by the Bantu dialect spoken in a specific region such as Karanga and the person who spoke that dialect would be called mukaranga and vakaramga in plural—this is numerically the dominant dialect in Zimbabwe today; Zezuru is the second common dialect and the speaker is muZezuru or maZezuru in plural, chiKorekore and the speaker would be muKorekore or plural makorekore, chiManyika muManyika and vaManyika being the plural, and finally chiKalanga the speaker being muKalanga and in plural form vaKalanga. These are the five main Shona dialects of Zimbabwean today, which are collectively called chiShona or Shona, and the speakers being va- or maShona in plural and the singular being muShona. See Doke, *A Comparative Study*; Kuper, *The Shona and Ndebele*.

24. Beach, *The Shona*, 66.

25. Ibid.

26. Mudenge, *A Political History*, 362.

The Shona generally lived under chiefs who did not wield a lot of political power or control over them. They could hardly be viewed as subjugated.[27] The chief was generally viewed as a senior elder who had to guide the community mainly in religious matters, and helped in resolving disputes that occurred between families and clans.[28] In some territories clans would have their own chief.[29] If people were not happy with a particular chief they simply moved from his area of influence and gave their allegiance to another chief.[30] This setting would act as a check on leaders who could develop despotic tendencies as well as in the exceptional cases where they found themselves under a leader like Munhumutapa who wielded influence over bigger sections of the Shona cluster communities.[31]

The Shona's social life was never organized around military expansion as later experienced towards the late 19th century by the arrival of the Ndebele.[32] Sociopolitical life for the Bantu in the Zimbabwean plateau was generally peaceful. It was the arrival of the Portuguese in the 16th century and their conflicts with the Arab traders over economic and religious interests that ignited large scale unrest among locals.[33] Although the Shona would have considered their pre-European and Asian intrusion peaceful it does not mean that skirmishes between various chiefs did not arise. The Shona generally would not fight in a war if they thought their chief was being an aggressor, but were open to offer their services in war of self-defense for their community.[34] It was first the arrival of the Ndebele in the mid-19th century, and then later the re-arrival of the Europeans in the same century, that would bring significant sociopolitical transformation to this territory.[35]

Ndebele Arrival and Their Traditional Socio-Political Organization

The Ndebele emerged in the geographical boundaries of modern day Zimbabwe between the 1830s and 1840s as a result of what has now become

27. Beach, *The Shona*, 79ff.
28. Beach, *The Shona and their Neighbours*, 59.
29. Ibid. 60.
30. Zvobgo, *Missions*, 101.
31. Ibid.
32. Carnegie, *Among the Matebele*, 15.
33. Bhila, "Trade," 25.
34. Sibanda, "Early Foundations, 26.
35. Ibid. 25

commonly known by Southern African historians as *Mfecane* or *Defacane*.[36] A number of Nguni groups heading north had passed through the Zimbabwe plateau fleeing from Shaka's Zulu armies and European attacks in present day South Africa.[37] They fled as far as the southern parts of modern day Tanzania and spreading as far as the south-western parts of Zambia.[38] Some Nguni also scattered around various parts of modern day South Africa. Mzilikazi had been Shaka's general before he defected with most members of his Khumalo clan. Upon heading north-east and then north-west, Mzilikazi had a series of settlements south of the Limpopo River. He finally moved north of the Limpopo after the October 1837 defeat, at Mosega, by some Voortrekkers who had moved out of the Cape Colony with the hope of carving their own state north of the colony.[39] When the Khumalo people arrived north of the Limpopo they completed the destruction of the Changamire state which had already been weakened by several attacks from other Nguni groups which had passed north through its territory. They then established their new state under Mzilikazi now known as the Ndebele.[40]

Their name emerged from the Sotho and Tswana people who called them *matebele.* It meant those who disappeared behind their shields.[41] It is highly likely that the term was coined in reference to their fighting techniques which were different from and superior to all the non-Nguni African groups. Since then they have been known as the Ndebele or amaNdebele rather than the Khumalo. By the time they established their state north of the Limpopo they had absorbed other non-Khumalo people. The name Ndebele created a sense of oneness among these people from different ethnicities, as the name Khumalo became reserved for those who were specifically of the Khumalo clan.[42]

The Ndebele state roughly occupied the same area as that once covered by the Changamire state.[43] Some local people began to adopt Ndebele

36. Fage, *A History of Africa*, 319.

37 Eldredge, "Sources of Conflict," 123.

38. Ibid. 278.

39. Thompson, *A History of South Africa*, 90. These Afrikaners were able to establish the Orange Free State and Transvaal, which were eventually incorporated into the Union of South Africa of 1910.

40. Douglas, *Zimbabwe Epic*, 65.

41. Samkange, *Origins*, 13.

42. Omer-Cooper, "The Mfecane," 286.

43. Beach, *Shona and Neighbours*, 136.

language and culture, and in the long run became part of them. Those that did not embrace the language and culture of the Ndebele and kept their culture, if not hostile to the Ndebele, were made to pay tribute to the state and were exempted from raids.[44] Those who resisted or were hostile to the Ndebele were in turn attacked.[45]

There were major sociopolitical organizational differences between the Ndebele and Shona. Ndebele villages were made of up household units, villages were part of a ward, wards were part of a territory and these territories made up a state.[46] The village units relied on agriculture, with a strong herding component, trade, raids and hunting-and-gathering. The king was theoretically the supreme ruler although he had advisors.[47] The political trials that ended in the death of the king's enemies who were accused of tyranny were distinct to these newcomers into the Zimbabwean plateau.[48] Another major difference between the Ndebele and Shona was on military organization. The Ndebele had military regiments called *Amabutho*.[49] These were young men called into separate residential areas when the king saw fit, but especially in times when he was faced with external or internal threats.[50]

Amabutho were units of a military system that was both offensive and defensive. In times of peace they spent most of their time herding state cattle.[51] These young men were later allowed to marry. As they married, their military bases turned into normal civilian residential villages. These military villages also gradually evolved and became part of the larger state.[52] There were various villages at different developmental levels at all times in the Ndebele state. In terms of this sociopolitical organization the Ndebele had modified Shaka's military oriented and offensive social system into a family and communal friendly system.[53] Those who refused to be incorporated into Ndebele state and accept its authority, the Ndebele treated with ruthless brutality.

44. Carnegie, *Matebele*, 15.
45. Beach, *Shona and Neighbours*, 134.
46. Carnegie, *Matebele*, 70.
47. Ibid.
48. Samkange, *Origins*, 16.
49. Douglas, *Zimbabwe Epic*, 102.
50. Hamilton, *Mfecane*, 286.
51. Beach, *Shona and Neighbours*, 135.
52. Ibid.
53. Sibanda, "Early Foundations," 28.

Birth of the Church and European Presence

In the 16th century the Portuguese missionaries had made contact with the local people of the Zambezi area and the eastern parts of Zimbabwe.[54] These early Portuguese missions failed to succeed in the conversion of the locals, but not as a result of hostility to their efforts by the locals.[55] Dominican missionaries lacked sufficient material support from Portugal and Goa, where their superiors were stationed, which limited their religious duties to being chaplains to Portuguese traders in the Zambezi area.[56] They then spent much of their time involved in trade. Jesuit missionaries who had seen some measure of success were expelled from the region by the Portuguese crown in 1759.[57] The Franciscans, who took over from the Jesuits, were forbidden to trade and at the same time were inadequately supported by the sending institution.[58] This state of affairs marked the end of successful Roman Catholic missions in the north-eastern Zimbabwean plateau until the re-emergence of Christian missions about a century later.[59]

The emergence of another force in the 19th century significantly changed the Zimbabwean plateau and ultimately defined the country's geographical location into what we know today as Zimbabwe. This force was made up of people drawn from various nations but the core element was of British origin primarily driven by a combination of economic and religious interests. By the mid-1850s Protestant missionaries from what is now South Africa[60] and Britain began working among people living north of the Limpopo River.[61] For almost half a decade Protestants tried to evangelize without much success.[62] Even though the first leader of the Ndebele, Mzilikazi, was fond of the missionary Robert Moffat who worked among the Tswana, the conversion of his people by other missionaries proved illusive.[63] In 1859 the London Missionary Society (LMS) established the Inyati

54. Mudenge, *Munhumutapa*, 47.

55. Parrinder, *Religion in Africa*, 122.

56. Rea, "The Economics," 15.

57. Ibid., 23.

58. Ibid., 24.

59. Ranger and Weller, *Themes*, 218.

60. The Union of South Africa came into being in 1910. Before then various provinces were independent states.

61. Zvobgo, *Missions*, 1.

62. Beach, *Shona and Neighbours*, 161.

63. Samkange, *Origins*, 103.

Mission followed by Hope Fountain in 1870[64] but still the evangelization of the Ndebele saw limited success. Despite this difficulty a few missionaries both Roman Catholic and Protestant continued to work among the Ndebele. In the early 1870s missionaries came from south of the Limpopo to work among the Shona.[65]

In 1872 Gabriel Buys a member of the Dutch Reformed Church (DRC) from the northern province of what in now South Africa left his home to evangelize the Shona people of the Zimuto area.[66] Around the same time Stephanus Hofmeyr, who had ministered to the Buys family, realized the need for more missionaries and missionary work if there was to be a lasting impact of the Christian faith among the Shona. In 1873 he made contact with the Paris Evangelical Society in Lesotho who a year later sent two African evangelists called Asser Sehahabane a Sotho and Jonathan a Pedi.[67] They concentrated their missionary efforts not only among the Zimuto people but also among the Chivi people to whom they promised to establish a mission center in their midst. Sehahabane and Jonathan went back to Lesotho to look for more support. Four Sotho evangelists escorted by a French missionary, Francois Coillard, left Lesotho once again to establish a mission among the Chivi people of southern Zimbabwe in the winter of 1877.[68]

In 1880 Gabriel Buys set out again for Zimuto country with another Sotho, Petrus Kolkodo, and found some people still open to the idea of having a mission among them, but some were skeptical since several years had passed from the initial promise. Others were reported as having been excited by the prospect of having Transvaal Afrikaners settling in some parts of their country. They viewed this as good news since the presence of the Afrikaners would have to a considerable extent guaranteed them some protection from Ndebele attacks, because the Ndebele and Afrikaners had signed a non-aggression pact.[69]

Around this period a war between the Zimuto and some Afrikaners broke out which disturbed missionary efforts among them. Afrikaners accused the Zimuto people of having stolen their cattle. Gabriel Buys who

64. Zvobgo, *Missions*, 1.

65. Atkinson, *Teaching Rhodesians*, 25.

66. Beach, "The Impact of Christianity," 25.

67. Ibid., 28

68. Ibid.

69. Phimister, *An Economic and Social History*, 20.

had been doing missionary work among the Zimuto was forced to join the war on the side of the Afrikaners, and was killed in the war. Even if he had survived the war he would not have continued with his missionary work among the Zimuto. By his selection of which side to join in the skirmish Buys had shown to the local community that he valued more his ethnic loyalties rather than his African "brothers in Christ." Many missionaries to follow would also take the Buys position whenever circumstances demanded that they make a choice between the two.

The desire to start a mission in the Shona territory did not die with Buys. After the war Africans within the DRC and Berlin Missions redirected their evangelistic efforts towards the Shona of the Save valley. Christians at the Berlin Mission in the northern part of South Africa started sending African evangelists to minister in the Matibi area in 1886. This eventually led to the establishment of the Matibi mission among the Shona of the Matibi area in 1888.

In 1890 Johannes Madima, an African evangelist from Tshakoma in South Africa,[70] who earlier had been responsible for founding the Matibi Mission was asked by Chivi people to provide a missionary to work in their area. More requests were made by other Shona chiefs in the Mberengwa area of southern Zimbabwe. Among these Shona groups of southern Zimbabwe it was evident that the newcomers and their religion were finally being embraced. This pattern of steady progress, which could have led to widespread acceptance of Christianity, was halted by the intervention of the British South Africa Company (BSAC).

In 1890, as the British South Africa Company's "Pioneer Column"[71] was on way into Mashonaland, in Matebeleland the Ndebele king was Lobengula. He had inherited the throne after the death of his father Mzilikazi in 1870.[72] During this period the pioneer column was in the process of constructing a road from South Africa into what had been carefully termed "Mashonaland."[73] This was land located to the west and north of Ndebele territory or Matabeleland. Because of military, and hence political domination, the Ndebele regarded the land occupied by the Shona as theirs.

70. Beach, "The Initial Impact," 31.

71. These were men, mostly Europeans, who had been gathered by Cecil John Rhodes's company to pioneer his mining ventures in Mashonaland. They became the first group of whites to enter Zimbabwe at a bigger scale with the intention to settle.

72. Douglas, *Zimbabwe Epic*, 65.

73. Ranger, *Revolt*, 3.

Fig. 4 Portrait of Lobengula
Courtesy of NAZ

Occupation of Mashonaland

Before 1890 the few foreigners that had frequently visited Mashonaland and Matebeleland were mainly missionaries, hunters and traders, but that radically changed in 1890. These traders, hunters and missionaries had whetted the economic appetites of whites south of the Limpopo River with tales of the economic potential of the territories of Matebeleland and Mashonaland. Stories about vast gold fields in Lobengula's Matebeleland as well as the surrounding Shona territories were common among the white community in South Africa.[74] All that was needed to prove whether this wealth of mythical proportion was real was someone with sufficient wealth or influence to venture into these lands north of the Limpopo River, and that person was Cecil John Rhodes.

At the age of seventeen Cecil Rhodes, the son of an English country vicar, had left England on the advice of doctors that living in a sunny country would improve his health.[75] Upon arriving in South Africa he made his fortune through dealing in diamonds and later gold.[76] Rhodes' capitalistic appetite to venture into Mashonaland was also spurred by stories of vast amounts of gold and other minerals in the region. Furthermore, he was motivated by a dream to create a British controlled empire from the Cape to Cairo. In order to realize his dream in Mashonaland, Rhodes through his company had to seek Lobengula's permission, but Lobengula was not prepared to grant mining rights to anyone for a significant period. Lobengula was also suspicious of foreign presence because he believed they had the potential to depose him; hence he was reluctant to promote any activities that would increase their presence in Matebeleland or Mashonaland.[77]

Rhodes's company representatives made use of several people to obtain Lobengula's consent to mine in Mashonaland. They also made use of some missionaries whom Lobengula trusted. Two such trusted missionaries were John Moffat, the son of Robert Moffat the missionary who had commanded a lot of respect among the Tswana of Botswana and Mzilikazi,[78] and Rev. Charles Daniel Helm of the LMS who had fruitlessly toiled among the Ndebele.[79] Since the negotiations were conducted in two languages Lobengula assumed that Helm and Moffat, whose father Robert had been a great family friend, would represent his interests in his dealings with the concession seekers. Helm was trusted by Lobengula but later records revealed that he

74. Samkange, *Rhodesia*, 68.

75. Clements, *Rhodesis*, 8.

76. Phimister, *An Economic and Social History*, 5.

77. Ibid.

78. Clements, *Rhodesia*, 10.

79. CD Helm was born in 1844 and died in 1915. A greatgrandson of Helm, Charles Helm, believed that his great grandfather, Helm, was solely driven by his commitment to Christianity and did not ascribe to the colonialist agenda, thus his motives were pure and selfless. January 1999, in unpublished family manuscript donated to the author by Charles Hepburn at Mowbray Presbyterian Church, Cape Town, South Africa, 9 September 2012.

was on Rhodes' pay-roll.[80] The church historian Mark Shaw[81] and the social historian Samkange[82] believed that Helm might have undermined Lobengula's interest in favor of an imperialist agenda whilst Ngwabi Bhebhe perceived Helm's position as that of a neutral translator, who sincerely believed the concession seekers' interests would be restricted solely to mining.[83] Rhodes was never present at these negotiations as he still lived in the Cape Colony. Consciously or unconsciously a complex web of connections between missionaries and exploitative colonial policy had been woven.

Before Rhodes' company managed to gain Lobengula's consent to operate in Mashonaland, representatives of the British government based at the Cape had managed to get John Moffat to convince Lobengula to agree to what became known as the "Moffat Treaty."[84] In this treaty Lobengula agreed that he would not grant any mining concession or sell part of his land to any foreign power without the knowledge and sanction of the British high commissioner at the Cape.[85] The first major step towards colonial subjugation was taken. It was on the basis of this treaty that all other European powers were kept out of what is now Zimbabwe during "The Scramble for Africa."[86]

On the 30 October 1888 another significant treaty was signed. This time it was between the representatives of Rhodes' company and Lobengula. It became known as the "Rudd Concession," after Charles Dunell Rudd, Rhodes' business partner, friend and representative.[87] Besides Rudd, Rhodes was also represented by Rochfort Maguire and Francis Robert Thompson. Rev. C.D. Helm served as the translator, and was presumed by Lobengula to be on his side or neutral. When Lobengula, who could not read nor write, put an "x" symbol as his signature, on a document drafted in English, he had granted Rhodes and company major concessions that included "the exclusive rights to extract all metals and mineral in Lobengula's kingdoms; full power, including their heirs to do all things necessary to win and procure the same, to hold, collect and enjoy the profits and revenues, if

80. Samkange, *Rhodesia*, 117.

81. *Shaw, The Kingdom of God*, 214.

82. *Samkange, Rhodesia*, 117.

83. Bhebhe, *Christianity*, 87.

84. Clements, *Rhodesia*, 10.

85. Ibid., 11.

86. Ibid.

87. Douglas, *Zimbabwe Epic, 182.*

any, derived from the same metals and minerals subject to the fulfilment of their contractual agreements."[88]

In return Lobengula and his council were to receive a hundred British sterling pounds every lunar month; one thousand Martini-Henry breech rifles with one hundred thousand suitable rounds of cartridges; and a steamboat with guns on the Zambezi river or in lieu a payment of five hundred pounds on the day the presents were to be executed.[89] While the Moffat Treaty protected British interest in Matebeleland and Mashonaland from other European competitors, the Rudd Concession secured political and economic protection for Rhodes and his companions from other competitors. The two treaties became the fertile seed bed on which colonialism was to germinate and take root, and in both missionaries had been complicit.

Initially Rhodes faced strong resistance in Britain about his plans to colonize Lobengula's territories.[90] Joseph Chamberlain, Earl Grey and Sir I. Fowell Buxton offered strong opposition.[91] Samkange writes of how Lobengula received valuable but belated advice from a member of the House of Lords in a letter on how to deal with concession seekers like Rhodes. The Lord advised, "As a way of expressing hospitality a host does not give his whole kraal to a visitor but he gives them a cow."[92]

Although many people in England were opposed to what they perceived as an intention by Rhodes to subjugate Lobengula and his kingdoms moral arguments began to be presented to justify such a move.[93] The wanton killings of the Shona by Ndebele armies and Lobengula's heavy handedness and what seemed to be crude forms of punishment given to offenders in his kingdoms were cited as necessitating change of leadership.[94]

Most Protestant and Roman Catholic missionaries seemed to have been certain that Lobengula's influence over his people was what made their conversion extremely difficult. Therefore they believed that in order for Christianity to progress especially among the Ndebele and the surrounding Shona areas there was also need for leadership change. Missionaries saw their spiritual success connected to a white political victory over

88. Clements, *Rhodesia*, 11.

89. Ibid.

90. Ranger, *Revolt*, 54.

91. Phimister, *Economic and Social History*, 30.

92. Samkange, *Origins*, 120.

93. Zvobgo, *Missions*, 3.

94. Clements, *Rhodesia*, 10.

Lobengula. Hence most missionaries during this era were eager to promote efforts that contributed towards change of leadership among the Ndebele. The tide of support in this respect turned in favor of Rhodes. Various Christian groups and individuals began to present Rhodes as a lesser evil, if not a greater good. He sought for a Charter from the British government that would authorize him to officially conduct business in Mashonaland under the British crown.

The Charter was granted to Rhodes' company the British South Africa Company in 1889.[95] Upon being issued a charter his company could officially venture into Mashonaland. A telegram sent to the colonial office at the Cape shows that the BSAC's pioneer column under a Colonel Pennefather had reached their destination by the 23rd of September 1890.[96] Their final destination was around the present day Harare Kopje.

The pioneer column included Canon Balfour of the Anglican Diocese of Bloemfontein and a Jesuit missionary Fr. Andrew Hartmann as its chaplains. Rhodes, as a sign of good will to the Anglicans who were part of the pioneer column, gave them on behalf of BSAC £600 towards the establishment of missions in Mashonaland.[97] By February 1891 Mashonaland was made part of the South African diocese which was headed by G.W.H. Knight-Bruce. Knight-Bruce had been deemed fit for this post because after his 1888 visit to Mashonaland and Matebeleland he had called for an establishment of a British protectorate in Mashonaland as a way of protecting them from what he viewed as inhuman cruelties of Ndebele control. At first, the Anglican mission was solely directed towards the settlers but, soon after Knight-Bruce took charge, and his staff increased, services were geared towards the locals.[98] He accepted significant amounts of land annexed in Mashonaland offered to the Anglican church by BSAC. One of his reasons for accepting the land being that when need arose it could be used to sustain the locals' livelihood.[99] Knight-Bruce may have by then envisaged that it was just a matter of time before the locals would be left landless by fellow settlers.

The arrival of the BSAC opened the flood gates for missions in Mashonaland and later Matebeleland. Besides the Anglicans, various Roman

95. Bull, *Rhodesian Perspective*, 11.

96. Samkange, *Origins*, 235.

97. Zvobgo, *Missions*, 3.

98. Latourette, *A History of the Expansion*, 383.

99. Ibid.

Catholic missionaries were part of the pioneer column, including Jesuit priests and Dominican sisters who offered, among other services, nursing and spiritual care. A number of Roman Catholic mission stations were established, including missions to the Zezuru of Domoshawa and Chishawasha areas as well as to the Manyika of the eastern part of Mashonaland.[100] Roman Catholic presence was further augmented by the Trappists from Mariann-hill.[101] In 1891 the Wesleyan Methodists arrived and received, like the Roman Catholics and Anglicans, sizeable land grants from the BSAC. The arrival of settlers strengthened the Dutch Reformed Church's resolve to establish a major mission station over the smaller ones that they had already initiated among the Shona of southern territories. In 1891 they established Morgenster Mission. Loyal to his adage, "One missionary is worth a hundred policemen,"[102] Rhodes and his BSAC gave generous financial gifts and loans as well as land for mission work. The budding state and budding church were in harmony, one leaning on the other when help was needed.

By 1895 the Seventh Day Adventists had also been established in the territory joined in 1897 by the American Episcopal Methodist Church and the Brethren of Christ. By 1907 the Berlin Missionary Society, which had started its work before the occupation had three mission stations, and by 1914 the Presbyterian Church of South Africa, the Church of Sweden and the Salvation Army were all part of Mashonaland and Matebeleland's religious, social and political melting pot. Besides having gained ground figuratively, in its mission of winning converts, the church also had literally gained much ground in Matebeleland and Mashonaland. By 1960, almost half a million of acres were classified as mission land, and more than a quarter of the local population claimed to be Christians.[103]

Invasion of Matebeleland

Success in mining was initially illusory for the pioneers in Mashonaland and new speculations quickly emerged that the gold was in Matebeleland. The settlers now needed an excuse to get into Matebeleland in search of the elusive second Rand, hence the need to depose Lobengula became

100. Kane, *The World's View*, 130.

101. Ibid.

102. Linden, *The Catholic Church*, 116.

103. Bourdillon, *Christianity*, 70.

urgent.[104] Seeking for an excuse to invade Matebeleland, in 1890 Rhodes was reported saying, "As soon as they interfere with our rights, I shall end their game . . . and when it is all over I shall grant farms to those who assist me."[105] Leander Starr Jameson, Rhodes' henchman, was also reported to have written to his brother saying, "Next year I shall be on the move as this map making enterprise includes not only Mashonaland but the surroundings of the Chartered's possessions, which I shall do my best to increase, in fact all of the so called Zambezia or as it will be called 'Rhodesia.'"[106] In these two individuals' words the fate of Matebeleland had been sealed.[107] An opportunity arose for the settlers to attack the Ndebele in July 1893.[108] Lobengula sent his army to punish the Shona of Karanga dialect living in what had come to be known as the Victoria area, now called Masvingo, and reclaim the cattle he accused them of having stolen. For this transgression, Ndebele armies killed a number of Shona, some of whom by then were working for some of the settlers who had chosen to settle in and around Fort Victoria. What seemed to be a moral high ground held by settlers should be counter balanced by some practical considerations. The Shona were a source of cheap of labor for the settlers, and furthermore through trade they provided the settler community with the much needed grain and other local products.[109] These were commodities that they desperately needed for their survival in the early days of establishing themselves. Therefore Ndebele raids and their killing of the Shona would have negatively impacted the well-being of the early settlers. Missionaries as far as Khama III's country, Botswana, made long journeys to 'Makalaka[110] of Shashi and Tati' to procure grain for themselves and Khama's people.[111] Although no settler was attacked Jameson used the massacre of these Shona people as an excuse to attack the Ndebele. Upon hearing the settlers' intentions to attack him, Lobengula sent envoys to arrange for a peace settlement. He did all he could to avoid confrontation even to the extent of presenting gold to the

104. Phimister, *Zimbabwe*, 10.
105. Clements, *Rhodesia*, 20.
106. Ibid.
107. Loney, *Rhodesia*, 40.
108. Beach, *The Shona*, 167.
109. Makalaka are the Shona of Kalanga dialect.
110. Hepburn, *Jottings*, 50ff.
111. Ibid.

settlers as a peace offering.[112] Nonetheless, the settler army attacked and defeated some Ndebele regiments on their way to Bulawayo, the Ndebele capital. On the 15th of November 1893 the army reached Bulawayo but only to find it deserted. Lobengula and the Ndebele had fled.[113]

Upon the defeat of the Ndebele, their cattle which had been the backbone of their wealth were divided as booty among the BSAC and the members of the army that had fought the Ndebele. Most parts of Matebeleland were divided into farms for the settlers and the BSAC. The church was also granted some land in the conquered territory, further entrenching links with the colonialists. After the fall of Lobengula a BSAC employee, reflected the general feeling among the settlers of their invasion of Matebeleland: "The whole affair had been a good piece of business."[114] From thence Matebeleland and Mashonaland were amalgamated. Rhodes preferred this acquired territory to be called "Zambesia," and his right-hand man Jameson wanted it to be called "Charter-land." Most settlers believed Rhodesia was a suitable name for these territories, in honor of the visionary Cecil John Rhodes. Out of Mashonaland and Matebeleland Rhodesia was born.[115]

British South Africa Company Rule

After the defeat of the Ndebele, Mashonaland and Matebeleland came under the jurisdiction of the BSAC. Bulawayo which had been Lobengula's capital was thrown open in 1894 as a trading location. It became the main center of settler focus. Within two months of its official opening about 400 gold-seekers had acquired licenses and made 11000 claims.[116] Not all gold-seekers were of European origin, a few were of Asian descent and some Africans.[117] These few Africans from South Africa and Asians had been part of the pioneer column. Rhodes had granted them some of the rights and privileges he had granted to whites.[118] When the settlers realized that even in Matebeleland there was no Second-Rand they began to direct their efforts primarily towards various agricultural activities. This development

112. Loney, *Rhodesia*, 40.

113. Clements, *Rhodesia*, 8.

114. Phimister, *Zimbabwe*, 10.

115. Morris-Jones, *Rhodesia to Zimbabwe*.

116. Gann, *Southern Rhodesia*, 120.

117. Ibid., 120.

118. Clements, *Rhodesia*, 27.

brought the need for labor, but neither the BSAC nor most settlers were willing to pay fairly for that labor. The BSAC worked towards turning the local people into wage workers.[119]

The Company devised ways of accessing cheap labor by offering token incentives and by disguised or even at times open compulsion. The economic advancement of the colony was to depend on African labor in all sectors. The BSAC also realized that by making the locals work they would contribute to the colony's economy through paying taxes. The tax system was viewed as a two way tool since it stimulated the need for employment and also managed to inject the required revenue.

In 1894 a hut tax was sanctioned which the locals abhorred. The hut tax demanded that every African man should pay 10 shillings in respect of every house he occupied. At first in cases where the locals could not pay in cash payment could be made in kind, but by 1895 this provision was withdrawn in preference for having locals contribute towards the payment of their tax through offering labor.[120] A money tax and insistence on money tax ensured that locals entered into the money market if they were to meet their obligations. They needed to sell goods for cash or they had to work for the settlers in order to get cash for tax payment purposes.

The BSAC also exerted more economic pressure on the locals by insisting that the headmen and chiefs had to ensure that a certain number of their people worked for settlers in return for board, lodging and a 10 shillings a month salary.[121] These orders were enforced by the police. The Ndebele had already borne the brunt of the economic consequences of the defeat. Most of their cattle, a major source of their wealth, had been taken. The imposition of the hut tax further added to their levels of discontent. The whole Ndebele way of life was thrown into disarray by the manner in which the cattle and land division was conducted by the BSAC.[122] The Ndebele were moved from the fertile lands and which became the property of settler farmers, this further created resentment.

In Bulawayo the gender imbalances among settlers, which stood at a ratio of 502 men to 154 women, led some settlers into seeking sexual relief and fulfillment from local women, including instances of rape.[123]

119. Gann, *Southern Rhodesia*, 121.

120. Ibid., 123.

121. Hodder-Williams, *White Farmers in Rhodesia*, 21.

122. Blake, *A History of Rhodesia*, 118.

123. Keppel-Jones, *Rhodes and Rhodesia*, 381.

This incensed the Ndebele. In addition to these problems, the BSAC administration was viewed as oppressive and its settler police, the British South Africa Police (BSAP), were accused of often operating as gangs as well as being a law to themselves. They were known for looting the possessions of locals.[124] In Mashonaland the sociopolitical state of affairs was equally gloomy. The Methodist Rev. John White, one of the early critics of colonialism in Zimbabwe, believed that the uprising against settler rule that was soon to follow "was a direct result of Shona oppression by Company officials."[125]

Natural disasters, in the form of plagues and droughts, followed the occupation of Matebeleland and Mashonaland. The rinder-pest significantly depleted the local herds of cattle. In trying to curb this disease, the BSAC shot thousands of infected as well as some healthy cattle. Locals attributed this act to malevolence. Before the rinder-pest there were 250,000 cattle in Matebeleland alone but after 1897 there were only 41,000.[126] These developments became some of the major reasons that led to the 1896 Ndebele and Shona uprising against the settlers.[127] This rebellion known as *Umvukela*[128] in Ndebele and *Chimurenga*[129] in Shona, came as a surprise to the settlers who had assumed that the locals, especially the Shona, were happy under their rule.

Mission stations[130] that had mushroomed throughout the country and other institutions that locals believed represented settler interests were attacked. Bernard Mizeki,[131] an African Anglican catechist and teacher who had arrived in Mashonaland from Cape Town in 1891 was killed, with other church helpers.[132] Before the BSAC could quell the uprising, a few missionaries and settlers as well as their African converts who lived away from the emerging major settlements were also killed. The execution of two influential Shona spirit mediums Nehanda (female) and Kaguvi (male), on

124. Ibid.

125. Zvobgo, *Missions*, 25.

126. Ibid. 23

127. Ranger, *Revolt*, 1.

128. Ndebele and Shona for revolution.

129. Keppel-Jones, *Rhodes*, 473.

130. For the scale of missionary activities during this period consult Zvobgo, *Missions*.

131. For a detailed biography on B. Mizeki, see Farrant, *Mashonaland Martyr*; he is considered in the African Anglican community as a hero of the Christian faith .

132. Zvobgo, *Missions*, 45.

the 2nd of March 1898 marked the end of the uprising.[133] After the uprising Rhodes promised the locals administrative justice, and as a sign of good will among the Ndebele he began to occasionally invite some Ndebele leaders to his personal parties.[134] At least for the next 50 years settlers were able to pacify the locals. In that period Christianity grew with mixed fortunes in the first 15 years and in leaps and bound in the next 35 years and onwards.

Responsible Government

During its early years Rhodesia did not fare well economically. Several mines mushroomed throughout the country. In the mines, although the locals did not have the name of slaves, they were to a high degree treated as such. The wages were low and the working conditions inhumane. The laborers were accommodated in overcrowded dormitory-like conditions away from their families. It was common practice to have men work 6 or 7 days per week with shifts of 14 hours per day. Safety conditions in the mines were reported as dismal and diseases were rampant. On the other hand the labor laws had been tailor-made to protect the interest of the settlers. Phimister, a historian on Rhodesia's socio-economic history, recorded a case where: "For kicking a black worker to death, at the Old Chum mine in 1916, FE West was sentenced to a £25 fine or six months in prison."[135] He continued, "Gustav Peer, who drowned an employee in a bucket of hot water for dropping a valve they were working on, was to pay a fine of £50 or face six months of hard labour in prison."[136]

In the farms the wages were low and child labor was rampant. Gertrude Page, a settler living on a farm observed, "In Rhodesia you grow lots of things by chiefly looking at niggers."[137] The farm workers, besides verbal abuse, also suffered physical abuse.[138] In due course, though at the expense of locals, the agricultural focus of the settlers paid-off.

133. Ranger, *Revolt*, 309.

134. Keppel-Jones, *Rhodes*, 495.

135. Phimister, *Economic and Social History*, 87ff.

136. Ibid.

137. Ibid., 130.

138. Ibid.

Fig. 5 African women laborers at a farm carrying tobacco leaves. Courtesy of NAZ (Settler farmers standby chatting and enjoying a smoke-pipe)

Rhodesia quickly changed into a family-oriented, predominantly farming and trading community. By the time when Cecil John Rhodes died, on 26 March 1902, Rhodesia's white population induced by agricultural prospects had risen to about 11000.[139] By 1911 this population had increased further as a result of the influx of South Africans, who preferred the rule of the BSAC rather than the government of the newly created 1910 Union of South Africa.[140] The influx of South Africans increased the rate of marriages among settlers. The white population by 1911 doubled to about 24000.[141] Between 1907 and 1917 the BSAC intensified its agricultural efforts, and this led to steady economic growth. The increased settler population growth and the general economic growth propelled the need for self-government among settlers. They believed Rhodesia could be turned into another South Africa, Australia or New Zealand.[142]

Dominated by farming and family interests the settlers lobbied for a representative and responsible government. In 1918 the judicial committee

139. Kane, *World's View*, 232.

140. Thompson, *South Africa*, 157.

141. Jollie, *The Real Rhodesia*, 28.

142. Kane, *World's View*, 232.

of the Privy Council ruled that un-alienated land in Rhodesia belonged to the British crown rather than to the BSAC. As a result of this ruling the company lost interest in administering the country.[143] The BSAC, in an endeavor to protect its business interests, campaigned to have Rhodesia amalgamated into the Union of South Africa. In 1922 a referendum was conducted giving settlers the opportunity to choose their preferred destiny of the colony.[144] The choice was between joining the Union of South Africa or forming a government of their own. 59% opted for responsible government and the remainder for union with South Africa. On the 12th of September 1923 the BSAC was relieved of its administrative duties. With a population of about 870 000 Africans and 35 000 whites, on the 1st of October of the same year, Rhodesia was handed over to be governed by settlers under what they termed a "responsible government."[145] In all this African opinion was never sought.

Charles Coghlan, of Irish Catholic background who had been born at the Cape, became Rhodesia's first prime minister in 1923.[146] Clements a Rhodesian historian offered a window into the nature of the political system in the 1920s in Rhodesia. He wrote, "[T]here was no strong party system; personalities counted for more than policies and there was a constant forming and reforming of the groups of individuals who exercised power."[147]

The group that controlled the government was known as the Rhodesian party. It was more of a council of settler elders who administered the affairs of the country. The first opposition political party emerged in the 1930s. The Labor Party that emerged remained eager to cooperate with the governing council of the Rhodesian Party, operating as no more than a pressure group to preserve the interests and privileges of the settler working class. The Labour Party constantly backed down on any of its policies or ideas that it believed might encourage Africans to seek economic and political advancement.[148] Little was possible among Africans during this period in terms of political organization.

143. Bull, *Rhodesian Perspective*, 12.

144. Jollie, *Rhodesia*, 85ff.

145. Bull, *Rhodesian Perspective*, 13. The term "Rhodesian government" will also be employed to refer to Rhodesian or white governments and "Zimbabwean government" will mainly be employed to refer to the African government.

146. Jollie, *Rhodesia*, 84.

147. Clements, *Rhodesia*, 44.

148. Ibid., 45

The Early Tensions

From the beginning of settler occupation most missionaries, Roman Catholic and Protestant alike, shared the racial and cultural attitudes prevalent among the settler community. They saw their task not just as bearers of the Christian message, but also as cultural role models. It was often unclear whether they were in fact missionaries, or chaplains to the white settler community who took some services amongst the African populace. Varieties of western cultural norms, depending on the origins of the missionaries, were taught to the locals as if they were a key component of the Christian message. Because of, on the one hand, a lack of European education and, on the other hand, an admiration of European education, among locals a strong uncritical dependency on missionary theology and practice developed. Together with this came a desperate need for approval from missionaries. In their leadership of this uncritical and dependent church it was common practice for some missionaries to dictate social and cultural policies.[149] As Brand comments, "They thought they knew what was good for the Africans and were determined to impose it with or without the consent of the Africans."[150]

The church that developed in Zimbabwe during the first seven decades rarely offered administrative responsibilities to Africans.[151] Its attitudes and practices began to reflect those of the settlers. Despite holding views different to those of the Dutch Reformed Church (DRC), churches had been founded in Zimbabwe by missionaries of the Nederduits Gereformeerde Sending-kerk van Suid Afrika (NGK) which held a theologically-based understanding of the fundamental differences between the races. Both the Protestant and Catholic missionaries effectively upheld social separation of the races no different in practice from those of the NGK.[152] They preserved the social distance between blacks and whites.[153] As in the Rhodesian political system, the church protected white missionary privileges and interests. The missionary led church defended its position by claiming

149. Gray, *White Missionaries*, 81.

150. Brand, "African Nationalists," 69.

151. Scholz, "The Catholic Church," 201.

152. The NGK of South Africa provided the theological basis for South Africa's apartheid governments and its Dutch Reformed missions in Rhodesia were also bound by its theology.

153. Scholz, "The Catholic Church," 210.

that cultural differences necessitated social distance and justified economic discrepancies.

The relationship between the church and state from inception was cordial.[154] It was tied together with the seemingly unbreakable umbilical cord of race, and the desire by both church and state to civilize the locals they generally regarded as heathen.[155] The church worked closely with the government and urged its converts as well as other locals in general to abide by government laws. The BSAC from early days had largely handed over the responsibility for African education to missions. As a result of this arrangement many missionaries became the unavoidable stepping stones for Africans who had the ambition to succeed in the new order of things.[156] To most Africans, missionaries became the highway not just to heaven but also to socio-economic success. It was not only with regard to education that missionaries were influential. They also worked closely with the government in the development of legislation.

In 1901 with the blessing of the church the governing authorities introduced the Polygamous Marriage Tax Ordinance.[157] The law demanded the paying of taxes for people in polygamous marriages, and it restricted the amount of *lobola* (dowry) to be paid. The law also outlawed the practice of *Kuzwarira*. In this practice Shona girls were given for marriage at a young age, even before they had the ability to consent. As soon as they matured, usually judged by the beginning of their menstrual cycle, they would be taken by their husband to fulfill their marital duties. The authority that the government gave to missionaries in the years that followed did not end within the school or mission parameters but also extended into the local communities within their sphere. This became a fertile ground for missionary social experiments. Brand observed, "In Africa a position of power and privilege permitted them (missionaries) to realize however imperfectly and microcosmically their own vision of the Christian order in a way which they would never have been in their own societies."[158]

Ideas which missionaries would not consider experimenting with in churches back home were implemented in Zimbabwe's African churches. In some cases western middle class values and virtues became required

154. Phimister, *Economic & Social History*, 146.

155. Ibid.

156. Brand, "African Nationalists," 70.

157. Phimister, *Economic & Social History*, 146.

158. Brand, "African Nationalists," 71.

aspects for conversion to be accepted as genuine.[159] Conversion was aimed at both religious and social aspects, and even to morally neutral cultural values and practices. This was due to a lack of both a clear understanding of the value and significance of the local customs and culture as well as the demands of Christianity on all cultures and traditions.

Furthermore, because of the position of the missionaries and their tendency to be heavy handed when applying discipline they became synonymous with the Native Commissioners.[160] The locals began to judge missionaries more harshly since their attitudes and behavior could be weighed against the principles they professed and taught. In the church Africans were dominated. At mission stations missionaries ruled supreme. They lived in segregated houses of better quality, earned higher salaries, and unfortunately most of them exhibited the same supremacist attitudes as those found among the settlers.[161] Yet, despite negative attitudes towards Africans by most missionaries, church and school enrolments continued to rise.

The settler population was about 40,000 by the mid-1920s and it was estimated that about 86% of this population viewed itself as Christian. Zimbabwe's African population was estimated to be around 900,000 by 1927 and about 100,000 within this figure were registered Christians.[162] By 1927, the gross African Christian population which included non-registered mainline denomination Christians and non-mainline denomination Christians was estimated to have been about 35%[163], in a country whose average annual African population growth rate was 4%.[164]

These figures excluded African independent churches that had also grown significantly in the 1920s,[165] and also African Christians who could not meet membership requirements but still attended church and

159. Phimister, *Economic & Social History*, 146.

160. The Native Commissioners had been established first in Matebeleland in 1894 by Order in Council. They were under the chief Native Commissioner in the Ministry of Native Affairs and were in charge of the Matebeleland Native Police and then later Mashonaland Native Police. The Native Affairs Ministry had the responsibility to recruit manual local labor, known then as native labour, to enforce law and tax collection.

161. Brand, "African Nationalists," 73.

162. Zvobgo, *Missions*, 336.

163. Because of the unavailability of membership statistics in several denominations in the 1930s and 40s it is not possible to satisfactorily establish the scale of church growth during this period in Rhodesia.

164. Soderstrom, *God Gave Growth*, 135.

165. Taber, *The Church in Africa*, 83.

believed they were Christians. Those that were excluded by the stringent membership rules significantly outnumbered those that were registered. For example, in the Salvation Army to be accepted into full membership a convert was to attend weekly training classes for at least one year and even at the end of that period membership was not guaranteed.[166]

For the London Missionary Society, as well as the Church of Sweden, converts had to go through at least two years of training before they could be admitted into membership. Anglican converts had to, among other requirements, learn to read before they could be admitted into membership.[167] Almost all major denominations in Rhodesia during this period maintained these strict membership requirements.[168] Despite these rules the church grew steadily.[169]

A rapid numerical growth averaging 15% per year was experienced by the African section of the Zimbabwean church between 1933 and 1963. In 1960, more than 50% of the African population was believed to be Christian.[170] On the other hand the majority of settlers, and even their political establishment, also claimed to be Christians. They further claimed that Zimbabwe was in fact an embodiment of a Christian civilization.[171] Most within the church establishment, predominantly missionaries and settlers, seemed to have been both in agreement with the claim, and also seemed to be at peace with the sociopolitical status quo in which they served. Hence the events that were to unfold in the development of this nation from 1957 caught them in a state of moral, theological and prophetic slumber.

What should also be noted is that during much of the period under discussion in this chapter protest against colonialism from the African community was very limited. The few Africans that protested largely sought increased economic privileges in the colonialists' economy rather than outright demand for sociopolitical equality and the ending of colonialism. Historical events of church and state relations in Zimbabwe to the 1950s seem to justify the claims made by Ali Mazrui that "Christianity became linked with the whole vision of '*Pax Britannica*' and became 'associated

166. Zvobgo, *Missions*, 319.

167. Ibid.

168. Ibid.

169. Sundkler and Steed, *A History of the Church*, 453.

170. Soderstrom, *God Gave Growth*, 135.

171. Skelton, "They Shall . . . Persecute You, Luke 21:12," NAZ, GEN-P/SKE.

with colonization.'"[172] With the church closely tied to the colonial ruling elite, it was going to find it hard to see the need for, or support, demands for political and social emancipation. The churches would need to make significant changes in order to break free from long-established and inherited patterns of thought.

172. Mazrui, *Towards a Pax Africana*, 198.

3

The Development of Radical African Politics in Zimbabwe, ca. 1960–1964

The development of African politics in Zimbabwe came later compared to other southern African countries. Its development was a product of various factors within as well as beyond the country's borders. In the late fifties several factors brought about political consciousness as well as a mood change to that of radicalism among Zimbabwean Africans. Events elsewhere, and particularly in Africa, brought a sense of self belief that Africans could determine their own political destiny. The independence of Ghana in March of 1957 was both a wake-up call and a source of inspiration for many African nations and more so for British colonies. Ghana's independence gave hope to Africans living in British colonies that independence was possible and achievable.

During this period the Mau Mau revolution in Kenya provided colonized communities with another possible avenue for independence besides round-table political negotiations.[1] By engaging in an armed struggle, the Mau Mau had provided another model which Zimbabwean Africans could follow in their pursuit for self-rule. These developments became a symbol of hope for pioneers of Zimbabwean African political consciousness and nationalism who by early 1957 had not developed a spirit of national political consciousness or even a political party that had the support of Africans nationally.[2]

1. Chennells, "Rhodesian Nationalism," 134.
2. Zvobgo, "Southern Rhodesia," 482.

The Bulawayo African National Congress and the Salisbury based City Youth League were the only groups that voiced some of the issues that affected African residents of the two cities,[3] but their role was no more than that of small pressure groups. Their activities did not even demand the attention of the settler authorities because they were not viewed as political threats. They were simply viewed as little beggars agitating for a few crumbs from the settlers' sociopolitical buffet. Perhaps inspired by Ghana's independence in that year these two groups merged on 12 September 1957 to form the Southern Rhodesia African National Congress (SRANC).[4] The day was also significant for settlers as they celebrated it as "Occupation Day."[5] The merger came under the leadership of Joshua Mqabuko Nkomo.[6] As radical African politics in Zimbabwe was in its infancy in the late 50s, in Malawi, South Africa and Zambia nationalist movements were already established.

In the early years of African politics in Zimbabwe nationalists from the northern territories of Malawi and Zambia became a valuable source from which Zimbabwean nationalists could learn.[7] Hence it was common to have African politicians from the northern territories share the political podium with Zimbabwe's nationalists.[8] Therefore as political attitudes and philosophies of nationalists north of the Zambezi became radical they also advised and shared these experiences and political philosophies with Zimbabwean nationalists. The radicalism of African political activities and philosophies before the independence of the territories north of Zambezi then applied *mutatis mutandis* in these early years of the formation of African nationalism in Zimbabwe.[9]

By 1959 it was clear that nationalism had gathered momentum in Zimbabwe. Even the rural population that had been at the fringe of things

3. Nyangoni and Nyandoro, *Zimbabwe*, XVI.

4. Brand, "African Nationalists," 75.

5. Occupation in reference to their invasion of Mashonaland and eventually Matebeleland.

6. Nkomo became the first Vice President of Zimbabwe and was affectionately known as "Father Zimbabwe."

7. The term "nationalist/s" will assume a broader meaning in this work. It will include all Africans whose efforts were geared toward the ending of colonialism and the creation of an independent Zimbabwe in which Africans would participate in the sociopolitical life of the country as equal citizens.

8. Bhebhe, *Simon*, 135–37.

9. Linden, *Catholic Church*, 50.

as the African urban elite took center stage had joined the fray.[10] Before being proscribed when a state of emergency was declared in 1959, in the Federation of Central Africa, the Southern Rhodesia African National Congress had paved a way for the birth of a national party for Africans. Some of its leaders were imprisoned along with other 500 members in various towns and cities throughout Zimbabwe.[11] Those in the leadership who had not been imprisoned revived SRANC under a new name; the National Democratic Party (NDP).[12]

The NDP was officially launched on 1 January 1960 with Michael Mawema as its interim leader.[13] The rebirth of Southern Rhodesia African National Congress as NDP brought with it a different mood from the old party. It moved from the old stance of seeking administrative and sociopolitical justice for Africans to an outright demand for self-rule by Africans.[14] The NDP demanded that there be adult universal suffrage in Zimbabwe. Taking advantage of the mood of the time of anger among most Africans as a result of the imprisonment of the Southern Rhodesia African National Congress leadership—during the state of emergency—the NDP campaigned for members throughout the country and it quickly grew into the first nationalist movement. The state of emergency which had been declared with the added intention of choking African nationalism failed to achieve this purpose, but instead it achieved the opposite. Africans felt their leaders in prison were being treated unjustly and hence were further agitated.[15]

The Adjustment Period

From the late 1950s, the churches in Zimbabwe increasingly faced the problem of how to respond to the challenge of African nationalism, especially in the light of the long-standing peaceful relationship between the churches and government. It was to prove a key issue on which the political theology of the churches was to be shaped and tested. In this the missionary movement was closely tied to government policy. As Sundkler observed,

10. Ibid., 48.
11. Zvobgo, "Southern Rhodesia," 483.
12. Bhebhe, "The Nationalist Struggle," 70.
13. Ibid.
14. Ibid.
15. Day, *International Nationalism*, 16.

nowhere in British Africa was this as pronounced as in Zimbabwe, "The ordained missionary served as a superintendent of schools supported by government which paid the travel expenses of the missionary's inspection tours. Church interests were provided for in that the ordained superintendent of schools was, at the end of the school inspection, free to call together a church meeting . . . this meant that the missionary was virtually tied to the government system with links provided by comparatively generous government grants."[16]

African nationalism brought a challenge to both the philosophical foundation on which settler philosophy was based and the political structures from which they drew their authority. Whilst both African non-Christians and the African Christian laity lent their support to nationalism, the church leadership, which was predominantly white, took a different view. Although there were a few prominent white church leaders, such as Todd, who spoke on behalf of Africans the majority of these representatives of the church were unable to readily embrace African nationalism at its inception, and instead spoke out against it.

There are a range of reasons why most church leaders did not embrace African nationalism in Zimbabwe, but at the heart was a mistrust of nationalists. Their general suspicion of nationalists matched that of other settler communities elsewhere in Africa. In Kenya the Mau Mau (1952–56) uprising had led to much bloodshed and had also deepened the fears of white authorities and communities elsewhere.[17] Social upheaval had ensued in places like Burundi, Congo and even Ghana under nationalist leadership, which led some church leaders in Zimbabwe to reject nationalism from the outset,[18] but comparisons with other struggling countries that were under white control were not made. Nationalists were often viewed by the white church leadership as a small but subversive group of Africans who were bent on causing social anarchy.[19] The fear of what might happen to Zimbabwe under a nationalist government stopped some church leaders in the early sixties from being open to the positive outcomes under nationalist governments such as those in Malawi and Zambia where the church had continued to operate and grow.[20]

16. Sundkler and Steed, *Church in Africa*, 803.

17. Gordon, "Decolonization and Development," 37.

18. Khapoya, "Zimbabwe," 41.

19. Linden, *Catholic Church*, 60.

20. Linden and Weller, *Mainstream Christianity*, 190.

The difficulties in missionary work in the past had left older church leaders with a feeling of being indebted to the state.[21] According to D.J. Maxwell, "The correspondence files received from missionaries in Rhodesia show that a number of the older ones who had cut their teeth in the 1950s were hostile to the early nationalist movement."[22]

The church leadership was also predominantly white, with close personal ties in the rest of the white settler community.[23] All this created an atmosphere which was not conducive to challenging prevalent racial or political attitudes.[24] In 1961 a group of Roman Catholic leaders dismissed nationalism as "fundamentalism" and asserted that, "Nationalism, as opposed to patriotism, has no room for either of these two fundamental principles of love. Nationalism as Christ constantly pointed out to the Pharisees, places the will of man before the will of God."[25] Charles Mzingeli,[26] a leading nationalist in the late 1950s and early 1960s and a Roman Catholic layman, was denied communion by his church for protesting against its inhibiting of Africans from joining the Reformed Industrial and Commercial Workers Union (RICU).[27] RICU although being a workers union had a reputation of being a platform for voicing nationalist grievances in Zimbabwe. Though a large section of the church hierarchy seemed not to support nationalist grievances there were some members within its leadership structures that identified with the nationalist cause in the early 1960s.

Ranges of Responses to Political Challenges c.1960

In 1958 Reverend Fred Rea, of the Methodist church, looked to a time of union in the Zimbabwean Christian community believing that the country was destined to be a multiracial society.[28] Rea argued that with increasing urbanization there was growing need both within the general Zimbabwean

21. Maxwell, "Christianity and the War," 62.

22. Ibid.

23. Sundkler and Steed, *Church in Africa*, 803ff.

24. Brand, "African Nationalists," 82.

25. "Nationalism versus Patriotism," *The Shield*, May 1961; Linden, *The Catholic Church*, 60.

26. His father who was converted to Christianity after the fall of the Ndebele in 1896 helped to co-found the Roman Catholic Mbakwe mission in Zimbabwe

27. Shamuyarira, *Crisis in Rhodesia*, 32.

28. Rea, "The Need for a United Church," 87.

urban and Church communities to manage and encourage partnership between the races.[29] He contended that the church should stand as a "training ground for fellowship" and as a guide for interracial relations, especially among its own members. Rea believed that this could not be accomplished at "congregational level of regular weekly worship" but it could be further promoted in "the councils and committees of the Church, in its theological training, in the fellowship of the ministry, in the fact that the youth organizations and adult groups have both black and white branches and that these meet together at conferences and on similar special occasions."[30]

In highlighting the polarization that existed within the churches, Rea drew up categories which outlined the general racial composition of the mainline Zimbabwean church membership and the missions which were most affected by ethnic and political polarization. Although the categories were formulated in the late 1950s they still applied in much of the period under discussion in this chapter. Canaan Banana believed the categories were only basic,[31] and noted that they omitted the Pentecostal and indigenous churches.[32] This omission of African initiated churches is serious, but it does not affect much the understanding of the nature of polarization within the church since African initiated churches, or indigenous churches, were predominantly if not exclusively African in terms of their composition.[33] As an overall outline Rea's categories are useful ways of illustrating the issue of polarization.

The two church categories that were least affected by ethnic tensions were missions or denominations that were largely mono-ethnic.[34] These denominations were least susceptible to polarization because they had predominantly white members or almost exclusively black members.[35] The predominantly white missions in his first category were composed of the Presbyterian Church of Southern Africa with a membership of about 6 000, the Dutch Reformed Church with a white-only membership of about 15 000, the Baptist Church, the Apostolic Faith Mission and few other smaller

29. Ibid., 86.

30. Ibid., 87.

31. Banana, *Church and Struggle*, 104.

32. Ibid.

33. Sundkler and Steed, *A History of the Church*, 814ff.

34. Notable among whites was the South-African-founded Dutch Reformed Church and among locals the African Independent Churches. Linden, *Catholic Church*, 298–99.

35. Rea, "The Need for a United Church," 84.

denominations and churches had a total white membership of about 35 000.[36] Since their membership and the leadership was white and was being protected and favored by the settler political system they were often silent on matters of political repression, and generally followed the official line on matters.[37] Since they were also protected from contact with Africans and their realities by settler-government laws, that did not permit racial integration by means such as creating separate residential and recreation areas, they were generally unaware of the world of Africans both in and outside the church.[38] Hence their section of the church said little on behalf of those that were oppressed by the system.

The second of Rea's categories consisted of missions with a predominantly African membership and these were the Salvation Army with a membership then of about 60 000;[39] the London Missionary Society; The American Board; The Church of Central Africa Presbyterian, whose membership was mainly composed of Africans from Malawi; The South African General Mission, The Brethren in Christ with about 2 000 registered members; The American and Free Methodists, The Churches of Christ and the Church of Sweden that had a membership of about 18 000.[40] By 1963 there were about 133 000 official Methodist members.[41] It should still be noted that although they were predominantly African in membership most of them were headed by white leadership[42] until the appointment in 1968 of the outspoken Bishop Abel Muzorewa by the American Methodists.[43] Churches in this category may have earlier seen the need for Africanizing their leadership, especially responding to the political events around

36. These figures were based on church registered members only and on figures supplied by Linden based on 1976 statistics, *Catholic Church*, 298–99.

37. Banana, *Church and Struggle*, 48.

38. Linden, *Catholic Church*, 95.

39. Sundkler and Steed, *Church in Africa*, 809.

40. Soderstrom, *God Gave Growth*, 134.

41. Ibid.

42. It should be noted that Rev. Andrew Ndlela had been appointed in 1965 to be chairperson of the British Methodists / Wesleyan Methodists. Although his decision making powers were curtailed, his role as chairman was limited almost to rubber stamping decisions made by the dominantly-white Methodist administrative board. Nationalists did not regard him as a credible leader with African interests at heart, Sundkler and Steed, *Church in Africa*, 806.

43. Mungazi, *Honoured Crusade*, 117.

which Africans were clamoring for self-rule.[44] One such forward looking Christian leader was Garfield Todd, former Premier of Zimbabwe when it was "Southern Rhodesia" and missionary turned settler-rancher and African nationalist supporter, of the Church of Christ New Zealand, who warned fellow settlers in 1963 of the consequences of racial and political polarization:

> Our white minorities must recognise the danger of the developing dichotomy which would destroy our generation. This urgency is stressed in Mr. Justice Snyman's comment: "If the white man should fail to regain the confidence and trust of the Bantu, a dangerously antagonistic nationalism is almost certain to develop." My criticism of that comment is that it is a prophecy 20 years too late—a prophecy unaware that the developed antagonism is today a threatening force in the life of our two countries—the dichotomy is there—we are confronted by dangerous division—we are divided—and our policies are designed to widen the gap.[45]

A few missionaries who were part of this category, like Todd, were sympathetic to the African cause of ending colonial domination. Hence it was not surprising that from this category the first African bishop or person holding a significant leadership position in Zimbabwean mainstream Christianity emerged.[46] The process was less traumatic than it would have been in a predominantly white denomination or a denomination with an evenly distributed membership of blacks and white such as was to be found in Rea's third category.[47]

This third category consisted of denominations with large bodies of members from both sections of the racial divide. These included the Anglican Church with about 75 000 white members and 120 000 African members, the Roman Catholic Church with about 32 000 white members and 350 000 African members, and the Wesleyan Methodist with about 17 000 white members and 35 000 African members.[48] It was in this third category that social tensions were constantly exhibited within the church.[49] The Anglican Bishop of Mashonaland Cecil Alderson observed, "The po-

44. Ibid.
45. Todd, "Challenge for Today."
46. Dodge, *Revolutionary Bishop*, 169.
47. Rea, "The Need for a United Church," 85.
48. Linden, *Catholic Church*, 298–99.
49. Banana, *Repression*, 13.

litical situation of Rhodesia necessarily affects the church in many ways. There has been inevitably a tragic division of opinion between those of our white churchmen who believe, not always from the worst motives that Mr. Smith is right, and those who don't. This division covers the clergy quite as much as the laity."[50] In this politically volatile context ministers and lay people in racially mixed denominations increasingly found themselves faced with the challenge of political issues that in the end forced them to choose sides.[51] Some ministers in order to keep both sides of the political divide in their congregations happy, which by and large represented the ethnic divide, compromised, stayed silent, or procrastinated.[52] As we shall see, Bishop Alderson of Mashonaland was one example who appeared to avoid taking decisions in the Zimbabwean crisis so as not to cause offence to the colonial government.

By 1960, the ruling white population was largely convinced in its belief in racial superiority.[53] Its position was preserved and enhanced by various legislative acts designed to protect settler privileges and ensure the perpetuity of African subservience.[54] Attempts made to reform these acts had met resistance from the majority of settlers.[55] These legislative and philosophical developments polarized Zimbabweans, and fuelled the rise and consolidation of African nationalism.[56]

An African Perspective

"Black labour . . . created a white social group that enjoyed one of the highest standards of living in the world . . . Christianity . . . encouraged the African to accept his defeat and humiliation."[57] James Mutambirwa argued that Christian theology or teachings by missionaries were counter liberationist during the colonial era in Zimbabwe. Similar claims are made in another African context by Claire Robertson who added, "Thus the missionary

50. Alderson, "My Dear," 1 January 1966, NAZ, GEN-P/ALD.

51. Ibid.

52. Ibid.

53. Todd, "Challenge for Today."

54. Ibid.

55. Ibid.

56. Ibid.

57. Mutambirwa, "The Impact of Christianity," 69.

played a critical role in perpetuating the idea of "the white man's burden" as a justification for white conquest."[58]

According to Mutambirwa, Christian beliefs of "equality" and "brotherhood of man," identified by some as being formative for African nationalism, were discriminatory instead of liberating, since Christian equality was only espoused through these doctrines for fellow Christians and not non-believers who are not allowed into heaven and are ostracised socially by Christians. Mutambirwa argued that the ideas were already embedded in traditional Shona philosophy before the arrival of Christianity.[59]

Mutambirwa also pointed to the role of ATR in African nationalism. He noted how at the beginning of nationalist political rallies throughout much of the country in the 1960s, a prayer was usually offered to Nehanda—a female spirit medium who in the mid-1890s called upon the Shona to drive the settlers out of the country. Now in the 1960s she was implored to give religious sanction and success to the struggle. Mutambirwa questioned how, if Christianity was so influential, could Christians hold the Bible in one hand and implore Nehanda with the other when Nehanda was considered by the missionaries as "nothing more than an evil witch."[60] Lawrence Vambe also observed, "The church has failed because it has not been able to influence the heart and the mind of the European in that unfortunate country into accepting his fellow African citizen as full human being, a child of the same God that the white Rhodesian believes in and prays to in his churches."[61]

In contrast Ndabaningi Sithole sought to differentiate between the Christian philosophy and those who transmitted it, the missionaries. Sithole argued that the latter were largely a negative force in relations to the sociopolitical aspirations of Africans but Christianity was positive. Sithole believed that the African nationalists' worldview was significantly shaped by Christianity. He also proceeded to give credit to missionaries for their role in the education of most African nationalists and also for molding their worldview. Sithole himself being a beneficiary of both mission education and the Christian ideology wrote, "Practically all important African

58. Robertson, "Social Change," 314.

59. Gelfand, *Genuine Shona*, 12. Some of these moral and traditional philosophical tenets Mutambirwa alludes to are mentioned in the following works of Gelfand: *The Spiritual Beliefs of the Shona*; *African Background*; and *Growing Up in Shona Society*.

60. Mutambirwa, "Impact of Christianity," 77.

61. Vambe, *An Ill-fated People*, 234.

politicians went through the Christian Church School. The African politician may turn his nose up in derision, and twist his lips by way of deprecation, when he hears it said that the Christian Church laid secure political foundations for African nationalism . . . Christian and non-Christian Africans have reaped, in varying degrees, the blessings of the Christian faith."[62]

No easy consensus emerged in response to the changing political context, which descended into an armed struggle. Even within theologically homogenous communities, sharp debates were to emerge on fundamental issues such as who to pray for, and what to pray for, especially whilst the armed struggle was going on. The polarization of views largely matched the division between the African and white sections of the populace. Events at an interdenominational evangelism conference held in Bulawayo in the 1970s illustrate this well. The "Evangelism in Context" event was attended by Michael Cassidy, from South Africa, and Ralph Bell, one of Billy Graham's associates. Henry Mugabe, the principal of Gweru Baptist Seminary and a participant at the conference, recalled how a member from a white singing group from a Baptist church in Bulawayo had already caused offence by praying: "save our African brothers from witchcraft and superstition."[63] He then went on, "We pray for the destruction of the vicious and murderous terrorists."[64] Henry Mugabe reported that after this there was uproar, "I tell you people were crying, even older men[65] and one of the persons there who was a pastor said, "Look, I have a son who is fighting in the liberation struggle and one of my sons is a soldier fighting in the Smith regime, I want both of my sons and I want them alive." I think it was Phineas Dube[66] who said, 'How can you call me a brother and at the same time pray for the destruction of my son?'"[67] To Henry Mugabe, this represented a fundamental divide between the attitudes and understandings of African and white Christians. He continued, "I think then that the lines were clearly drawn and for many people it was like this, an oppressed people do not tell those

62. Sithole, *African Nationalism*, 57.

63. Henry J. Mugabe, Personal Interview, Gweru Baptist Seminary, Gweru, December 28, 2006.

64. Ibid.

65. The reference to older men also crying shows the seriousness of the situation, because culturally African men and elders do not easily break into tears in public as it is regarded as a sign of weakness.

66. Phineas Dube, a Baptist who runs a Christian leadership training program called the Green House, in the Mount Pleasant suburb of Harare.

67. Henry J. Mugabe.

in power what they think. You just keep it inside and that is how many of us related to many white people we interacted with, missionaries and so-forth. We could not say what we really, really, thought."[68]

Timothy Tavaziva, another leading figure in Zimbabwe's evangelical community witnessed the same event, and gave a similar account, varying only in some small details, recalling the prayer of a white pastor: "Lord! Destroy these terrorists." it typified the real polarization among Christians. Tavaziva went on:

> The black Christian would secretly say liberation is coming. Whites would go with the government and often Romans 13 was quoted saying, "let everyone be subject to governing authorities," it's there in the book, but others would argue saying that the government is there for the common good of the people but if it is oppressing the people what good is that . . .
>
> A heated debate broke as all the Africans there insisted that *vakomana*[69] should never be referred to as terrorists and if one prayed for the security of Smith's soldiers they also had to pray for the security of the freedom fighters. Most whites that were there pointed out *vakomana* were killing innocent people and fighting government authorities therefore they could be called terrorists. We insisted that they were involved in a just war therefore it was not right to call them terrorists.[70]

The incident suggests that two irreconcilable political philosophies represented by nationalists and the settler government had now largely come to represent either the collective expression of Africans on one side and settlers on the other,[71] and this division was reflected in the churches. In consequence, both Protestant and Roman Catholic churches' capacities to bring reconciliation were deeply affected, with members divided on ethnic lines, and neither racial side viewing attempts at political engagement as impartial.[72] It will be seen that even those who claimed to be neutral were distrusted by those on all sides who believed that a middle of the road

68. Ibid.

69. *Vakomana* is a Shona word that means boys. It was used both as an affectionate term and as code term for guerrillas in conversations between Africans that they did not want settlers or African children to comprehend.

70. Timothy Tavaziva, Personal Interview, Scripture Union Offices, Harare, January 16, 2007.

71. Todd, "For *Moto*," May 1968, NAZ, GEN-P/TOD.

72. Ibid.

stance was impossible;[73] no form of political comment was viewed as impartial.[74] There was a clash of paradigms and something had to give both in the church and the wider social context.

A Liberal Perspective

> My Lord,
>
> For years we have pleaded with our Governments to extend the franchise so that we might enjoy political stability in Central Africa. The United Federal Party governments, however, have chosen to play politics with the even more reactionary Dominion Party and have paid scant attention to the voice of eight million of voteless people. When protests have been made our Governments have used the pretext of maintaining law and order to stamp out criticism and dissent, and have not hesitated even to use their military might to do this. Government policies are now maintained by force of arms and are directly responsible for the present unrest.
>
> Ranged against the great mass of our people are 200, 000 whites with police, an army and air force: four percent of our population, in the name of civilisation, have ranged themselves against the great body of people of our country, refusing liberty denying justice and flouting the lessons of history . . .[75]

In 1960 a group of African nationalists and Todd set out their demands in a letter to the British Secretary of State for Commonwealth relations setting out the need for restitution of Africans' political rights. African nationalists during this period were increasingly becoming impatient and frustrated having continuously failed through non-violent means to have Africans' civil liberties fully granted by successive settler governments.

This frustration in the non-confrontational strategies of political change could be heard through the voices of nationalists such as George Nyandoro[76] who challenged fellow Africans who worked at the African

73. Henry J. Mugabe.

74. Banana, *The Church*, 53.

75. Enoch Dumbutshena, Paul Mushonga, Joshua Nkomo, and Garfield Todd were the signatories in a letter addressed to The Secretary of State for Commonwealth Relations after the riots within the Federation by Africans seeking political control in late fifties, 26 July 1960, NAZ, GEN-P/TOD. In Malawi these riots eventually set the country toward self rule after a period of a State of Emergency.

76. An Anglican and nationalist.

Daily News, "Nobody wants to go to jail. You all just want to sit here on your bottoms, theorizing about your rights."[77] These words reflected a gradual change of attitude among patriots that would fully take root in the later part of the sixties. This change of attitude was further reflected in the exodus of Africans from interracial societies such as Capricorn, nests for liberals, and this led to their speedy collapse in the early sixties.[78] Nyandoro as early as 1954 had negatively labeled interracial societies as "cooling chambers" for those that intended to vigorously seek political equality for Africans.[79] Some political liberals in the early sixties also took a back seat having come to the conclusion that, "What is the use of extending your hand of friendship to the Africans if you receive in turn a face-slap."[80] Hence a combination of these factors ultimately defined the destiny of the interracial societies and to a large extent the general social influence of liberals in Zimbabwe.

In 1964, Zimbabwe's liberal statesman Garfield Todd and the parliamentarian, Hardwicke Holderness[81] wrote to Sir Alec Douglas-Home warning of the deepening political tensions in the country:

> Successive governments, working on the assumption that political control must be kept in the hands of the white minority, have become involved in a sort of running war with the African leaders . . . African opinion has become consolidated behind African nationalist leaders now in detention without trial . . . White Rhodesians, having little contact with Africans except on a master and servant basis, have generally accepted the official view that Africans are not fundamentally interested in politics and that stability can be achieved by a show of African representation in parliament combined with a firm policy towards agitators comprising an excrescent minority.[82]

77. Shamuyarira, *Crisis in Rhodesia*, 19.

78. The word liberal was generally used in "Rhodesia" to refer, especially, to whites of liberal political leanings. Hence "liberal" in this work does not have any theological connotations. In a few cases the term radical will be used to differentiate those who held liberal attitudes toward the political establishment but who also supported African nationalists and the armed struggle.

79. Ibid., 22

80. Shamuyarira, *Crisis in Rhodesia*, 166.

81. Holderness was a member of parliament during Todd's premiership of the eighth parliament of "Southern Rhodesia" and the two were friends.

82. Todd and Holderness, letter to Sir Alec Douglas-Home, 15 May 1964, NAZ, GEN-P/TOD.

Guy Clutton-Brock, an Anglican, liberal sociologist and anti-colonial activist, observed how in the early 1950s, from school children to Chiefs, African people began to react strongly against racial discrimination.[83] Todd and other liberal statesmen in the country were convinced that the illiberal policies of the white minority had driven blacks into the hands of the African Nationalists. Anthony Verrier argued that Todd implemented retrogressive measures to nationalist aspirations during his days as premier.[84] Todd's government deported the Malawian political activist Dunduzu Chisiza back to his home country in 1957 for his activities as he gave impetus to both the Southern Rhodesia African Congress (SRANC) and the Nyasaland African Congress branches in Zimbabwe.[85]

In the late 1950s liberals had lost political control to settler radicals and that largely marked the end of their influence on the settler society and politics. In the 1960s the rise of African nationalism also saw a gradual splitting of ranks between liberals and most Africans as they joined nationalists. Hence their enviable position in the 1950s of being the middle ground and being able to significantly influence both settlers and Africans was gone. In a warring and polarized community their message of moderation and gradualism was no longer accepted by either side as most Zimbabweans had concluded that there was no middle ground to the political problems of their country. The liberal multiracial societies dwindled in the sixties and so did much of their influence except for those that were associated with the church.

A figure within the church that became unmistakably identifiable with the African cause was the former missionary turned settler, Todd. Todd had arrived in Zimbabwe from New Zealand as a missionary of the Church of Christ. He took charge of the Daya-Daya Mission and was later invited into joining politics by Godfrey Huggins, hence becoming the Zimbabwean premier of the Federal government in 1953.[86] He was viewed as the liberal representative par-excellence. Todd had called for the inclusion of African nurses and teachers on the electoral roll and wanted inter-racial marriages to be legalized among a few other changes.

Judith Todd, his daughter, believed that it was the issue of the legalization of interracial marriages advocated by her father during his

83. Clutton-Brock, "Thoughts on Zimbabwe."

84. Verrier, *Road to Zimbabwe*, 87.

85. Shamuyarira, *Crisis in Rhodesia*, 22.

86. Todd, *The Right to Say No*, 92.

premiership that led to his ultimate downfall.[87] Settlers viewed this change among a few others as radical and called for his resignation. He was forced to step down on 17 February 1958.[88] After his removal from office Todd joined the then newly formed Central Africa Party (CAP) in 1959 and was elected as its president.[89] Hancock described the CAP as follows, "The CAP was the last multi-racial party in white Rhodesia to be supported by respected African nationalists. It also constituted the last resting-place within white-led politics for those liberals who were making the transition to white radicalism."[90] On 2 September 1962 Todd officially retired from formal politics having failed, as he said, "to persuade the white community to revise its attitudes."[91] It was also during this period that the once popular liberal multi-racial societies began to drastically decline. Educated Africans broke ranks as a very few liberal whites who were radical, such as Todd, joined the nationalist movement upon his official retirement from settler party, and began to identify fully with the African nationalist cause.[92] Probably it was Todd's double humiliation by settlers, being forced to resign as premier in 1958 followed by an electoral defeat, as leader of the Central Africa Party in a Rhodesian Front landslide win in 1962, that forced him to identify strongly with the nationalist camp despite the movement having become radical.[93]

The nature of protest by a few members of the church's politically liberal community needs to be understood in light of the composition of the general leadership within mainline denominations. Mainline denominations until the later years of the sixties hardly had any Africans at the echelons of power. A few liberals filled in that gap to champion and to support the African cause. Hence they were derogatorily referred to as "kaffir lovers" by settlers.[94] A few liberals in the church at first had fulfilled the dual task of acting as bridges and encouraging continued dialogue between the polarized Africans and settlers. Liberals had the privilege, by virtue of ethnicity and association, of knowing the concerns of the settlers and on the

87. Chanaiwa, "The Premiership of Garfield," 92.

88. Ibid.

89. Hancock, *White Liberals*, 84.

90. Ibid., 85.

91. Ibid., 86.

92. Todd, "Southern Rhodesia" (Speech), 28 December 2006.

93. Megahey, *Humphrey Gibbs*, 69.

94. Todd, *Rhodesia*, 50.

other hand by virtue of association the aspirations of Africans especially the educated Africans.[95]

Hence they began to act as a vehicle of information between the two communities and at the same time transferring their own ideas and seeking to influence both groups towards what they believed to be the solution to Zimbabwe's problems.[96] They tried to influence the two groups to join them in what they believed to be a middle of the road solution.[97] At first, the liberal solution had been to ease the fears of the settlers of being swamped by African advancement that they feared would have eventually have them lose their economic and political privileges by promising gradualism in embracing Africans; and for the Africans they extended an invitation for the selected group that merited it into a Eurocentric future according to their own set standards.[98]

Their message was at first accepted by most Africans as well as by a few settlers.[99] When it later became obvious especially after losing in the 1962 elections to the Rhodesian Front that the majority of settlers were not willing even to accept moderate integration policies advocated by liberals, most Africans parted ways with liberalism and adopted the nationalists' demands for immediate and unqualified integration. This left most liberals feeling sidelined and they stepped back as advocates for change.[100] Only a few, mainly within the church, continued advocating change, but now solidly behind the nationalists in their rhetoric. These began to give, especially from the mid-sixties, their support to the nationalist camp as resource persons. Although liberals were happy to offer material support, and to be used as resource persons, there is no evidence yet to light of any white liberal joining the guerrilla forces when the armed struggle commenced in the mid-sixties.[101] This led to their being viewed as fair-weather partners by nationalists. The nationalists, however, seemed grateful for the other forms of help they got from and through liberals could not completely forsake them.[102]

95. Megahey, *Humphrey Gibbs*, 45.
96. Ibid.
97. Ibid.
98. Shamuyarira, *Crisis in Rhodesia*, 22.
99. Megahey, *Humphrey Gibbs*, 54.
100. Shamuyarira, *Crisis in Rhodesia*, 175.
101. Megahey, *Humphrey Gibbs*, 45.
102. Ibid.

As previously discussed Todd was accused of having not done much during his premiership to repeal unjust legislation,[103] and in 1962 he acknowledged to some degree some of this criticism.[104] His errors had been more of omission than commission. In his premiership years Todd had been largely guided by the white liberal ideology that shunned revolutionaries in preference to political moderates and gradualism or "evolutionaries," hence the deportation of Chisiza who fell into the revolutionary category. Contrary to Verrier's claim that Todd was "a complete hindrance" to the Africans' struggle for political rights it was his advocacy for Africans' political rights, though arguably moderate, that eventually led to his removal from office.[105]

At the end of his premiership, proving how popular he was among many Africans, an African musician composed in his honor a song mourning his removal from office. Its lyrics were basic but made the point, "*Hamba Kahle Mudhala*[106] (Go well old man). We will miss you."[107] The song proved he was popular among Africans; it became a best seller in Zimbabwe. Nathan Shamuyarira—*The African Daily News* editor form 1956 to 1963, a nationalist and Methodist layman—further noted that Todd always kept in contact with educated Africans and these were the chief architects for nationalism in Zimbabwe and led the call for restitution of Africans' political rights.[108] During this period Todd was fully identifying with Zimbabwe's African nationalist movement and also like Sithole acknowledged the significant role played by the church in sub-Saharan Africa and Zimbabwe specifically in nationalist politics: "The church in Africa started the great movement towards freedom which has already broken the bonds of serfdom for twentyfive [sic] nations south of the Sahara."[109] Todd continued, "The great issue which is at stake in our land is the freedom and rights of the individual. Until these are established, until they are respected by the majority and undergirded by our laws, . . . the very existence of every other association of free men, remains in jeopardy."[110] Above all, in contrast to Verrier's analysis, the continued invitation of Todd by Africans as the main

103. Verrier, *Road to Zimbabwe*, 87.

104. Todd, "Southern Rhodesia" (speech), 20 October 1962, NAZ, GEN-P/TOD.

105. Verrier, *Road to Zimbabwe*, 87.

106. Ndebele language.

107. Shamuyarira, *Crisis in Rhodesia*, 25.

108. Ibid., 23.

109. Todd, "R.A.T.U. Meeting" (Speech), 1 September 1962, NAZ, GEN-P/TOD.

110. Ibid.

speaker at functions and events in support of the nationalist struggle such as the African ministers' fraternal;[111] and the RATU, in place of Nkomo and other senior nationalists in prison,[112] serves to prove that Africans regarded Todd as sympathetic if not a champion of their political rights. After one such visit to the African ministers' fraternal Todd wrote, "I enjoyed the visit to Highfield[113] but what has made me particularly happy since seeing you is the fact that the churches have made this appeal to political leaders. They have highlighted the danger of the country and to the outside world this is of especially great significance. The next year or two are not going to be easy but I do hope that the Christian church, in all its branches, will take an increasingly active part in the life of the country."[114]

The identification of Todd and a few other whites that were being now identified as radicals with the uncompromising call for the restitution of Africans' political rights began to gather momentum. In May 1964, Holderness and Todd advocated a new constitution and franchise which they believed was essential for political stability in Zimbabwe; and further advocated the need for negotiation and agreement between the "two power blocs" into which the population was divided—the whites, on the one hand, with a small section of Africans still prepared to go along with them, and the Africans on the other with their handful of white liberal supporters.[115]

They contended that the question of the future had now become one for the white population, rather than the African one: "Wisdom should lead white men to seek a genuine, honest and therefore non-racial plan for the future, but let us remember that "the preservation of a country's system of government must depend on the acquiescence, if not the consent, of the governed." It would be safer to seek the consent."[116] This letter, written during the cessation of the Federation, sought to turn the tide of British support towards Africans. When Britain insisted, presumably as having responsibility over the future of the colony,[117] that settlers cede political

111. Todd, A letter to Rev. Herbert Chikomo, 27 August 1962, NAZ, MS 1082/1/14.

112. Todd, "R.A.T.U. Meeting" (Speech), 1 September 1962, NAZ, GEN-P/TOD.

113. Highfield was and is still a predominantly African suburb. By then it was a haven of nationalist politics in Salisbury.

114. Todd, A letter to Rev. Herbert Chikomo, 27 August 1962, NAZ, MS 1082/1/14.

115. Todd and Holderness, letter addressed to Sir Alec Douglas-Home, 15 May 1964, NAZ, GEN-P/TOD.

116. Ibid.

117. Ibid.

power it led to a political stalemate. To Todd and Holderness, the policy of token African political representation would not work, when whites in Zimbabwe only related to Africans on the basis of a "master and servant" relationship.[118] The denial of Africans' political rights was envisaged by Todd as a ticking time bomb which was waiting to explode, from the sporadic acts of sabotage in the early 60s as a result of frustration into a hot confrontation or hot war if Africans' political rights were not granted or restored in Zimbabwe.[119] By the late 1960s, as we shall explore in the coming chapters, "patience" ran-out. Many Africans began to seriously consider the armed struggle and entertained radical ideas that they envisioned as being able to transform the status quo.

118. Ibid.

119. Todd, "R.A.T.U. Meeting" (Speech), 1 September 1962, NAZ, GEN-P/TOD.

4

Growing Nationalist Frustration

FRUSTRATION WITH A LACK of more overt endorsement for nationalist support from churches began to grow in the 1960s, despite the commitment of a few leading liberals to the cause. In 1962 the Anglican priest, Rev. L. Machiha, highlighted these concerns: "People are measuring Christianity with the standards of this world. They say Christianity has failed to make brotherhood of men. Going to church is considered by some as going to be told to close your eyes, ears and mouth.[1] The church hinders all aspirations of the masses of people who want freedom."[2] With a predominantly white church leadership the churches began to be viewed as representing settler interests.[3] Critics of the churches were quick to misrepresent it as a white institution that any self-respecting African needed to avoid.[4] Kenneth Skelton, an Anglican minister, to a similar effect observed, "We who belong to a Church which proclaims its Catholicity, and yet is almost entirely officered and led by Europeans, have we any idea how difficult it is for Africans to be loyal to this Church—which in spite of all its protestations must inevitably seem to justify the title of a 'white Church'?"[5]

1. An expression meaning puppet.

2. "Why Educated Africans are Leaving the Church in Rhodesia," *The Link*, August 1962.

3. Mutasa, *Black Behind Bars*, 106.

4. Linden, *Catholic Church*, 69.

5. Skelton, "They shall . . . persecute you. Luke 21:12" (sermon), 19 April 1964, NAZ, GEN-P/SKE.

For the older guard of missionaries the rise of nationalism and its turning to radicalism had reawakened thoughts of the first Chimurenga[6] when the church had been viewed as a settler institution and had been attacked, bringing its first martyrs both white and black.[7]

To Brand, the old guard were products of a generation raised with an ideology of African inferiority and white superiority, and they could not envisage a "Southern Rhodesia" ruled by Africans.[8] Mutasa believed that the church leadership were also swayed by their need for socio-economic security and staying within their comfort zone despite the suffering of the majority of church members who were Africans,[9] preferring to side with the white settler community rather than upset the system by offering political protest.[10] Highlighting such problems with the Anglican Church, Mutasa wrote, "It is hypocritical to claim to be a Christian if the criminality of the Rhodesian way of life is overlooked. Black and white Christians should not kneel together before an altar receiving Holy Communion, pretending to be equal children of God, and come out of the church and immediately accept separate development as way of life."[11] White Christians in Zimbabwe and the church leadership benefitted from the privileges and protection offered by the state to whites who found it difficult to comprehend the resentment of Africans towards the political system in which they were both comfortable and beneficiaries.[12]

Some church leaders in the late fifties and early sixties claimed that Africans were not yet ready to rule and that the Zimbabwean state was too sophisticated for Africans to rule. Bishop Donal Lamont who was later to be a leading voice of protest against the white settler government among the Roman Catholic clergy wrote in 1959 that Africans were "to recognise in realistic humility, that however high his thoughts may aspire to complete independence, he is as yet equipped neither academically, nor technically, nor economically to assume complete control over . . . a highly complex and industrialized country."[13] Nationalists believed that this attitude by

6. Shamuyarira, *Crisis in Rhodesia*, 227.

7. Linden, *Catholic Church*, 60.

8. Brand, "Missionaries and Nationalists," 80.

9. Mutasa, *Black Behind Bars*, 106.

10. Ibid., 122ff.

11. Ibid., 122.

12. Brand, "Missionaries and Nationalists," 73.

13. Quoted in Scholz, "Catholic Church," 200.

the church leadership to Africans resonated of settler ideology,[14] and that instead their capacity to rule the country was warranted. There were about 17 000 Africans regarded as qualified to vote even by the stringent demands of the settler government's 1962 electoral system;[15] and some within this number were more educated than Members of Parliament of the settler governments.[16] Many other Africans with college and university education were not qualified to vote.[17]

Nationalists did not just feel patronized by this attitude but they also believed the church leadership like the settler political establishment was a stumbling block to a fair or just African participation in Zimbabwe's political life[18] Shamuyarira observed, "Nine out of ten nationalist leaders have been educated at mission schools, and owe a great deal to missionaries; yet nearly all would say today that they mistrust the church as a whole."[19]

Muzorewa believed that although the scriptural hermeneutics of the churches were at times open to question, Christianity was definitely influential on African nationalism in Zimbabwe: "One day I sat with a young man who said, 'We should destroy the Bible and find some Africans who can write our own Bible.'[20] He thought that the Bible had been written by people like the Prime Minister of Rhodesia, Ian Smith. The fact that so many whites in Rhodesia claimed to be Christians (although few attended churches) and the vast majority, including some missionaries, supported white minority rule, made my witness to African students extremely difficult."[21] Shamuyarira believed that the churches were tarnished by being white-led, like the government: "In African eyes the two institutions became in many respects indistinguishable. They have too many common features: racial discrimination, European domination and a despising of the African people."[22]

14. Ibid., 200.

15. Shamuyarira, *Crisis in Rhodesia,* 175.

16. Ibid., 169.

17. Alderson, "In the Event of UDI," *Rhodesia Herald*, 29 October 1965.

18. Mutasa, *Black Behind Bars*, 123.

19. Shamuyarira, *Crisis in Rhodesia*, 141.

20. Banana, "The Case of a New Bible," 17ff., was proposed almost two decades from the time the incident recorded here occurred; perhaps the origins of this thesis should not be attributed to Banana

21. Muzorewa, *Rise and Walk*, 62.

22. Shamuyarira, *Crisis in Rhodesia*, 143.

The greatest struggle for the church was to learn to identify itself with the people and to find the required humility to be a true friend.[23] Sithole also observed that "missionaries, working in a colonial atmosphere, also adopted a colonial attitude towards the African and stood between the latter and his big dream of independence."[24] Cecil Alderson recognized that this lack of understanding was fuelled by the fact that social relations between the majority of the church leadership and their African flock were usually at an artificial level.[25] So too did Garfield Todd, who argued that except for a few liberal missionaries who worked alongside the educated Africans, contact between whites in general and Africans was limited,[26] usually being during Sunday services and for a few hours. The Methodist Rea also believed that weekly congregational worship services could not suffice to build an interracial community in Zimbabwe.[27] At mission stations, where there was usually more contact between Africans and whites, missionaries were the bosses and Africans the servants,[28] with limited social interaction at an equal level between the two groups. Rea observed that on Sundays missionaries at most mission stations preferred to have their own services, which they attributed to the language barrier.[29] These limited relationships meant that most whites did not know what Africans really thought about the political crisis in Zimbabwe.[30] Bishop Alderson recognized this: "What Africans are thinking about it all [the political situation in Rhodesia] is nearly impossible for a white man really to know. Our priests get on with their jobs as best as they may."[31]

Although a few missionaries like Alderson honestly admitted this, most other church leaders believed that they knew what Africans thought,[32] and claimed that nationalists did not represent African opinion and that

23. Ibid. Cripps and White were noted for their advocacy for African rights within a missionary and European political culture that was apathetic to protecting African rights in early 1900s.

24. Sithole, *African Nationalism*, 57.

25. Alderson, "My Dear," 1 January 1966, NAZ, GEN-P/ALD

26. Todd and Holderness, letter to Sir Douglas-Home, 15 May 1964.

27. Rea, "The Need for a United Church," 87.

28. Brand, "Missionaries and Nationalists," 72.

29. Rea, "The Need for a United Church," 87.

30. Linden, *Catholic Church*, 55.

31. Alderson, "Letter to British friends," NAZ, GEN-P/ALD.

32. Linden, *Catholic Church*, 56.

the general African populace was content.[33] Nationalists were only thought to represent the African elite, and not the interests of the majority.[34]

When nationalists questioned the impartiality of the "church," their focus was upon the church leadership, which had remained silent when Africans suffered and continued to suffer various forms of abuse from the settler government.[35] Nationalists believed that the church should not only be a peace broker, but an advocate for those who suffered injustice.[36] Suspicions grew as they failed to condemn the settler government for its policies and abuse of Africans.[37] As early as 1960 a letter addressed to missionaries by the National Democratic Party (NDP) had expressed and highlighted these concerns: "We have noticed your acquiescence, for more than 70 years in a system which has reduced us to nothing more than hewers of wood and drawers of water. We have seen you supporting evil practices."[38]

Nationalists came to declare that instead of responding to their moral obligation to support their cause, the long-standing history of cooperation between the missionary-led church and the settler government had blinded the church leadership to this issue of social justice.[39]

Signs of growing frustration by 1961 with this lack of support were becoming apparent. Doubt and questioning turned to severe criticism of the missionary-founded churches,[40] seen as the guardians of teachings on justice and equality, for not being prepared to speak out against injustice.[41] Mutasa was convinced that the churches only encouraged passivity and compliance amongst its leaders: "The Church may allow white politicians to meddle in its religion but it forbids black political and religious leaders to take part in a religious act. Black people in the Anglican Church are only made suffragan bishops when they have no obvious political aspirations and agree to be stationed at centres which keep them out of sight."[42] Mutasa believed that a time for action had come: "One cannot see one's friends

33. Ibid.
34. Ibid., 60.
35. Mutasa, *Black Behind Bars*, 122.
36. Ibid.
37. Banana, *Church and Struggle*, 83.
38. Quoted in Brand, "Missionaries and Nationalists," 75.
39. Ibid.
40. Ibid.
41. "Letter to the Editor," *Bantu Mirror*, 15 July 1961.
42. Mutasa, *Black Behind Bars*, 123–24.

suffering under the political evils of the illegal regime and stand aside, claiming that one's duty as a Christian is not to help but to look on. That kind of attitude is both cowardly and unchristian."[43] The focus of criticism was directed at the white Christian leadership, rather than at the content of the bible as proclaimed by Joshua Nkomo, "The Christian philosophy is good, but the men preaching it are bad."[44] The complacency of church leaders to protest and the socio-economic gulf between church leaders and their people was strongly attacked by Mutasa, "Do some churches not lay treasure in Rhodesia where thieves steal black people's land, side by side with starving and unclothed people? And recently how many Christian chaplains have been sent to the illegal army and prisons? Have any been sent to pray for freedom fighters?"[45]

During this period some educated Africans especially in the cities, felt the need to prove that they were not subservient to whites, and began to leave the churches.[46] Hostility was directed towards selected institutions within the church that were openly supporting the settler government such as the Anglican and the Dutch Reformed Church.[47] African Christians who were members of such institutions were warned about attending Sunday services and missionaries from such denominations were sent threatening letters.[48] If they were not sure where a particular missionary's allegiance lay they corresponded with him requiring him to clarify his political allegiance.[49] Furthermore, African Christians were scorned as puppets. They were viewed as puppets of the church leadership that had sold its soul to the government, which nationalists viewed as evil.[50]

Others went further. In 1962 nationalist activists vented their anger at political repression by the settler government by burning and damaging 10 churches and 18 mission related properties.[51] Persuasion and threats were employed to gain support from the churches.[52] Although most Africans

43. Ibid.

44. Quoted in Shamuyarira, *Crisis in Rhodesia*, 141.

45. Mutasa, *Black Behind Bars*, 106.

46. Linden, *Catholic Church*, 69.

47. Bhebhe, "African Nationalists," 108.

48. Brand, "Missionaries and Nationalists," 75.

49. Ibid.

50. "Church in Rhodesia," *The Link*, August 1962.

51. Bhebhe, *"The Nationalist Struggle,"* 108.

52. "Letter to the Editor," *Bantu Mirror*, 22 July 1961.

were sympathetic to the cause of nationalism, those who were reluctant openly to join the nationalist camp began to face intimidation, a foretaste of the way nationalist parties were later to treat their opponents. Bhebhe observed that by 1961, because of "NDP inspired outbreaks of violence, civil disobedience, strikes and intimidation of collaborators of the white regime . . . it was becoming apparent that the NDP could cause so much chaos as to prevent the implementation of the new constitution. Moreover, the chiefs were so frightened for their own personal safety, that they were urging the Government to ban the NDP."[53] Although nationalists during this period tried to differentiate attacks on missionaries, Christians and Christian institutions from attacks on the Christian religion, persuasion and threats failed to solicit widespread support for nationalists from white church leaders.[54] Indeed, the policy, borne of frustration, put an end to immediate prospects of gaining support from most of the church leadership and missionary community, and served to widen the gap between them and this influential section of the community.[55] Missionaries felt their work was being severely undermined and were personally under attack from a hostile philosophy.[56]

On the other hand, they had been reluctant to embrace nationalism because many in the Zimbabwean Christian leadership had come to believe that nationalism was simply Communism in disguise and they believed they were protecting the church from the evil of an atheist philosophy, which would prevail if nationalists seized power.[57] The Roman Catholic Bishops of South Africa claimed that the Roman Catholic Church was "the strongest bulwark against anarchy, indifferentism and communism. It is a pity that her most vital influence is being denied."[58]

To Linden, "Many a bush missionary saw himself as an outpost of the non-communist world struggling against unseen enemies, a silent soldier in the Cold War."[59] This was a further reason why most in the white settler

53. Bhebhe, "*The Nationalist Struggle*," 101.

54. Ibid.

55 Linden, *Catholic Church and Struggle*, 63.

56. Brand, "*Missionaries and Nationalists*," 74.

57. Linden, *Catholic Church and Struggle*, 48–49.

58. "The Role of the Church and the Rhodesia Society," *Rhodesia Herald*, 8 January 1959.

59. Linden, *Catholic Church and Struggle*, 49.

constituent of the churches concluded that Christianity and nationalism were incompatible.[60]

As a result of a combination of these factors only a few individuals with the Christian leadership remained convinced in the early 1960s that it was the duty of the church to speak on behalf of the oppressed alongside nationalists. These few individuals from the political liberal camp were to become one of the greatest contributions the Zimbabwean church would offer to the nation at its political crossroads. However, there were other factors that hindered the churches from significant political engagement.

The Problem of "Neutrality"

In order to retain some semblance of unity and avoid further polarizing the church many church leaders thought it prudent to take a position that became popularly referred to as that of "neutrality."[61] A member of the Dutch Reformed Church (DRC) which officially subscribed to the position of neutrality commented, "Church [DRC] policy was that you do not get involved in politics whether on the side of the government or the boys[62]. It was not an issue that you supported the white government or not. You simply had not to get involved, you had to be neutral. But on the ground, people in their individual capacities as Christians were actively supporting whoever they wanted."[63]

To some, a doctrine of political neutrality, of non-partisanship in a political conflict, could be seen as truly prophetic.[64] Gwemende observed that there was a strong tradition of this position within the history of the DRC in Zimbabwe, which predated even the 1948 apartheid government in South Africa. The missionary founder[65] of the DRC during the Chimurenga wars in the 1890s was able to continue staying at Morgenster mission by saying "I am not taking sides," until he was forcibly removed by the settler soldiers who warned him "*munovurawa kuno*."[66] He refused to

60. Ibid.

61. Maxwell, "Christianity and the War," 63.

62. Guerrillas.

63. Kudakwashe Gwemende, Personal Interview, Scripture Union, Harare, January 11, 2007.

64. Maxwell, "Christianity and the War," 62ff.

65. A. A. Louw founded the mission in 1891.

66. Shona for: you will get killed here, a number of whites, missionaries included, and Africans that assisted them were killed during the first Chimurenga.

sell chief Mugabe[67] guns and to allow soldiers to come to the villagers. Gwemende observed, "He was able to stay with blacks, negotiate with whites and sometimes negotiate with whites on behalf of blacks. In the years to come this position served missionaries well, they hardly condemned political injustice saying they were neutral. Neutrality served them well because they could continue operating indifferent to the situation around them and that is why they couldn't condemn apartheid."[68]

In the 1960s and 1970s neither supporters of the two sides of Zimbabwe's political divide believed that the position of neutrality was a genuine one. David Maxwell has argued that the inability by nationalist guerrillas to believe anyone, even the Elim Pentecostal Mission, could be truly neutral led to the murder of nine Elim missionaries and their four children.[69] Those that supported the African nationalist cause believed that the church leadership's general silence on political matters was neither neutral nor amoral. Robert Mugabe in the late 1970s commented to Sister Janice McLaughlin, "The missionary should not view himself as the man in the middle or he will be mistaken to be on the side of the oppressor."[70]

To many others neutrality meant a failure to make a difficult moral choice as to which side to support, and to need-fully speak out in a prophetic way against injustice, oppression, or physical abuse.[71] It implied that the churches had no right or need to comment on wider social or political matters. In general, it discouraged Christians from getting involved in issues of a political nature.[72] It raises questions over whether it was possible to have no view at all about the rights and wrongs of the Zimbabwean conflict. It would only be sustainable if the issue had no moral implications, or if both sides were equally right or equally wrong. African nationalists argued that the doctrine of neutrality in the 1960s played into the hands of the settler government as the oppressing group, leaving it not challenged or confronted by a united church as it implemented its sociopolitical policies no matter how unjust.[73] The Methodist bishop Ralph Dodge in a let-

67. Chief Mugabe, not related to Robert Mugabe, had contacted Louw seeking guns to arm his people for protection and hunting.

68. Kudakwashe Gwemende.

69. Maxwell, "Christianity and the War," 63.

70. Quoted in McLaughlin, *On the Frontline*, 33.

71. McLaughlin, *On the Frontline*, 33.

72. "Called to Serve," *The Link*, August 1962.

73. Shamuyarira, *Crisis in Rhodesia*, 143ff.

ter to Joshua Nkomo and Kenneth Kaunda who later became the Zambia President commented, "It should be clearly understood that the practise of non-violence often may not accomplish the desired purpose in this world of ours. It may mean that a ruthless enemy will take advantage of the spirit of love on the part of those who practise non-violence and cause harm to befall them."[74]

When the settler government was contemplating UDI, Dodge warned that such a move would be tantamount to rebellion against Britain. He threatened that he would advise members of his denomination not to take orders from such a government.[75] On the other hand, missionaries who thought that they were in the middle ground were perceived to be in acquiescence with the political authorities. By 1966 some Catholic Bishops were moving from their 1960 position of outright rejection of nationalism, and coming to recognize the complexity of the situation, a position similar to that reached by a few Anglican priests: "It comes as no surprise to us that many [Africans] are saying, 'So this is Christian Civilisation! This is what Christianity is' the preservation of privilege for the few and well-to-do, and the neglect of many who have nothing. It seems as if we have been deceived by the exponents of Christianity, the missionaries. These have come here only to prepare the way for the racist state where we shall remain permanently the hewers of wood and drawers of water."[76]

What the churches needed in this divided community was to be impartial not neutral, and not to be seen as simply wanting to perpetuate settler interests.[77] According to Canaan Banana, they needed to wrestle with the moral dilemmas in the Zimbabwean conflict, and having judged impartially who was in the right and who was in the wrong to make a stand on behalf of what was or who was right.[78]

A Remnant of Liberal Protestors

The words and actions of some white Christian leaders who sought to publicly voice the grievances of Africans challenges the view that the

74. Dodge, "Top Secret," 10 June 1963.

75. Shamuyarira, *Crisis in Rhodesia*, 142.

76. Ibid.

77. Hugh,"Luke 23:34; Father, Forgive them" (sermon), 27 February 1966, NAZ, GEN-P/SKE.

78. Banana, *Church and Struggle*, 318.

churches were an outright barrier to nationalism.[79] These white Christians were largely missionaries from a liberal political background. Any form of political protest was viewed with great suspicion and hostility, yet some resolutely believed that the churches in Zimbabwe were to be agents of reconciliation, and that they should actively work for the transformation of social structures.[80]

To some of them, the church's reconciliatory role was viewed as limited to dialogue and peace initiatives.[81] Any attempt to force the government to change its policy by any means other than non-confrontational words and prayer was regarded as unbiblical.

Those that viewed the church's role in Zimbabwe as that of promoting reconciliation argued for the need of continuous dialogue by the church on behalf of the African people. The Anglican bishop Cecil Alderson proclaimed, "[W]e must be true with our dealings, with all of our fellow-citizens . . . 'where there is discord let me sow peace.'"[82] Confrontation with political authorities was not viewed by this group as an option that Christians could pursue. Their belief that the prophetic task of the church was solely for reconciliation made them stand aloof or castigate the few that believed that Christians could be political activists.[83]

These tensions were highlighted in the Southern Rhodesia Christian Conferences.[84] The Christian conference had been formed in 1903[85] and was primarily a conference for missionaries held once in every two years.[86] On 22 August 1962 some members of the Southern Rhodesia Christian Conference suggested the forming of a separate council that would, among some of its duties, give a Christian voice on various sociopolitical issues.[87] This suggestion was given as a solution to tensions that had arisen as result of some of its members calling for the need of the conference to

79. Mutambirwa, *"Impact of Christianity,"* 69.

80. Muzorewa, *Rise and Walk,* 56.

81. Ibid.

82. Ibid.

83. Ibid.

84. The Christian Conference was an event where missionaries in Zimbabwe gathered and generally discussed and prayed for various matters concerning mission work in that country.

85. Falk, *Growth of the Church,* 196.

86. Muzorewa, *Rise and Walk,* 58.

87. Watyoka, 25 *Years,* 2.

address political matters as part of its mandate.[88] This threatened the unity of the Conference, as some believed that it was "dragging the church into politics,"[89] suggesting a theological dualism that compartmentalized issues into spiritual and temporal. The majority of the leaders and members of the largest denominations, Anglicanism and Roman Catholicism, still saw that political matters belonged to the government and religious matters to the church. Muzorewa observed, "It was (in 1963) disturbing to hear the conservative reaction of many church leaders . . . that a true Christian should not be involved in politics, nor be active in the national struggle."[90]

The disputes in the Christian Conference deepened, amidst initiatives from the Bulawayo and Salisbury African ministers' fraternal according to Muzorewa who, "longed for an inter-church body that could speak . . . on national issues as they arose,"[91] and had urged for a formation of a council that could deal with such matters. The eventual result was the formation of the Southern Rhodesia Christian Council and its formal launch on 29 July 1964. Article (i) of its first constitution read, "The Council shall participate in forming an enlightened public opinion on all issues affecting the people in the territory. It shall serve as the representative body which can, after study and investigation, express the mind of the Christian community on issues. The actions and pronouncements of the Council shall not commit any of the denominations or other agencies represented on it to any policy or line of action, or financial responsibility without the consent of their executive authorities."[92] The Christian council was therefore open to "actions," as well as pronouncements. The few liberals who had been willing to speak out against the resistance of the government to reconciliatory actions by the church were members of this body.[93] Not all members agreed with this position, believing that nonviolent action was the only appropriate prophetic stance for the church, and that there was no strong theological justification for use of violence as a means for social transformation. Those who called for action argued that non-violence had failed to dissuade the settler governments, especially after Smith's take over, from increased political repression against Africans.[94]

88. Ibid.

89. Ibid.

90. Muzorewa, *Rise up and Walk,* 59.

91. Ibid., 58–59.

92. Christian Council of Southern Rhodesia, "Constitution," NAZ, GEN-P/WOR.

93. Muzorewa, *Rise and Walk,* 58ff.

94. Watyoka, *25 Years,* 11.

Difficulties in Organizing Non-Violent Protest

As the mid-sixties dawned some within the white church leadership and a few Africans that were beginning to infiltrate into the Zimbabwean mainline churches' leadership ranks had come to believe that confrontation with the government was necessary, but that confrontation with the political authorities should be limited to non-violent means. Demonstrations against the government were acceptable but violent forms of attack were viewed as out of bounds for Christians. This was the position of many Christians within the Southern Rhodesia Christian Council at its formation.[95] Others were increasingly convinced that rhetoric and non-violent action had failed to bring about justice, and that violence could be adopted as a legitimate means to bring about social transformation by Christians in Zimbabwe, now all other possibilities had been tried and failed.[96] Some debated whether the churches in Zimbabwe had ever tenaciously tried to organize non-violent protest in a formidable way, and whether Skelton's ideas of non-compliance expressed as the settler government in 1964 contemplated a Unilateral Declaration of Independence (UDI) might work: "The idea . . . is so far from the truth as to be laughable if it were not so tragic. It might quite well be that if such a situation rose . . . the church might have to advise its people that they were under no obligation to carry out the commands of a government which had committed such an act; and what an agonizing position for this would be for us all."[97]

Garfield Todd also contemplated along similar lines, "If Africans stopped work then Rhodesia would stop also."[98] If the church or the African community had taken advantage of its numerical dominance in some form of passive protest they could have posed a formidable threat to the settler government since Africans outnumbered settlers at a ratio of 95% to 5%.[99] The American Civil Rights Movement offered a powerful contemporary model, and numerically Africans and the church in Zimbabwe were at a

95. Herbert Chikomo, Personal Interview, City Presbyterian Church, Harare, January 21, 2007.

96. Shamuyarira, *Crisis in Rhodesia*, 238.

97. Rev. Skelton, "They Shall . . . Persecute You, Luke 21:12" (sermon), 19 April 1964, NAZ, GEN-P/SKE.

98. Todd, "No Sudden Death," 30 December 1971.

99. Ibid.

more advantageous position than the African-Americans that were considerably fewer although well organized in their protests.[100]

The arrest of Rosa Parks on 1 December 1955 in Montgomery after having refused to give over her seat in the "black" section of the bus to a "white" male passenger ignited a new momentum in the civil rights struggle with Dr. Martin Luther King Jr. at the center.[101] The incident led to a campaign of bus boycotts and boycotts of other "white" owned businesses that lasted for thirteen months, and which ended in integration in Montgomery buses. Of this incident Dr. King Jr. commented, "Montgomery marked the psychological turning point for the American negro in his struggle against segregation."[102] Further protests followed in the rest of the southern part of the USA.[103]

Both were contexts of intimidation, so this was not an obvious reason why the Zimbabwean churches failed to organize in a similar way, although with more than twenty nationalists having been sentenced to hang under the Hanging Bill for minor political activities[104] perhaps not many Christians and their leaders had the courage to overtly protest and face a similar destiny.[105] To a considerable extant this proved Nyandoro's general observation to be correct that, "Nobody want[ed] to go to jail.,"[106] and that they seemed content just "to . . . sit . . . theorizing about [their] rights." with no action.

Shamuyarira suggested that there was a lack of "sympathetic conscience that needed to be pricked" and hence respond favorably in case of a non-violent demonstration.[107] He believed this was what made the American Civil Rights Movement successful, since they had political authorities in Washington sympathetic to their cause. He further argued that the same could be said in case of Mahatma Gandhi's India. Shamuyarira believed that non-violent protest carried the day in India in the mid-forties because political authorities in Britain were sympathetic to their cause.[108]

100. Cone, *Martin & America*, 22.

101. Slack, *Martin Luther King*, 111.

102. Carson, *Autobiography of Martin*, 13.

103. Fitts, *A History of Black Baptists*, 289.

104. Shamuyarira, *Crisis in Rhodesia*, 238.

105. Ibid.

106. George Nyandoro quoted in Shamuyarira, *Crisis in Rhodesia*, 19.

107. Ibid.

108. Ibid.

Perhaps self-sacrifice and a continued determination in face of intimidation and government brutality would have created sympathetic consciences elsewhere if nationalists or the church had organized similar demonstrations earlier, but it should be noted that demonstrations of that nature were contemplated but they were never seriously pursued.[109] "Kneel in" protests were organized, targeting denominations with an interracial membership, but practicing segregation. These flopped as only a few Africans bothered to join, so did attempts to boycott beer-halls, whose sole licensee in the urban areas was the government. Some nationalists had to end up intimidating and getting into skirmishes with fellow Africans over attending beer-halls.[110] These seem to have been some of the nationalists' limited efforts in the line of Gandhi and Luther King.

In the early 1960s, the Zimbabwean church leadership did not take advantage of their numerical size to bring about political change. But the numbers of African voices making clear protest were still few, despite a positive model being witnessed at this particular historical juncture in the African-American civil rights movement.[111] There was also a lack of organization and unity at a national level amongst the churches.[112] Yet, about half of the African populace were already estimated to be professing Christians in the early sixties and with the majority of the non-believing African populace ready to support initiatives that challenged settler political control, and the liberal section of the white community willing to support such initiatives, the church's failure to be a decisive voice or force seems notable.

The failure to formulate a clear non-violence protest stance may have represented a crucial failure of moral resoluteness. It may have pushed others to conclude that the only course that would produce results was that of committing acts of violence. Shamuyarira believed that, "The second course for a frustrated nationalist movement would be sustained terrorism. Although many African leaders do not like this desperate course, they are being forced by events to take it."[113] Some later began to define the nationalist war as justified under the theological position of waging a "just war."[114] Mutasa wrote, "It is generally regarded as more justified when a people uses

109. Ibid.

110. Shamuyarira, *Crisis in Rhodesia*, 189.

111. Carson, *Martin Luther King*, 13ff.

112. Rea, "Need for a unified Church," 87.

113. Shamuyarira, *Crisis in Rhodesia*, 238.

114. Mutasa, *Black Behind Bars*, 99.

it (violence) to defend their integrity, rather than to destroy that of others. We regard the force used by the rebel regime as a great evil and that used by the freedom fighters as defence of their rights."[115] Mutasa quoted seven conditions required to make a war "just" before concluding: "Our struggle for human dignity in our country can, and must be, seen by the rest of the world population as a struggle for human dignity in the world at large. This alone is a good cause for the struggle."[116] Because violence was continually applied by the settler government against Africans and other political prisoners that justified the need to take a radical stand against the settler government.[117]

ATR, Christianity and Nationalism

African nationalism was open to embrace African religious tenets, and appeared to promote syncretism, an approach believed by some to be inimical to Christianity.[118] The religious tendencies within nationalism in the early sixties in Zimbabwe created problems of political philosophical and theological adjustments for the missionary community.[119]

Though it is difficult to pin-point the exact time when openness to African traditional religious ideas within African nationalism began, nationalists began to include in their speeches references to African traditional religious expressions.[120] Brand observed: "As the tide of nationalist sentiment rose, prayers were said to the 'mhondoro'—spirits of the land—from political platforms and pressure was sometimes put on people not to attend church by, for example, arranging rallies on Sundays at service times."[121]

In 1961 the nationalist leader, and Methodist lay preacher, Joshua Nkomo made the overt declaration "[Africans] must look to their ancestral spirits for inspiration in the nationalist struggle."[122] For white church leaders it was easy to conclude that use of some African traditional religious

115. Ibid., 95.

116. Ibid., 99.

117. Ibid.

118. Verstraelen, "The Christian Bible," 231ff.

119. Brand, "Missionaries and Nationalists," 75.

120. Ibid.

121. Ibid.

122. Joshua Nkomo quoted in Linden, *Catholic Church & Struggle*, 60.

tenets meant only one thing; that African nationalism was anti-Christian.[123] Mutambirwa claimed that because of this issue, of employing African traditional religious expressions, "the Catholic Church even threatened to excommunicate its African members who took part in revolutionary politics."[124] Although Mutambirwa did not indicate the scale of the problem within the Roman Catholic Church, to him it was proof of the fundamental hostility of the Christian churches to the African nationalist cause.[125] As has been seen, Mutambirwa made instances such as prayer offered to Nehanda evidence that the Bible had no influence on African nationalism.[126] Mutambirwa argued that at rallies some politicians "used to ask the traditional African God to tell the Christian God, to instruct his followers the Europeans, to leave the country."[127]

The NDP is reported to have instructed some nationalists to memorize *Nehanda Nyakasikana*—a poem about Nehanda a Zezuru spirit medium–found in the Shona novel *Feso*,[128] and recite it at the beginning of nationalist meetings as prayer.[129] It goes, "*O Nehanda Nyakasikana!* How long shall we the *Vanyai*[130] groan and suffer? Holy tutelary spirit! How long shall we, the *Vanyai*, suffer oppression? We are weary of drinking our tears. How long shall we have forbearance? Even trees have a rest . . . How far will the tyrants go? In every house and every village our people are being pulled out and punished."[131] Although it cannot be disputed that this poem was employed at some nationalist meetings, it is difficult to ascertain how frequently this poem was rehearsed and how popular it was among the Ndebele nationalists and other Shona nationalists since it appealed to Nehanda a Zezuru spirit medium—Zezuru hardly being the largest Shona dialect. Certainly for those that heard and recited it its inspirational value could not be downplayed. The late Simon Muzenda, a nationalist and Roman Catholic

123. Linden, *Catholic Church & Struggle*, 60.

124. Mutambirwa, "Impact of Christianity," 77.

125. Ibid.

126. Ibid.

127. Ibid.

128. Mutswairo, *Feso*, 1956.

129. Bhebhe, *Simon*, 121ff.

130. Translated as your children or subjects.

131. *Feso* was later translated into English and included in an anthology published as Mutswairo, *Zimbabwe, Prose and Poetry*.

layperson,[132] was arrested after having recited it for subversion and inciting people to rise against the settler government.[133]

The inclusion of African religious tenets should not necessarily be seen as part of a conscious policy by African nationalism to alienate itself from the church. Nationalists were trying to reconstruct and assert what seemed to be a long lost collective African identity.[134] According to Bhebhe, this sheds light into some of the thinking behind this romanticization of the traditional African past. He described how—on Robert Mugabe's initiative—the National Democratic Party (NDP) in the early sixties tried to inspire the spirit of "self-sacrifice," marked by a rejection of European luxuries and habits and by emphasis on African culture in attire, music, diet, drinks and religion.[135] It was an attempt to inspire pride in African culture, and was calculated to cultivate a spirit of self-discipline and reduce unnecessary dependence on whites. Those who attended public meetings expressed this by attending such gatherings without shoes, socks, watches, hats and jackets.[136]

Mugabe at a political rally in 1961 proclaimed, "Today you have removed your shoes. Tomorrow you may be called upon to destroy them altogether or to perform other acts of self-denial."[137] However, traditional romanticists did not also resort to removing European shirts, trousers and inner garments and put on *mhapa neshashiko* or in Ndebele *amabetshu*[138] which was the traditional form of dress. If some leading members of the postcolonial government had exercised similar restrain from selfish accumulation of wealth and corruption—condemning millions of fellow Africans to sub-human living conditions and starvation—Zimbabwe could be in a better socio-economic state.

Besides the desire by nationalists to assert their African identity, adopting African traditional religious expressions was simply a cry-out for support that the church was not willing to offer.[139] Nkomo's words, "Afri-

132. Simon Muzenda was the first Vice-Prime Minister of Zimbabwe as well as her first executive Vice-President.

133. Bhebhe, *Simon,*121.

134. Shamuyarira, *Crisis in Rhodesia*, 62.

135. Bhebhe, "Nationalist Struggle," 101.

136. Ibid.

137. Shamuyarira, *Crisis in Rhodesia*, 67.

138. These were the two traditional main items of clothing, usually animal skins that simply covered one's bottom and the corresponding front area.

139. Brand, "Missionaries and Nationalists," 76.

cans must look to the ancestral spirits for inspiration,"[140] point to a belief that the spirits of the ancestors could help nationalists fight settler oppression, and nationalists were willing to embrace spiritual help from their ancestors which was not being rendered by the church.[141] White mainline churches failed to realize that the adoption of traditional religious expressions by nationalists also served to fill in the philosophical and religious void that had been left when the general church leadership had snubbed African nationalism.[142] It was with respect to this status quo of a lack of definite moral support from the church hierarchy in the early sixties that Bishop Abel Muzorewa later was to write, "The Christian church was in real danger 10 years ago of being rejected by the masses of young people as foreign, western and part of the system of white oppression."[143]

The embracing of African traditional religious expressions should be viewed in light of the apparent paradox in Zimbabwean nationalist philosophy, which borrowed from various religious and philosophical traditions, rather than as evidence of rejection of Christianity by nationalists. Nkomo who in one incident appealed to ancestral spirits, as previously noted, on another occasion in 1961 at a political rally in Bulawayo declared, "Ministers have preached to people that they are the same in the eyes of God, at the same time have supported a social system that divides these people into groups of unequals. It is here where the Christian churches have lacked moral courage. The Christian philosophy is good but the men that preach it are bad."[144] Nkomo sought to have his audience to salvage "the baby from the bath water" and not to judge the validity of the Christian message based on the behavior of its messengers.

As evidence that the two were not inimical, African Christian congregations continued to grow as simultaneously Africans rapidly embraced nationalism.[145] In the early seventies, as shall be explored later and as discussed in David Lan's significant work *Guns and Rain*, African traditional religion would take a more active role in Zimbabwe African National Union (ZANU) guerrilla camps outside Zimbabwe. Shamuyarira believed that the challenge, in this early 60s period was,

140. Joshua Nkomo quoted in Linden, *Catholic Church & Struggle*, 60.

141. Linden, *Catholic Church*, 60.

142. Shamuyarira, *Crisis in Rhodesia*, 69.

143. Muzorewa, *Rise Up and Walk*, 185.

144. Shamuyarira, *Crisis in Rhodesia*, 143.

145. Ibid., 146.

"for the church to satisfy the present African spiritual and moral base for African nationalism."[146] Embracing African religious expressions did not necessarily mean that Christianity was being excluded.[147] To this effect Shamuyarira in writing about this period observed, "The teachings of the church are revolutionary enough to provide such a base, if its leaders would make it clear that the neighbour you should love is of any race. If Jesus was to return to Rhodesia in flesh today, there is no doubt who would be his neighbours and where he would stand on the all-important question of political, social and economic equality."[148]

The Pervasive Influence of Christianity

Although African nationalism in Zimbabwe was based on the need for majority rule it did not have a static philosophical doctrine.[149] From its early years it fought for democracy within a liberal meritocratic framework, and then changed to a call for democratic rule within a liberal democracy framework. In the 1970s it adopted a multifaceted approach to the African cause. What remained constant within the movement was the demand for African rule but what was certain was that African nationalism in colonial Zimbabwe was not guided by a single political doctrine.[150] However, even in the late sixties most nationalists still professed to be Christians and a significant number of them had come out of mission institutions.[151] At this stage many others had received education in Christian institutions, and they began to challenge church leaders to make a stand based on Christian principles and teachings on justice and the equality of all humanity instead of racial and ethnic loyalty.[152] To this effect Sithole wrote, "One of the unique teachings of the Bible, especially the New Testament, is the worth and dignity in the sight of God, and there is a relation between this teaching and the present African nationalism . . .. If [the] Bible teaches that the individual is unique, of infinite worth before God, colonialism in many respects, says the opposite . . .. while African nationalism is strongly

146. Ibid., 69.

147. Halpern, "Polarization," 1ff.

148. Shamuyarira, *Crisis in Rhodesia,* 146.

149. Linden, *Catholic Church & Struggle*, 206.

150. Ibid.

151. Halpern, "Polarization," 1ff.

152. Brand, "Missionaries and Nationalists," 75.

motivated by African consciousness of an oppressed people seeking freedom, it is Christian consciousness that gives it proper direction and that self-sustaining creativity which makes for human progress."[153]

Ndabaningi Sithole argued that when nationalism emerged in Zimbabwe it was influenced by Christianity. The extent of this influence is open to debate, but the influence of Christian ideas cannot be denied. Biblical texts and doctrines were used by nationalists.[154] James Mutambirwa, though skeptical of the role and influence of Christianity in nationalist politics, in the mid-70s noted the use of Exodus stories and other biblical texts by Nationalists, although he argued that this was for the sake of "exploiting mass psychology."[155] Whilst there may be some truth in this, the same could be said about African nationalism's use of African traditional religions tenets. The use of *Nehanda Nyakasikana* could have produced significant psychological effects. Bhebhe wrote, "The poem expressed African outrage and bitterness against white people. It pointed out white humiliating, rapacious robbery of African wealth, and it underscored African yearning for the day that exploitative and oppressive burden of white would go away."[156] The poem was designed to inspire Africans to challenge colonial rule more than it being a call to embrace African traditional religions. Nowhere does Nehanda Nyakasikana call Africans back to traditional worship but it certainly does express Africans' political grievances and their need for liberation.

Strong connections between African nationalism and Christian thinking remained. Sithole, a Congregational Church minister, and the Methodist lay preacher Nkomo, despite his concessions to African religion, were the leading nationalists of the time, and argued that nationalism and Christianity were compatible and Christian principles were the base on which they argued for the nationalist cause. Yet they were aware of the limitations of the position taken by most Christian churches.[157] Shamuyarira writing on events in the early to mid-sixties commented, "God is not interested in just a part of human life, but in the whole of it. The church should never fail to raise the voice of conscience of fundamental principles of equality, human

153. Sithole, *African Nationalism*, 53.

154. Ibid., 171.

155. Mutambirwa, "Impact of Christianity," 77.

156. Bhebhe, *Simon*, 121.

157. Banana, *Church and Struggle*, 124–25.

dignity, and justice. It cannot support a qualified franchise, and the Land Apportionment Act, and still pose the question 'Who is my neighbour?'"[158]

In 1964 when the Methodist bishop Ralph Dodge was deported for supporting nationalist activities, as President of ZAPU Nkomo wrote, "In Church people have found in you a sincere Christian leader whose field of service was not bound by denominational barriers. In your Christian mission you have indeed preached the living Christ and have made the Christian religion something from which people find salvation here and now as well as in the life to come. In this country the type of your Christian mission is a novelty. We hope that it will not be long before you return."[159] Dydmus Mutasa an Anglican, who went on to hold a minister's position in the postcolonial ZANU government wrote, "The individual Christian must be the conscience of the nation. The Church must be such that she speaks fearlessly, against all evil, and supports fearlessly all good causes. She must be such that she will never hold her peace through fear, or favour of man."[160] Later imprisoned for involvement in the struggle for restitution of Africans' political rights, Mutasa further wrote of the comfort he found in the chorus, "I know who holds my future and I know He holds my hand. With God things don't just happen. Everything by Him is planned. And as I face tomorrow with its problems, great and small, I will trust the God of miracles. Give Him all."[161] Yet many Christians were to find no conflict between such pious thoughts and a willingness to embrace violence and bloodshed. As the ZAPU nationalist Shamuyarira, concluded in 1962: "My personal view as a Christian has always been a complete and utter abhorrence of violence as a political weapon. I believe that issues settled by violence are never solved. I hope that the duty will never fall on me to take someone's life. I would never do it. But, having said that, I must add that I cannot see any other effective way of bringing change in Southern Rhodesia."[162] Such notable evidence, supporting Sithole's claims that Christianity had a strong role in shaping early nationalist attitudes, without deterring them from resorting to violent outcomes, should not be ignored.[163]

158. Shamuyarira, *Crisis in Rhodesia*,142ff.

159. Dodge, *Revolutionary Bishop*, 157.

160. Mutasa, *Black Behind Bars*, 66.

161. Ibid.

162. Shamuyarira, *Crisis in Rhodesia*, 73.

163. Sithole, *African Nationalism*, 51.

The messages of the nationalists in these formative years of nationalism were mixed with Christian sentiment, such as the ethics of the beatitudes;[164] the dignity and equality of all humanity;[165] and love and fair treatment for one's neighbor.[166] Hence, this was part of the core values and beliefs of the nationalists at the time. The tendency to later downplay some of these Christian values and beliefs was as much a sign of frustration from African nationalist leadership with the lack of general support from much of the church, as it was genuine interest in other new ideas such as Communism.[167]

The development of radical African politics was not met by a warm reception by the Zimbabwean churches from 1957 to c.1964. Christian missions owed a historic debt to the white pioneers, whose victory over local ethnic leaders had opened the way for more secure mission activity. This legacy bred a tendency for churches to seek an accommodation with the governing authorities, and to adopt a non-critical stance to political developments. Lawrence Vambe in response to this development called the church to "re-examine its position."[168] Eventually, during the same period, as political events began to impinge much more directly on the Zimbabwean churches, they began to engage into the open political arena. The church's voice in opposition to colonial policies began to emerge. From the mid to the late 60s, as we shall examine in the following chapter, their voice became a significant one in response to settler political repression, though it was not a single or consistent voice.

164. Mutasa, *Black Behind Bars*, 65.

165. Sithole, *African Nationalism*, 53.

166. Shamuyarira, *Crisis in Rhodesia*, 142ff.

167. Mutasa, *Black Behind Bars*, 111–24.

168. Vambe, *Ill-fated People*, 234.

5

Zimbabwean Church in Protest

IN THE PERIOD 1964 to 1970 the Zimbabwean mainline churches which had largely been known for their political quiescence began to gradually shift from this position. This change of attitude which took more than half a century to evolve was due to a combination of factors some of which were due to internal pressures and changes within the church and some to external stimulation, and to both these factors I shall now turn.

Repression and Church Protest

From 1964 onwards, events pushed some in the churches into more overt political territory. From the time Ian Smith took over, the police could search homes at will. Government permission was needed for public gatherings. Newspapers that the government viewed as pro-nationalist were being banned and citizens could be detained without trial.[1] In 1963 under the Law and Order Maintenance Act (LOMA) the government introduced the Hanging Bill.[2] This bill was meant to have retributive and deterrent effects on those that sought to challenge the government authority especially by acts of protest. The bill made several political offences and acts of vandalism with political motivation punishable by hanging. One of those affected by this law in its early days of implementation was a Richard Mapolisa who

1. Todd, unpublished paper presented at the Que Que Lions Club Banquet, 29 August 1964, NAZ, GEN-P/TOD.

2. Shamuyarira, *Crisis in Rhodesia*, 132.

had thrown a petrol bomb into an unoccupied private house and caused carpet damage amounting to £17.[3] Mapolisa was tried and sentenced to hanging. A reprieve was granted after the Defense and Aid Fund financed an appeal to the Privy Council in London: "Everybody of goodwill will be grateful to the religious leaders in this country, including the Archbishop of Canterbury, the Moderator of the Free Church Federal Council and the Moderator of the Church of Scotland who, in response to a suggestion by Christian Action, appealed to the Prime Minister of Rhodesia for clemency. They will all be happy that the government of Rhodesia has responded to public and private representation of this kind. It is to be hoped that this reprieve may be indicative of a change in policy in Rhodesia."[4] Although Mapolisa was reprieved, political hangings continued. Once Ian Smith became Premier he extensively used the provision of the LOMA to deal with anti-government protest from within or outside the church.

It was within this political context and framework that in a consultation on race relationships in southern Africa held in Kitwe, Zambia on the 25th May to the 2nd June 1964[5] organized under the authorization of the World Council of Churches, Todd and other influential delegates within the Zimbabwean church came to conclude that violence was becoming an unavoidable alternative to pursuing peace within the southern African context and various forms of support from the church were needed to help augment the nationalist cause.[6] For these ideas Todd began to be viewed as not just a liberal but also as a radical.[7] Another significant liberal prophetic voice who was also viewed as radical and subversive during this period was the American Methodist Church bishop in Zimbabwe, Ralph Edward Dodge.[8]

3. Christian Care, "Richard Mapolisa," Case files for legal assistance for political prisoners, 18 February 1964, NAZ, GEN-P/CHR

4. Christian Action, "Press Statement: Canon Collins on Mapolisa Reprieve," Chairman: The Reverend Canon L. John Collins, 2 Amen Court, London, 29 April 1965, NAZ, GEN-P/CHR.

5. Bent, *Breaking Down the Walls*, 10.

6. Mindolo Ecumenical Foundation, "Southern Africa Christian Consultation on Race Relations," May 25-June 2 1964, NAZ, GEN-P/WOR.

7. "Questionnaire of men and women who visited, worked or lived in Zimbabwe between 1945 and 1980 and who experienced some or all of the Rhodesian crisis 1959–1979," Filled in by Reginald Stephen Garfield Todd, sent out by Tafataona Mahoso in partial fulfilment of a History dissertation, at Temple University, Philadelphia, NAZ, GEN-P/MAH.

8. For R Dodge's biography consult, Mungazi, *The Honoured Crusade* and his

Voices of Protest from Within the Church

Dodge's prophetic ministry had long evolved before his settling in Zimbabwe in 1956. He had been a missionary in Angola since 1936 where he had been part of a Methodist mission that was proactively involved in and promoted nationalist activities, especially among Christian students.[9] He had also been active in organizing scholarships for nationalists in Zimbabwe and the two former Portuguese colonies in the early 60s. Antonio Agostinho Neto (1922—1979) the nationalist and former Methodist minister, who became Angola's first President at independence in 1975 had once been Dodge's personal secretary.[10] He also continued to advise students in Portuguese East Africa, modern day Mozambique, on various nationalist matters in their territory as he began to be involved in African nationalist politics in Zimbabwe from its conception. Keen to put Africans at the fore of organization in either church related or political position he regarded his prophetic role as that of primarily advising the then emerging leading nationalists, such as the late father of Zimbabwean nationalism Joshua Nkomo.[11]

In the sixties Dodge was one of the first proponents within the church to consider the possibility of non-violent resistance to repressive political authorities, in American civil rights fashion, but he also realized that sometimes non-violence could not yield the desired results in an oppressive system. Thereby he left his position open to interpretation, with Winston Field's settler government suggesting that it was obvious that Dodge supported a violent revolution.[12] Dodge was also instrumental in organizing various conferences addressing issues such as, "how to combat oppression."[13] After the death of the first Zimbabwean medical doctor and nationalist, Parirenyatwa,[14] Dodge helped to conduct the funeral on 18 August 1962.[15] According to Shamuyarira, the inquest revealed that Parire-

autobiography; *The Revolutionary Bishop*.

9. Top Secret Papers, "Bishop Dodge," 13th June 1963.

10. Hastings, *A History of African Christianity*, 143.

11. Top Secret Papers, "Bishop Dodge," 13th June 1963.

12. Ibid.

13. Ralph Edward Dodge quoted in Top Secret, 10 June 1963.

14. Tichafa Parirenyatwa was also mission educated and he became the first African medical doctor who treated patients across the racial boundaries and supervised white staff in a period were racial integration was unlawful under settler laws.

15. Ralph Edward Dodge quoted in "Top Secret: Bishop Dodge Suggested

nyatwa and his driver, Sibanda,[16] were stopped a mile beyond Shangani and were both beaten up by some whites. The next thing Sibanda remembered was waking in hospital. He assumed "Pari" had taken over the wheel and, though injured, driven until he collapsed and died near the level-crossing. The account that "Pari" was taken to the level-crossing by whites who staged an accident with a train, is generally believed by Africans. The official Commission of Enquiry concluded he had died as result of an accident. "Pari" was viewed as a nationalist martyr and the blame for his death will always be put at the government's door. His death was met with truly national mourning,[17] making Dodge's participation in his funeral all the more significant.

Dodge was involved in demonstrations, notably early in 1963 when he was part of a group that demonstrated against security legislation by the government which he believed to be too stringent. His offices were used as the launch base for the demonstrations.[18] To Dodge the church was embarrassed by trying to uphold and encourage the enforcement of laws which "it sincerely feels should not be observed. The most common area the church finds itself in such a dilemma is in respect to discriminatory legislation."[19] He believed that: "The church should not fail to call the attention of those in responsible positions in government to the urgency required in replacing archaic and discriminatory legislation with legislation which is fair and just to all racial groups. The time is past when the minority can hope to legislate with impunity against the majority."[20] As the chair of the American Methodist Church he taught that the Church should be involved in politics.[21] He closely identified with his denomination's Social Concerns Committee who, on the 4th May 1964 at the Methodist Conference in their report said, "We urge the Rhodesian Government to lift the ban on the Zimbabwe African Peoples Union, so that African Nationalism may have a means of expressing itself. We urge nationalist leaders in addition, to be willing to

Deportation," File addressed to the Prime Minister by J. M. Greenfield (private secretary to the minister of economic affairs), 10 June 1963, NAZ, GEN-P/DOD.

16. Danger Sibanda was (Pari) Parirenyatwa's driver.

17. Shamuyarira, *Crisis in Rhodesia*, 75–76.

18. Ibid.

19. Ralph Dodge quoted in Mungazi, *Honoured Crusade*, 87.

20. Ibid.

21. Ralph Edward Dodge quoted in "Top Secret: Bishop Dodge Suggested Deportation," File addressed to the Prime Minister by J.M. Greenfield (private secretary to the minister of economic affairs), 10 June 1963, NAZ, GEN-P/DOD.

meet with Government leaders on this problem so that communication can be re-established between the leaders of the races in Rhodesia."[22] As a result of his stand on political matters Dodge would not settle long enough in Zimbabwe to be directly involved in its political life.

As early as 1963 the settler government had considered deporting Dodge for his role in nationalist politics but the then Premier Winston Field had stopped the deportation because of fear of the political damage that action would have caused. At this first suggestion of Dodge's deportation by his government Winston Field responded, "A nasty piece of work, but I think that Rhodesia, at this juncture will lose more than it will gain by deportation. There are lots of others just as bad."[23]

The dissolution of the federation and the political uncertainty which followed, and the British concerns about majority rule were serious considerations that Winston Field cited to his state security agents and ministers as reasons that militated against deporting Dodge at that period of Zimbabwean history.[24] It would have brought an international outcry and especially from the Christian community and it would have further highlighted the sociopolitical problems that the rest of the world needed to take notice in Zimbabwe. Hence his deportation at this juncture was viewed as counter-productive.

Field's conclusion that, "there were lots of others just as bad"[25] was simply hyperbolic. Certainly there were a few other critiques among the white community. The matter of deporting Dodge "the nasty piece of work" was suspended, perhaps serving to show that to some extent Field was a reasonable man, or had a "soft spine" as his successor accused him.[26]

The deportation of missionaries who spoke against the policies of the settler government commenced when Ian Smith became premier and Dodge became one of the first casualties on 17 July 1964 as he was served with a deportation order for his political stand.[27] Smith was beginning to show the reputation that would mark his years in office as a hardliner.[28]

22. Ibid.

23. Ibid.

24. Ibid.

25. Ibid.

26. Smith, *Great Betrayal*, 63.

27. Dodge, *Revolutionary Bishop*, 154.

28. Top Secret Papers,"Bishop Dodge Suggested Deportation," The Private Secretary to the Prime Minister, 13th June 1963, NAZ, GEN-P/DOD.

Dodge's unapologetic stance to the matter of his deportation and ministry activities in general was evident in his response to his deportation when he said, "If I am being deported because of what I have done and written, then I have no apology to make."[29] By this time, Dodge had made his contribution to African nationalism in Zimbabwe as well as in Angola and Mozambique. The American Civil Rights Movement and the experiences of abuse of African-Americans in his home country, and personal feelings of guilt on behalf of his compatriots, might have influenced his sternness to fight injustice on the side of Africans in his work as a missionary in Africa.[30] What cannot be taken from Dodge is that his influence had lasting significance especially within the American Methodist African community as he awakened their political consciousness and the early years of the rise of African nationalism.[31] Hence various Methodists generally became conscious of nationalist grievances under Dodge's leadership and some members from the seventies became leading nationalists.[32]

Another prominent voice within the liberal community that was emerging in the mid-sixties and that was to fully identify with the nationalist cause especially from the late sixties in Zimbabwe was that of the Roman Catholic Bishop of the Umtali diocese, Donal Lamont whose prophetic stand also stemmed, as stated by Diana Auret, from "his Irish background" and "the experience of the underdog."[33] Lamont was born in 1911 and grew up during the years of the Irish war of independence out of which he grew to support the Irish nationalists. Upon leaving school he joined the Carmelite Order and later spent time studying theology in Rome between 1933 and 1939. It was when he was in Rome that his doctrine and philosophy of social justice was substantially shaped by his superior, a German Carmelite. His superior taught him that priests had to promote God's justice on earth and that undertaking that task was the mark of being an authentic representative of Christ.[34]

These developments occurred in the context of escalating acts of Fascism and Nazism that eventually led to the Second World War. As if his childhood experiences and superior's instructions were not enough his

29. Quoted in Mungazi, *Honoured*, 94.

30. Ibid.

31. Muzorewa, *Rise and Walk*, 44.

32. Ibid.

33. Auret, *Reaching for Justice*, 12.

34. Lamont, *Speech*, 27.

dramatic encounter with Hitler as a student at the Vatican engrained his quest for confrontation with unjust state powers. Lamont wrote, "When he [Hitler] came to Rome we experienced the thrill of engaging in the conflict at close quarters."[35] When the Pope refused to meet Hitler, the student body of which Lamont was also part at the Vatican, protested against Nazi incursion by not going outside the college doors. After almost two days of stand-off their resilience was broken-down by the Nazi and Fascist coalition. Besides being, "thrilled" as Lamont put it by conflict,[36] these events seemed to have left a lasting impression in Lamont's life and hence prepared him for the challenges he would face later in Zimbabwe when he arrived in 1946 having volunteered to start mission work.[37]

Lamont's influential ministry in Zimbabwe gradually started after his appointment in 1957 as the Bishop of the Umtali diocese. With a denominational agenda instead of a nationalist one, he saw in June of 1959, the need for addressing race and civil rights issues. Contrary to the wishes of the majority of other Roman Catholic bishops Lamont wrote a pastoral letter titled, "Purchased People"[38] in which he addressed some of the grievances of the rural Africans such as problems posed in rural communities by urban migration for labor, the government's destocking policy as well as the need for land.

By 1961 a few liberal minded Catholic priests and Bishops had steadily begun to align themselves with the doctrine of social justice which Lamont was beginning to propagate within the Roman Catholic community which was then generally opposed to the nationalist cause. In responding to the proposed 1961 constitutional changes the few liberal elements within the Catholic Church wrote a joint pastoral letter in May 1961 advocating a just constitution. After this pastoral "Peace Through Justice,"[39] more younger liberal minded priests gradually began to be proactive in their prophetic rhetoric but largely on behalf of African Roman Catholic political interests.[40]

The weakness of Lamont's approach and that of the liberal Roman Catholics in the sixties in Zimbabwe was that they chiefly argued for justice

35. Ibid., 28.

36. Ibid.

37. Ibid., 29.

38. Lamont, "Purchased People." The majority of Roman Catholic laity who could not read or write had no access to it as it was published in English only.

39. Auret, *Reaching for Justice*, 10.

40. Linden, *Catholic Church and Struggle*, 58.

on behalf of Africans within the confines of Zimbabwe's existing constitutional boundaries. Hence in the early and mid-sixties they did not seek for the complete overhaul of the system but its modification. They also exhibited, as they slowly discovered their prophetic voice, paternalist tendencies emanating from pedagogical ideas of the day in their understanding of Africans and the Zimbabwean problems.[41] Hence Lamont insisted in the sixties that Africans with a population then close to five million did not have enough human resources to manage the country therefore they needed a settler led government. Another factor that restricted the Roman Catholic voice of protest in the sixties was their reliance largely on the Papal and Vatican pronouncements on social justice.[42] The Zimbabwean political realities were different from the original audiences and contexts to whom the original documents had been written.[43] One of the realities was that the African populace or to be specific the Roman Catholic African populace found some concepts from these writings not just far removed from their everyday realities but also intellectually unattainable even when translated into the vernacular languages as they were at times.[44] To this effect Lamont basing his authority on Rome in the *Purchased People* wrote, "The Bishops of the church, united under the leadership of the successor of St. Peter, are themselves corporately the successors of the Apostolic College and inherit its authority."[45] In language that would have been difficult for the general laity to fully comprehend he continued: "Terrible beyond all describing would it be, if so forgetting his apostolic heritage, he were to forget also the supra-national quality of the church, its divine policy of indefectibility, its nature as the Mystical Body of Christ, its timelessness, its divinely guaranteed permanence, its dowry of suffering and persecution and allow it to become the willing servant of any political party or of other temporary power."[46]

41. Ibid., 46.

42. Roman Catholic Bishops Conference, "Rhodesia-The moral Issue"—a pamphlet expressing the Catholic Bishops concerns over Zimbabweans' social problems, 28 November 1965, NAZ, GEN-P/CAT.

43. Linden, *Catholic Church and the Struggle*, 52.

44. Roman Catholic Bishops Conference, "Rhodesia-The moral Issue"—a pamphlet expressing the Catholic Bishops concerns over Zimbabweans' social problems, 28 November 1965, NAZ, GEN-P/CAT.

45. Lamont, "Purchased People."

46. Ibid.

Lamont, besides the use of Roman Catholic teachings also continued to employ liberal arguments against settler policies which, by the sixties were not just ineffective in dealing with the settler regimes, but no longer popular with the African masses as the majority completely turned for political guidance and thrust their hope in nationalist activities.[47] To his credit he was one of the early outspoken Catholic bishops and managed to change his ideas in the process when the older theories and strategies fell short of political transformative effects. He also managed to initiate the first protest steps within a denomination that had grown to be the largest numerically in terms of membership by the sixties but could not speak much on behalf of its oppressed Africans. After Vatican II, Roman Catholic participation in political protest increased significantly in Zimbabwe.[48]

Rev. Herbert Chikomo, a former office holder in the Christian Council of Rhodesia and a retired minister in the Presbyterian Church in Zimbabwe, was impressed by Lamont's prophetic stand, "He was a very courageous priest. He spoke out in dangerous times that some of us could not speak. Maybe because he was a bachelor compared to some of us who were married that is why he was so outspoken."[49] In the early and mid-sixties his role was more constrained but from late sixties and seventies Lamont proved certainly to be an outstanding and courageous prophetic voice. Perhaps in a sense his single status influenced him in being courageous but singleness was not the only explanation for this, since there were people like Dodge and Todd who were married but also equally courageous and outspoken. At least for missionaries like Lamont there was the realization from the late sixties that even if they were jailed they would not stay long in prison since the Smith government's main disciplinary measure for men of the cloth who engaged in sociopolitical protest was deportation. Africans and those that had become citizens of Zimbabwe like Todd knew certainly that long jail sentences or restrictions and other harsh sentences awaited them if they were judged subversive in their prophetic efforts.

Another liberal prophetic figure among Anglicans in the sixties was Kenneth Skelton, the Bishop of Matebeleland and the first President of the Christian Council. In his sermons he preached against segregation and

47. Verrier, *The Road to Zimbabwe*, 111.

48. For further reading on these changes within the Roman Catholic Church in Zimbabwe as a result of Vatican II, consult Gundani, *Changing Patterns of Authority and Leadership*.

49 Herbert Chikomo.

settler policies when his fellow Anglican bishop of Mashonaland Cecil Alderson was calling for moderation in denouncing the settler policies.[50] In his Zimbabwe ministry, Skelton was threatened at gun point by a settler woman who wanted him to desist from making his protest.[51] Skelton was unable to sustain his protest. Citing family reasons he resigned as Bishop of Matebeleland and left Zimbabwe for England in 1970. Some believe he left because he was afraid that deportation on account of being involved in politics would be scandalous for his future ministerial appointment and promotion in the Anglican Church in England.[52] The major downside to Skelton's departure, besides the loss of an important prophetic voice, was that his departure created doubts among Africans as to how far they could count on liberals' support since they could abandon the ship whenever they saw fit.

Despite their limitations, these liberals became instrumental in providing the church with some prophetic voice that had been largely absent from the Zimbabwean church. The efforts of these experienced leading figures in the church began to be gradually augmented by the arrival of younger missionaries.

These few sources of liberal ecclesiastical protest began to indirectly and directly provide various resources to nationalists. They provided insights to nationalists into understanding the fears and concerns as well as the general world of settlers. On the other hand they also helped to find international contacts for nationalists who would help them further their struggle. They became pivotal especially when the armed struggle commenced as they were able to access material support for war refugees and internationalized the Zimbabwean crisis.

For African Christians who embraced nationalism the few outspoken missionaries became a model they could draw inspiration and hope from within the boundaries of their faith. To Todd the African ministers fraternal wrote:

> Dear Sir,
>
> The Highfield Ministers have asked me to thank you very much for your most inspiring and encouraging sermon last week when you preached at a Home & Family service.

50. Bishop Cecil Alderson, letter addressed to Anglican clergy over Father Hugh Bishop's sermon that caused offense in the Salisbury Anglican cathedral, 3 March 1966, NAZ, GEN-P/ALD.

51. Chennells, Review of *Here to Stay*, 78ff.

52. Ibid.

> Although we are a poor group of ministers we realise we are not as poor as to fail to give a hand to a friend who has always sacrificed ever his own life for our sake. Please sir, herein enclosed find a sum of two (£2) pounds as our share in your travelling expenses.
>
> May God bless you in your struggle to liberate all the oppressed people in a country which you yourself have helped develop.
>
> Yours sincerely,
>
> Herbert Chikomo[53]

In Christian liberals that protested for African political rights most African Christians saw what they perceived to be models of Christian witness. These few Christians courageously refused to stand simply as spiritual leaders with no social duties. They rejected the course of remaining detached from the Africans' everyday concerns and sheltering behind the settler laager of political repression for Africans, and affluence and unmerited socio-economic privileges for whites.[54] To varying degrees, and without undermining their Christian faith, they had risked and suffered for the just cause of Africans.[55]

Few lay Christians joined voices with those of the liberal church leadership. These were people of moral courage and those that could summon an audience with influential diplomats at a national and international level that could speak and be heard through the colonial period. Due to these factors liberal proclamation was largely elitist, and was easily quelled by the settler government. Proclamation of the need for justice and change was not complemented by organized social action of people in the grass-roots as was happening during the same time within the American Civil Rights Movement.

In the Civil Rights Movement Christian leaders like Martin Luther King Jr. had been able to organize grassroots protest, as seen in the bus boycotts and other forms of demonstration including at times a refusal to spend their money in white-owned businesses.[56] Hence proclamation of protest was largely accompanied by action of protest, not just of the elite

53. Herbert Chikomo, letter addressed to the Hon. R.S.G. Todd, Houkoni Ranch, Dadaya, from Mufakose Township, Salisbury, 1 August 1962, NAZ, GEN-P/TOD.

54. Halpern, "Polarisation," 1ff

55. Ibid.

56. Slack, *Martin Luther King*, 111.

but of the masses. Instead of being, "a one man's revolution"[57] as Todd advocated, in the American context though headed at times by one man or a small committee, the church's protest had become a mass movement. As a result of the masses' stand when they came together to protest they were noticed. Since people like Todd and Lamont did not have a significant following among the grass-roots a "one man's revolution" was understandably appropriate compared to utter silence.

The deportation of those that believed that the role of the church included action for social change and the further implementation of policies that increased racial tensions by the Smith regime led to the conclusion that the time for rhetoric was gone and was to be replaced by acts of defiance from the church.[58] The embryonic signals that the church was becoming more impatient with the settler government's policies began to emanate when it became apparent in 1964 that the Smith government was mulling over the idea of a Unilateral Declaration of Independence (UDI).[59] With regards to Africans' civil rights, UDI would give Smith's government the leeway to implement separatist policies or flout basic human rights without the inconvenience of being made accountable to any external authority. Britain's reserve powers enshrined in previous constitutions as the colonial power that was supposed to safeguard Africans' rights would be made void by UDI.[60]

Although Britain had not in the past significantly insisted on her reserve powers their presence in the constitution had always somehow made both the settlers and Africans feel they were in different ways bound to Britain. The issue of independence was not the issue since the end of the federation had implied the coming of independence to the three former federal sisters. The question or the issue was what nature of independence was to be granted to Zimbabwe? The settler hardliners were determined to have independence but only on terms acceptable to them.[61] Tensions within the country increased at the threat of UDI. Some Church representatives that had not protested in the past began to seek dialogue with the

57. Todd, "Challenge for Today," July 2 1963, NAZ, MS 1082/1–14; Todd borrowed the phrase from Robert Frost.

58. Linden, *Catholic Church and Struggle*, 83.

59. Verrier, *Road to Zimbabwe*, 129ff.

60. Ibid.

61. Megahey, *Humphrey Gibbs*, 90.

government hoping to persuade it to change its course.[62] Radical liberal Christian voices uttered strong protest. In Bulawayo Cathedral, Rt Reverend Kenneth Skelton preached, "The idea of a UDI . . . is so far from the truth as to be laughable if it were not so tragic. It might quite well be that if such a situation rose—which God forbid—the church might have to advise its people that they were under no obligation to carry out the commands of a government which had committed such an act; and what an agonising position this would be for us all."[63]

In 1964 a joint press statement of caution was issued by the Methodists, Congregationalists, the Presbyterian Church and the Anglicans in which they warned, "No extreme act outside the constitution could be morally justified without the expressed consent of the peoples of the country and without the reasonable hope of promoting the common good."[64] Smith would not pay heed, on 11th November 1965 he declared: "We Rhodesians have rejected the doctrinaire philosophy of appeasement and surrender. The decision which we have taken today is refusal by Rhodesians to sell their birthright . . . We have struck a blow for the preservation of justice, civilisation, and Christianity and in this belief we have thus assumed our sovereign independence. God bless you all."[65]

For the clergy that had called Christians to an unqualified obedience of political authorities the declaration created for them a theological quagmire. Smith, the colonial authority, had rebelled from Britain the imperial authority. The dilemma was if all political authority was God ordained and therefore the church should submit to political authorities, which Caesar or political authority in this case deserved the church's obedience?

Others concluded that only force could bring justice.[66] The declaration of the UDI led those who believed that the church was an agent of sociopolitical change to the conclusion that confrontation with the state was now necessary.[67]

Though UDI was declared Skelton's words were not acted on. Even moderates such as Alderson condemned UDI but not so much with the

62. Ibid.

63. Skelton, "They Shall . . . Persecute You, Luke 21:12" (sermon),19 April 1964, NAZ, GEN-P/SKE.

64. *Rhodesia Herald*, 21 April 1964.

65. Smith, "Unilateral Declaration of Independence," 18 November 1965.

66. Todd, "White policy and politics," 121.

67. Mutasa, *Black Behind Bars*, 63ff.

passion to see a restitution of Africans' political rights but more as a result of the loyalty of some settlers to Britain.[68] However, even at such a defining moment, moderates were highly critical of subordinates who took a more robust stance. One such was the Anglican Father Hugh Bishop, Superior of the Community of the Resurrection, who castigated the Smith regime for having declared a unilateral independence. He spoke of the insensitivity of whites, who were unaware of how Africans felt or thought, and of the suffering their actions caused: "Well, perhaps might we include insensitivity among the headings of our self- examination when we are preparing to make Easter confessions . . . 'We have struck a blow' said Mr Smith on November 11th last year, 'for the preservation of Christianity.' How insensitive do you have to be to believe that?"[69] Cecil Alderson, the Anglican bishop of Mashonaland, in disapproval responded, "[T]he preacher's own sensitivity deserted him. Insensitive, I think, to the courtesy owed to the Dean of at least consulting with him about matters of great public feeling . . . I trust no preacher in this diocese will use the expression 'the illegal regime' which contradicts this principle of charity."[70]

In 1966 Alderson again reprimanded Father Hugh Bishop,[71] who had in a Lenten sermon called the settler government under Smith a "tyranny" that did not want to introduce universal suffrage.[72] Hugh Bishop likened the suffering of the Africans to a crucifixion, with the settler government in the form of the Roman oppressor: "Somewhere, not far away, a cross is being set up and the nails are being driven in. For 'inasmuch as you have done it unto one of the least of these my brethren'–for each one of them is His brother or sister, His kith and kin,[73] whatever their colour—'you have done it unto me.' One of the most frightening things about the Passion of Christ is that it was planned by and executed by average humanity. They

68. Alderson, "'Long live the King! (1 Sam. 10:24)'"—sermon preached at the Salisbury Cathedral, three days after the Unilateral declaration of Independence (UDI),14 November 1965, NAZ, GEN-P/ANG.

69. Hugh, "Luke 23:34; Father, Forgive them," sermon preached at Salisbury Anglican Cathedral, Rhodesia, 27 February 1966, NAZ, GEN-P/SKE.

70. Alderson, "My Dear," 1 January 1966.

71. Cecil, "My dear Brother," 88–89.

72. Hugh, "Luke 23:34," 85–87.

73. By referring to all races as "kith and kin" Father Bishop Hugh had attacked directly the heart of settler nationalism which limited the usage of the phrase only in relation to whites. Smith, *Great Betrayal*, 63, passim.

were ordinary people committing their ordinary everyday sins, who crucified Jesus."[74]

> Hugh Bishop applied this directly to the Zimbabwean situation, quoting a statement issued at the beginning of the month and signed by the Anglican Archbishop of the Province, as well as the Roman Catholic Archbishop and the leaders of the different Christian communities in Zambia: "We are deeply concerned," they say, "about the continued denial of the right of self-government to the African community under the illegal regime in Rhodesia. We believe that in the sight of God all men are of equal value in Rhodesia and should be treated as our brothers. Conditions in Rhodesia today flagrantly violate this conviction. The tyranny of a police state produces widespread fear among African population and threatens the freedom of all, both black and white, who oppose the regime . . .
>
> "Indiscriminate beatings, the use of torture, and even the killing of Africans are reported. The court case concerning an African prisoner beaten to death by a police officer in gaol suggests that there is substantial truth in at least some of these reports."[75]

He justified this direct political reference by arguing the issue was instead, "not about political but moral issues. Can the Christian conscience be silent when the average wage of an African is £16 per month, the subsistence level of an average family £20 per month, and the average wage of a European worker £100 per month? Or has the Christian conscience nothing to say when government expenditure on the African child is one-tenth of that spent on a European child?"[76] To these direct and indirect references to the political situation, Bishop Alderson responded severely, "It is the latter, with its reference to 'the illegal regime in Rhodesia,' 'one man one vote,' and 'indiscriminate beatings, the use of torture, and even the killing of Africans'—'are reported,' which caused great hurt . . . I trust no preacher in church will within this Diocese use the expression 'the illegal regime' which contradicts this principle of charity . . . In my judgement, 'indiscriminate beatings, the use of torture and even the killing of Africans are reported' is simply not good enough. Unless the preacher had very sure information, this was an improper quotation to make."[77] Although arguing for a

74. Hugh, "Luke 23:34," 85–87.

75. Ibid.

76. Hugh, "Luke 23:34," 85–87.

77. Alderson, "My dear Brother," 3 March 1966.

"no politics" line from his clergy, Alderson appeared to have little time for nationalist claims: "'One man one vote' I have many times said that this dictum is not part of the Christian religion. Christianity is concerned with justice in human affairs, and must judge political devices and arrangements by the standard of justice . . . 'one man one vote' is not in itself a Christian or Anglican principle."[78] Instead Alderson preferred an approach where the Anglican clergy steered clear of political matters deemed subversive, and "insensitive," and lacking in courtesy to the dean of the church in which he preached.[79]

For Alderson "sensitivity" and "courtesy" ultimately meant that critical political issues were to be avoided.[80] The rebuke to Hugh Bishop shows how those who sought to make political protest in this polarized community were constrained. Whether it was fear of upsetting senior clerics, or ordinary parishioners, fewer and fewer ministers chose to speak out on political matters.[81] Alderson's defensiveness sprang from fear of stirring up further division: "The task of the preacher in Rhodesia today is a bitter one indeed. There is nothing he will say, and nothing he will not say that will not wound and grieve and anger greater numbers of his fellowmen and fellow-Christians. God has entrusted to me hundreds of thousands of African Christians and tens of thousands of white Christians, all equally precious to Him and dear to me. Today they are stunned, perplexed, separated, deeply divided. How can I help them all? How can I not hurt them all?"[82]

The mid to late sixties became an era in which the church's voice and the efforts of the few protesting figures began to grow in significance. Despite the tense political climate in Zimbabwe and UDI having brought the nation speedily towards a hot war, there was a continued steady arrival of young missionaries within the mainline denominations. From 1966 to 1975 the number of protestant missionaries increased from 402 to 533.[83] This generation of missionaries was more open minded to ethnic matters in the light of civil rights in America and especially to nationalist rule than their older counterparts. They were prepared to work alongside Africans, unlike many of the older generation, having been products of the old sys-

78. Ibid.

79. Ibid.

80. Ibid.

81. Ibid.

82. Alderson, "Sam. 10:24," 81.

83. Hastings, *African Christianity*, 227.

tem where Africans had always been subservient and at best assistants. Some within the new brand of missionaries was also more open to African nationalism, being largely influenced by western social liberal ideas, they were able to distance themselves from the thought trends of their older co-workers. However, although some actively supported the existing socio-political transformative initiatives, many of these newcomers did not take an active role in protest over political issues. The intolerance and the settler government's policy of repressing dissent acted as a deterrent to all but the most courageous, but compared to the older guard they did not seek to discourage those who wanted to do so. This new generation of missionaries was quick to see parallels of how the church could co-exist with nationalist parties as exemplified in Zimbabwe's two former federal sisters, Zambia and Malawi.[84] When these two territories had become independent nationalists had not prohibited worship. Some of these progressive thinking missionaries, according to Maxwell, are said to have at times visited Malawi to learn from the situation there.[85] Hence a few among these new arrivals with courage added their voice behind the few older protesting counterparts.

Those who wanted change, both the African clergy and liberals, concluded that such laws and UDI were evidence that the settler government was not prepared to listen or prepared to change by persuasion. After Smith's declaration, on 11 November 1965, a special council meeting took place on the 26th November, 1965 at the Trinity Methodist Church Hall in Salisbury, to review "The Position of the Church in the Present Circumstances." At the meeting a statement was made available to each Church Head and every delegate for study. UDI was condemned. From that day onwards running battles between the Council and the minority government were fought,[86] as the Christian Council became more outspoken in their criticism, condemnation and defiance of the Smith regime. Although most opponents of the regime were deported, imprisoned, detained and restricted, according to Watyoka: "The "dark days" had indeed descended upon the country. Those who watched the happenings from close quarters were left in no doubt that the churchmen and women of our country rose to the occasion and held the torch of salvation." Watyoka concluded, "History had thrust the banner upon the nation individually and collectively through their churches and Council . . . Indeed "the spirit" was the source

84. Skelton, "Luke 21:12," 19 April 1964.

85. Maxwell, "Christianity and the War," 63.

86. Watyoka, *25 Years*, 11.

of their life, they let it "direct their course." It was a gruelling contest and the acquitted behaved themselves well."[87] It is to this major factor, acknowledged above by Watyoka, that brought this significant change and brought impetus to the way mainline churches in Zimbabwe began to protest with regards to the country's sociopolitical status quo from the mid-60s that I will now turn to explore.

African Presence in Leadership

The lack of vibrant protest against the colonial government that characterized the Zimbabwean church was to be further countered by the gradual Africanization of the church leadership from the mid-sixties. Reflecting the ethnic problems, churches had not done much in appointing Africans into positions of denominational leadership. It was only with the founding of the Christian Council of Rhodesia in 1964 that Rev Herbert Chikomo was given a role with a good measure of responsibility and some considerable measure of influence as the Secretary General.[88] Three more Africans were chosen to be part of a six member assisting committee. These became the Christian Council's executive committee. Although still numerically dominated by whites, for the first time there had been an effort to include Africans in meaningful posts in one of Zimbabwe's significant church organs.[89]

Although in 1964 wheels of Africanization seemed to have started rolling, the pace for the general Africanization in various denominations was very slow. In 1965 Rev. Andrew Ndlela was appointed chairperson of the British Methodists. His decision making powers were curtailed and his role as chairman was seen as limited almost to that of largely rubber stamping decisions made by the predominantly white Methodist administrative board.[90] Sundkler observed, "the nationalists did not regard him as a credible leader with African interests at heart.[91]

Only in 1968, with the appointment of Abel Tendekai Muzorewa as the American Methodist bishop, did the first mainline denomination have an African as its leader or as part of its national leadership team. The

87. Ibid.

88. "Christian Council of Zimbabwe," Minutes from the Christian Council of Rhodesia Meeting, 17 July 1964, NAZ, GEN-P/WOR.

89. Hallencreutz, "Council in Crossfire," 53.

90. Banana, *Repression*, 13.

91. Sundkler & Steed, *History of the Church*, 806.

Zimbabwean Church leadership had invested little energy in developing or encouraging locals for leading the church without white supervision. According to the Zimbabwean historian, Ngwabi Bhebhe, the Lutheran Church was affected in similar respect, "In spite of all this phenomenal growth by 1963 the church was still run by missionaries and its mother agent, the Church of Sweden Mission . . . Such a situation, coincided with the height of the African nationalist demand for majority rule as well as the crucial decision by Africans to resort to the armed struggle . . . The Church of Sweden responded by shifting responsibility for much of the local affairs to the local Church and by granting a constitution which met the wishes of missionaries."[92]

In most mainline denominations, the Lutherans included, poor salaries paid to African ministers ensured that they remained at the mercy of the better paid missionary workmates or superiors. Poor salaries further prohibited African church personnel from acquiring educational qualifications that were required for them to assume the major leading roles within the church.[93] Furthermore, in a number of denominations as the clamor by African personnel for their need of assuming important leadership roles became louder, fuelled by a new found confidence being propagated by nationalists that Africans were capable of running things without white supervision, most denominations from the mid-sixties began to consider the theory of Africanization or indigenization.[94] Although the white led church began to consider Africanizing, other developments within the church demonstrated that the missionary leadership was not yet fully prepared to let go their stranglehold on the leadership reins.[95]

As the clamor for Africanization gathered momentum most denominations formalized dual payment structures for church personnel. In this system African Ministers were to be paid by the local church even though many missionaries knew that the local congregations certainly had no capacity to pay ministers sufficiently.[96] On the other hand missionary personnel were funded from abroad and hence assured of decent salaries. In some denominations, like the Evangelical Lutheran Church, realizing the importance of evangelists who were in most cases African and were

92. Bhebhe, *ZAPU and ZANU*, 132.

93. Sithole, *African Nationalism*, 15.

94. Hallencreutz, "Policy of Religion," 11.

95. Ibid.

96. Soderstrom, *God Gave Growth*, 162ff.

largely responsible for the numerical growth of the denominations, mission boards offered to have them paid from abroad.[97] Although paid from abroad they were also underpaid since their salaries had to be drawn below those of ministers by virtue of the latter's superior educational qualifications and job classification.[98] This sorry state of African personnel's salaries whether by design or coincidence was generally understood as a missionary conspiracy against Africanization by most African ministers. Financial domination meant continued domination of Africans over the decisions that the church made. Finances were perceived as a weapon of control.[99] The negative effect of poorly paid African ministers, evangelists and other service personnel was that they ended up spending time looking for ways to sustain themselves rather than paying for an education that was needed to provide them with essential skills to enable them to be both effective personnel and eventually being equipped to become part of the echelons of the church's structures.[100]

Mission agencies were satisfied with the dual payment arrangement since they felt it encouraged the African church to be self-reliant.[101] Some viewed the lack of dependence of funds from abroad by the local ministers as the first step towards establishing a self-supporting church. Africans seemed not to believe this line of thinking since there was no evidence that missionaries were beginning to delegate major responsibilities and decision making on major issues pertaining to the running of denominations to Africans.[102] They insisted on having a self-supporting and self-propagating church but without accepting Henry Venn's third requirement–the need for a self-governing African church.[103] Matthew Rusike who served as United Methodist minister shared his financial concerns in a letter to a fellow African Methodist minister. He complained, "The money you have been giving me from 1960 works to 5/- per week and my wife 5/- per week. Can a married person live on 10/-? Garden boys live on more than that plus ration."[104] Even by 1976 the church's treatment of African ministers had not changed

97. Ibid. 166.

98. Ibid.

99. Banana, *Church and the Struggle*, 86.

100. Ibid.

101. Soderstrom, *God gave Growth*, 165.

102. Ibid.

103. Warren, *To Apply the Gospel*, 26.

104. Banana, *Church and Struggle*, 85.

much. The Reverend Canaan Banana[105] complained to the Rev. Hugh Thomas of the Methodist Missionary Society, "I was shocked to the point of a heart attack when I saw the salary scale for our white ministers. How can anybody, let alone the Christian Church ever justify such gross disparity in salary? African ministers earn less that 1/5 (one-fifth) of their white counterparts. This makes a mockery of the church's outbursts against apartheid and racial discrimination . . . If this trend is not checked, I am afraid the church is going to be eroded of its qualified indigenous personnel."[106] Some missionaries further justified the paying of lower salaries by arguing that an offer of poor salaries would ensure that no Africans would be enticed into Christian ministry for financial reasons.[107] Therefore the belief was that only Africans committed to ministerial work would consider entering into Christian ministry. What made this claim untenable was the fact that most missionaries were not living on the paltry stipends that they expected Africans ministers to live on.[108]

There was failure to realize that poor pay was far from being a guarantee that African recruits would not take up ministerial jobs for financial reason. The system ended up ensuring that less educated and uneducated Africans who offered their services for paltry pay were recruited.[109] The African Christian intellectual cream and those few who sacrificed and advanced their education while in ministry looked elsewhere for employment. The lack of jobs for Africans meant that others opted for ministry not motivated simply by a desire to serve.[110] Meager salaries ensured the continued control of the church by missionaries on the pretext that the church did not have Africans qualified enough to efficiently run the church.[111] The system therefore had simply ensured that many of the African intellectual cream did not offer their services to the church and the church received ineffective African personnel.[112] Hence the void of African representation

105. Banana was a Methodist Minister and nationalist, and later he became the first ceremonial President of Zimbabwe.

106. Banana, Letter addressed to H Thomas of the Methodist Missionary Society, London, May 1976, Harare, Methodist Connexional Archives (MCA), CS Banana File.

107. Soderstrom, *God Gave Growth*, 170–171.

108. Banana, *Church and Struggle*, 84ff.

109. Soderstrom, *God Gave Growth*, 171ff.

110. Ibid.

111. Ibid.

112. Muzorewa, *Rise and Walk*, 47.

in the top church leadership structures had been perpetuated.[113] For some Africans the solution to this whole problem was a call for a moratorium, as it certainly ensured self-governance, self-reliance and self-propagation, and on the flip-side a moratorium may have had detrimental effects on these three major aspects caused by both lack of qualified personnel and resources which the missionaries offered and was badly needed by the African church.[114]

In the mid-sixties a new epoch began to dawn. A few Africans who had gone abroad to further their theological education began to return.[115] These had been beneficiaries of the rise of African nationalism which had forced a few liberal dominated denominations to speedily realize that the nationalists' demands for political African rule had also implications on Zimbabwe's white led church. They had earlier realized that an African takeover of the church leadership was inevitable.[116] Ralph Dodge was one of those early realists. Hence the American Methodists provided a few scholarships in the late fifties and early sixties for some of its young able ministers.[117] Those that returned, though few, began to be absorbed into various leadership positions and hence a very slow Africanization of the church leadership ensued.[118]

The early roots of the philosophy of bringing Africans generally into leadership of institutions lay in the liberal multiracial communities such as the Cold Comfort Farm where Africans were given experience by white liberals of leadership.[119] Educated Africans believed to be responsible were generally thrust into some positions of influence where liberals were in charge.[120] At first Africans were given positions of leadership mostly in institutions that offered services to fellow Africans and especially over fellow Africans.[121] This was done as a way of assessing Africans' capabilities and if they were deemed capable by their liberal mentors they would be given an opportunity to handle more challenging positions mostly over fellow Afri-

113. Soderstrom, *God Gave Growth*, 171.

114. Ibid.

115. Dodge, *Revolutionary Bishop*, 138.

116. Ibid.

117. Ibid., 126.

118. Mutasa, *Black Behind Bars*, 42.

119. Ibid., 39.

120. Ibid.

121. Chung, *Second Chimurenga*, 33.

cans.[122] There were hardly any opportunities elsewhere that opened up for Africans to manage whites bearing in mind that Zimbabwean legislation and social structuring would not permit that kind of scenario.[123] Liberals besides their philosophical convictions of equality were also motivated by the desire to challenge the prevailing assumption among settlers that Africans were generally incompetent.[124] This idea was peddled in the settler community where it was also used to instill a sense of fear that if Africans were to take charge things would fall apart hence giving the settlers justification for their continued hold on power.[125]

In the church and its other institutions the ethnic composition of mainline denominations in the sixties seemed to confirm this assumption. The heads of denominations of all mission established or mainline churches were whites even in mainline denominations that had predominantly an African membership. Even most rural mission centers were headed by whites. Roman Catholics defended the all-white composition of their leadership by blaming it on their institution's bureaucratic leadership appointment procedures.[126] The reality still was almost three-quarters of a century from the birth of the nation and a seemingly thriving church there were no Africans in the overall mainline denominations' top leadership positions before 1968. The installation of Abel Tendekai Muzorewa as bishop of the American Methodist Church in 1968 was the beginning of a process that catapulted several Africans into top positions within mainline denominations.

There are several factors behind the installation of Muzorewa as the American Methodist bishop in 1968. The American Methodists in Zimbabwe were predominantly African in terms of their leadership and therefore the appointment of an African leader would have not caused as much of a stir as it would have in predominantly white denominations or those denominations that shared an almost equal number of members from the white and African communities. Dodge, whom Muzorewa replaced as bishop in Zimbabwe, had also been at the forefront of the liberal struggle for African rights, hence his influence on who was to succeed him.[127] The

122. Shamuyarira, *Crisis in Rhodesia*, 18.

123. Mutasa, *Black Behind Bars*, 39.

124. Shamuyarira, *Crisis in Rhodesia,* 22ff.

125. Verrier, *Road to Zimbabwe*, 74ff.

126. Hallencreutz, "Council in Crossfire," 53.

127. Dodge, *Revolutionary Bishop*, 126.

choice was intended to make a dramatic and symbolic point to the settler regime that these leadership positions whether in church or government would eventually be taken over by Africans no matter how much they tried to fight against the liberation of Africans.[128] Furthermore, Muzorewa in his own right was a capable and hard-working man.[129]

He had returned in 1966 from America where he had successfully acquired a Master's Degree in Theology. The Civil Rights Movement which was at its zenith during his time of studies in America left a lasting impression on Muzorewa: "In those years Dr. Martin Luther King gave inspired leadership in the civil rights movement. It was plain that he was trying to change an unjust, segregated system, but he always spoke without hate, in a steady, convincing way. That was something which I never would forget."[130] Muzorewa's style of preaching was similar to that of Baptist African-Americans,[131] but slightly toned down by a less enthusiastic reception to that style of preaching from an African Methodist audience whose church experience had been, by and large, shaped by a generally less exuberant western Christian conservative experience, though still more lively than the general western Church experience.[132] His stance on non-violence, in the early years of his ministry, was also similar to that of America's civil rights era: "By nature I am a non-violent person. Since childhood I have recoiled at the sight of blood, and the presence of violent death . . . I believe . . . in the principle of non-violence. Christianity teaches us to love and forgive our enemies. Harmony in any society is preferable to violence. Even where pressures must be brought to bear on those in power to achieve greater justice, I would prefer using direct non-violent action."[133]

Upon Muzorewa's return he was offered the position of Youth Secretary in the Christian Council of Rhodesia where he excelled in organizing various church based youth and women self-help projects.[134] Upon his resignation in 1968 to take over as the American Methodist bishop they had to employ three people to undertake his duties. It seems as if the two years

128. Ibid.

129. Brand, "African Nationalists," 78.

130. Muzorewa, *Rise and Walk*, 49.

131. J. Mubaiwa, Persoanl Interview, City Presbyterian Church, Harare, January 16, 2007.

132. Ibid.

133. Muzorewa, *Rise and Walk*, 175.

134. Hallencreutz and Moyo, *Church and State*, 57.

that he worked for the Christian Council had also given people like Dodge, who recommended him for the position, and others within their Methodist leadership, confidence that he was capable of running their Methodist denomination.[135] His installation further encouraged other denominations to think seriously about the Africanization of their own leadership structures. The paternalistic missionary church leadership was assured by Muzorewa's conduct of duties that Africans were capable. His early years in that office were as important to the Methodists as they were to the general Zimbabwean community.[136] Settlers would have delighted in his failure since it would have affirmed their presumptuous belief that Africans were incapable of effectively running big organizations. On the other hand the African populace and their white liberal companions were eager to see him succeed as that would have proved a point to settlers that the major problem Africans had was lack of opportunity not capability.[137]

As the sixties headed towards their end the process of Africanization was hastened by the intensification of the armed struggle that had commenced in the mid-sixties. The guerrillas and the government forces targeted African civilians, missionaries and white farmers in rural areas as a deliberate action of their political strategies.[138] Although there were a few settler farmers that supported the nationalists, white farmers were usually indiscriminately attacked by guerrillas on the basis that they supported the settler government.[139] Africans in the rural areas suffered the most as they were attacked by both settler and guerrilla armies often being accused by either side of being sell-outs.[140]

Missionaries in the rural areas found themselves in a precarious position. The guerrillas wanted their support and on the other hand the settlers required the same. A lack of cooperation with either side usually led to

135. Ibid.

136. Muzorewa, *Rise and Walk*, 61.

137. Ibid., 64.

138. Ibid., 202.

139. Janice McLaughlin, Personal Interview, Avondale, Harare, January 20, 2007.

140. Some estimate that at least 30,000 lives were lost during the liberation struggle and only about thirty-one missionaries died. These figures serve to show that if more missionaries had spoken in protest against the settler government the number should have been significantly higher bearing in mind that the Roman Catholics alone had more than 880 white priests, sisters, brothers, and seminarians by the end of the war; Roman Catholic figures in Linden, *Catholic and Struggle*, 310.

grave consequences.[141] Killing of missionaries though not frequent is believed to have been orchestrated by both warring sides. Both the settler army and guerrillas targeted missionaries and blamed it on each other.[142] The killing of missionaries was used by the government forces to confirm to the outside world and their home supporters the claims they made that guerrillas were communists who were bent on destroying what the western world was believed to stand for; that is capitalism and Christianity.[143]

Guerrillas on the other hand, although it was not official policy, targeted missionaries because besides a strong belief that they represented settler interests there was also a belief that the outside world listened when white blood was shed.[144] Shedding African blood seemed not to have the same alarming effect on both the settler government and the international community. Hence as the armed struggle intensified most missionaries left the rural areas and headed for urban areas and some as the war progressed left the country.[145] This development left open at mission stations and other rural projects and ministries positions that had been once a sole privilege for missionaries. Africans were hastily installed to fill in the positions but some missions closed down completely.[146] Hence for Africanization the commencing of the armed struggle had a positive side. Rural Mission founders and their descendants, who would have found it difficult to share authority of their own volition, were forced for the first time to solely trust their fellow African Christian workers to assume vital responsibilities of running the church.[147]

This emergence of an Africanized church leadership helped to give expression to a Christian voice of protest that ranged from strong sympathy to full identification with the nationalist cause. Muzorewa wrote:

> I was sick and tired of hearing missionaries and African pastors preaching for the conversion of souls and promising a heavenly reward to those who would repent and be saved. Our people needed to hear a total gospel-that God created a man, or a woman, as a total person, having a body, a mind and a spirit; and that our

141. Hallencreutz and Moyo, *State and Church*, 73.

142. Ibid.

143. Ibid., 87.

144. Meredith, *The Past*, 342ff.

145. Soderstrom, *God Gave Growth*, 147.

146. Ibid.

147. Ibid.

> Heavenly Father would save that total person. I believed, and preached that to love as God loves means to be in total service to the total man. That includes politics. Participation in politics is not a "secular" activity. It is part of the Christian's duty if he is to serve as Christ served.[148]

Some of the educated Africans who returned were given opportunities to preach in white congregations and they used the opportunity to address Africans' political grievances. Max Chigwida of the Presbyterian denomination and a nationalist addressed such a congregation, the Trinity Presbyterian congregation in Greencroft. He preached, "Whether you like it or not we are going to rule this country."[149] In the midst of addressing Africans' national grievances in his sermon some walked out in protest.[150]

These few Africans who assumed influential roles in the late sixties and early seventies in the church became nationalists in their own right as they began to exercise significant influence. In the absence of vibrant African political representation due to detention and various restrictions imposed on nationalist parties and nationalist politicians, the Africans who had assumed influential positions in the church also began to gradually fill the political void created as a result of the imprisonment of nationalists.

Land Tenure Act

"Sir, Last June, all the Christian Churches, with one notable exception, pleaded with the people of Rhodesia to reject the proposals for the new constitution. The churches had every right to do this. This state may determine what it considers to be legal but, in a Christian country, it is for the Church to say what is right or wrong . . . men who framed that document are the real terrorists in this country. Remember physical violence or physical terrorism is as real but it is a much more terrible thing."[151] These were the words of Lamont the Roman Catholic Bishop of Umtali to Mr. Partridge a Catholic minister in the Rhodesian Front government after the adoption of the constitution which incorporated the Land Tenure Act of 1969.[152] This act triggered a general social accord and consensus for protest

148. Muzorewa, *Rise Up and Walk*, 55–56.

149. Quoted by Rev. Hebert Chikomo.

150. Ibid.

151. Lamont, "Christian Country," 20 March 1970.

152. Palley, *Constitutional History*, 267ff.

for the first time from both the white and black leadership of the Zimbabwean church. Legislation had been passed before that was similar to that of apartheid South Africa,[153] but the 1969 Land Tenure Act in no uncertain terms was meant to entrench apartheid and enhance ethnic polarization within Zimbabwe and above all this it both indirectly and directly curtailed freedom of worship.

Its preceding sister Act, the Land Act of 1930, had divided the country into racial segments of European, African, Unreserved and Crown land. The Land Tenure Act of 1969 consolidated this further as it legislated for the establishment of racially segregated schools, hospitals, churches, residential areas, cemeteries and business areas.[154] On 2nd March 1970 Smith declared "Rhodesia" a Republic with a new constitution that included the provisions of the Land Tenure Act which he described as, "the death-knell of African political advancement"[155] and that it was designed, "to entrench Rhodesia's government in civilised hands for all time."[156] The government decreed in the 1969 Act that no race would be allowed to buy land in an area designated by law for another race except by special government permission. Hence the implications of the act to the church were that believers of one race could no longer worship with believers from another race since the act restricted various racial groups to particular territories. Religious ministers also could no longer serve across the racial barriers brought by the law. Ministers of the same denomination but different races could not live in the same communities based on racial differences. Missionaries under the act would have been forbidden to minister in rural areas since they were designated as tribal trust lands.[157] In church established institutions such as schools, old people's homes and hospitals the church was no longer allowed under the act to admit people outside a particular prescribed racial group depending on the geographical territory in which it was located.

153. Todd, "White Policy and Politics," 119. Some of the laws that were already in place that were similar to South Africa's apartheid laws included: The Immorality and Indecency Suppression Act, forbade sexual congress between black men and white women; The Vagrancy Act; The Unlawful Organisations Act. For a detailed analysis of these laws consult, Palley, *Constitutional History and Law*

154. Palley, *Constitutional History and Law*, 267.

155. Muzorewa, "Speech to National Affairs Association," 29 May 1973, NAZ, GEN-P/MUZ

156. Halpern, "Polarisation in Rhodesia," January 1971. This article further exposes the injustices brought by the 1970 "Rhodesian" constitution to the African populace.

157. Rural territories allocated for the local people were called Tribal Trust Lands.

Furthermore for its various racial members to congregate the church had to seek authorization from the state.[158]

The demands of the Act had dire consequences for the operations of the church, especially on denominations that were involved in cross-ethnic missions, and for the first time the consensus of Zimbabwean church leadership threatened the settler government with civil disobedience. The government sought to establish a society that was confined to specific racial territories and crossing which required state authorization.[159] Although settler nationalism had desperately sought to distinguish itself from the apartheid system south of the Limpopo, its legislation had over time and especially through this Act come to resemble that of South Africa. For the first time in Zimbabwe a united outcry was heard that called for various sections of the church to protest against this act.[160] The Christian Council of Rhodesia (CCR) protested: "The Church has been called by God to be a community in which race, like all other human distinctions, loses all divisive significance. We should not stand silent when injustice is being done to those who have a right to expect our support, nor when freedom to assemble peacefully together and to meet as friends irrespective of skin colour is being threatened. We believe that the living together of persons of different race as Christian brothers is the best way to eliminate racial friction in this country."[161] From the Roman Catholic camp Bishop Lamont summed up the attitude of the church on this particular matter, "The men who framed such a constitution are no friends of Rhodesia."[162]

This act seemed to have been met with hostility by the church not because the church had finally crossed the "Rubicon" into being a vibrant prophetic mission but because its institutions were now being directly threatened. Hence out of the need for self-preservation and to defend its sovereignty which was now being directly curtailed, the church had to take a stand for what it believed to be right, if it wanted to remain autonomous. The 1969 Act directly infringed freedom of worship and association of believers.

158. Rea, "To Heads of Churches and Representatives," 31 October 1969, NAZ, GEN-P/REA.

159. Banana, *Repression*, 123.

160. Rea, "To Heads of Churches and Representatives," NAZ, GEN-P/REA.

161. CCR quoted in Hallencreutz and Moyo, *Church and State*, 68.

162. Lamont, "Christian Country," 20 March 1970.

The Salvation Army abandoned their policy of neutrality and silence on political matters, and the Rhodesian Christian Conference that had the reputation of avoiding confrontation with political authorities and were viewed as largely sympathetic to settlers also protested.[163] The Christian Conference wrote, "I am enclosing reports of the progress of recent conversations with the Ministers of, Lands, Local government and Internal Affairs, on the subject of the Land Tenure Bill in so far as it affects not only Mission lands but also freedom of worship. It is likely that certain concessions will be granted, notably a change in clause 73. Refusal to alter clause 3 (1) is a matter for grave concern, and the question arises whether further steps should be taken to voice our dissent."[164] The contentious clause (3) gave government ministers statutory authority to forbid occupation of a building in one racial area by members of the other race. For two days in October 1969 the Christian Conference's deputation met with the settler ministers of lands, internal affairs and local government outlining the difficulties of the Act in relation to church worship and its ownership of land. At the meeting, "The minister was asked to consider the device of creating non-racial ecclesiastical areas as a special category alongside those already created for non-racial residential, commercial and industrial purposes."[165]

The main concern of the Christian Conference delegates was the overall implications of the 1969 Act on the ethnic relations in Zimbabwe on a day to day basis, and the effects of the Act on inter-ethnic worship. If the government had allowed interethnic worship and left its policies on racial segregation in other social spheres unchanged, seemingly, the Christian Conference would not have protested.

Leaders of the Anglican Church which represented the denomination attended by most settlers and which also officiated at state ceremonies held a secret meeting with Ian Smith and some of his cabinet ministers to try and resolve the matter.[166] In the meeting the Right Reverend JP Burroughs

163. Rea, "Heads of Churches and Representatives," NAZ, GEN-P/REA.

164. Ibid.

165. Rhodesia Christian Conference, "Government ministers minutes," of meetings held on the 20th and 27th of October 1969, in documents dispatched to heads of churches and representatives of church leaders for review by the organization's secretary general F Rea, 31 October 1969, NAZ, GEN-P/REA.

166. Burroughs quoted in, "Confidential Notes of a Meeting between the Prime Minister and Representatives of the Anglican Church in the Prime Minister's Office, Milton Building, Salisbury," 13 May 1970, NAZ, GEN-P/BUR. These notes can also be found in Lapsley, *Neutrality or Co-option?*, 90–94.

the Anglican Bishop of Mashonaland requested to have churches allowed to operate as they had done in the past without having to seek a minister's permission as required by the Land Tenure Act. He further pointed out that if someone hostile to the church was to take over the premiership position the Act could be used to oppress the church.[167] The implication of Burroughs' comments was that Smith was not hostile to the church. The government's response was to assure the Anglican Church representatives that, "the Act was not meant to create problems for the church but to ensure law and order."[168] Smith further admitted in the meeting that the same law could be applied to deal with some people who worked against the government under the disguise of the church.[169] It was eventually agreed that, "The government would consider amending the constitution to allow the church largely to operate and gather across the racial boundaries, but the whole act would not be changed."[170] On the 8th September 1971 the Christian Council further protested against the Land Tenure Act: "We cannot acquiesce in the removal from the churches of the right to decide who shall live on land belonging to them. To ask us to evict people because of their race would be asking us to deny our basic principle of unlimited love."[171]

Church leaders under the banner of "Heads of Denominations"[172] also opposed the Land Tenure Act.[173] They sought to speak as both non-partisan and authentic representatives of the majority of Christians in Zimbabwe, since the general belief then was that the ecumenical Christian Council was pro-nationalist hence it was perceived as partisan. The "Heads of Denominations" believed that their voice was more inclusive compared to the Christian Council since it was predominantly a Protestant board.[174] Although Roman Catholics were present at most Christian Council meetings they were not official members of this ecumenical body. They simply sat through the deliberations as observers. There were other Protestant groups

167. Ibid.

168. Ibid.

169. Ibid.

170. Ibid.

171. *Moto*, November 1971.

172. The "Heads of Denominations" were the leaders of most Protestant and Roman Catholic denominations in Zimbabwe, which had a leadership responsibility of about twelve denominations. The heads usually added up to seventeen as some denominations provided more than one head such as the Roman Catholics and Anglicans.

173. Heads of Denominations, "Press Statement," October 1969, NAZ, GEN-P/CAT.

174. Ibid.

who were not represented in the Christian Council such as the Dutch Reformed Church who had pulled out citing that it was too political.[175]

Therefore the "Heads of Denominations" were regarded by the Zimbabwean community as the Christians' final voice of authority and regarded as the most influential Christian voices in the land.[176] A forceful press statement was suggested by one head of denomination which outlined the various policies that were being implemented by the settler government which violated the law of love but this was rejected by other heads.[177] Instead, the heads unanimously accepted a milder resolution that simply condemned the Land Tenure Act and called upon all people to, "strive for the removal of legislation that accelerated racial animosity."[178] They were firmer in their press statement as they insisted that, "The church was going to carry its work in all racial territories as it saw fit rather than as required by the state."[179]

Although the "Heads of Denominations" called people to strive to remove racist legislation they never outlined the course of action that was needed to achieve that greater national goal. However in response to the Act's implications for land owned by the church, church leaders resolved to do three things; firstly, that they would assure registered tenants on such land of full support in retaining their rights of occupation as against the Land Tenure Act; secondly, that the churches would not in any way assist the government in its unjust attempt to evict registered tenants; and finally, that the churches would oppose the government and support the registered tenants in any attempt at compulsory removal.[180]

The 1969 Act challenged the church hierarchy to contemplate and threaten the government with the possibility of civil disobedience. The Roman Catholic Bishop Lamont further threatened that his denomination in protest would shut, or run-down its institutions, that catered for the elderly

175. Maritz, "Church-State Relations," 352. Maritz gives an account which suggests that DRC was active in political protest. The evidence from this author's research and most scholars points to a different conclusion from the one reached by Frans Maritz.

176. Hallencreutz, "Council in Crossfire," 64.

177. Heads of Denominations, n.d., date could be estimated around 1970, NAZ, GEN-P/CAT.

178. Heads of Denominations, "Minutes on meeting held in Salisbury," 20–21 October 1971, NAZ, GEN-P/ TOD. Seventeen church leaders representing twelve denominations in Zimbabwe attended.

179. Hallencreutz and Moyo, *Church and State*, 63ff.

180. Ibid.

and children.[181] Some within the Roman Catholic bishopric had distanced themselves from Lamont's threats saying that, "they were not representative of the Roman Catholic position."[182] Jack Halpern in, *The World Today*, contended that it was primarily due to the negative effects of the Act on freedom of worship that invoked the church leadership's desire to contemplate defiance rather than their defiance being action stemming from the burden and desire to act as voices of prophetic protest against wider issues in society.[183]

The 1969 Act also made it evident that the argument that the church should not be involved in politics was unsustainable, especially if politics decided to directly involve itself with the church. The 1969 Land Tenure Act impinged upon both the sacred rights and constitutional rights of the church. The response of the churches had shown what could be achieved. With the threat of civil disobedience, the government was forced to reconsider its legislation. Whether out of self-interest or not the church's involvement with politics was beneficial. Without wanting to lose face before the public for having backtracked in the face of the churches' threat of defiance and of diplomatic efforts, with regards to the facet of the Act that affected the church, the government announced that churches would not be required to register under the proposed legislation citing that the churches were already registered under the old Voluntary Organization Act.[184] Hence the church had its first taste of success in opposition.

The realization that several attempts, such as the talks on the *Tiger* in 1966 and on the *Fearless* in 1968,[185] since UDI had failed to persuade the Smith regime to change its political philosophy and course; and then the adoption of so extreme a piece of legislation as the 1969 Act swayed some moderates to believe that drastic action was needed to curtail the activities of the settler government. Other Christians, who had been on the fence, came to the realization that even the apolitical church was not

181. Lamont quoted in Confidential Notes of a Meeting between the Prime Minister and Representatives of the Anglican Church in the Prime Minister's Office, Milton Building, Salisbury, 13 May 1970, NAZ, GEN-P/BUR.

182. Ibid.

183. Halpern, "Polarisation in Rhodesia," January 1971.

184. Lapsely, "Anglican Church and State," 118.

185. The *Tiger* and *Fearless* are names of vessels where Harold Wilson and Smith held, in 1966 and 1968 respectively, unfruitful meetings to resolve the Zimbabwe crisis; for a reading on these talks consult Smith, *Great Betrayal.*

after all immune to attacks from the settler government.[186] Some began to actively support various protests from the early seventies. Although the government had not repealed the whole act the fact that the Smith regime had shifted its position gave confidence to the church that if it leaned on the government as a unity or exerted pressure demanding justice, policies could be changed. Some Christians began to believe in the possibility of change. Hence the position taken by the church on the Land Tenure Act of 1969 was both an important stand and a significant stimulant that awakened much of its leadership into more vibrant protest for the restitution of Africans' sociopolitical rights. Linden aptly observed that Rhodes' favorite dictum "One missionary is worth a hundred police" was no longer true.[187]

The crop of African church leaders who emerged in the sixties fully understood the problems of Zimbabwe from a nationalist perspective; in fact they were nationalists in their own right. They shared the aspirations of the leading nationalists who were imprisoned, being among the marginalized and directly affected by injustice. This reality became epitomized in the ministries of people like Bishop Muzorewa, Canaan Banana and several other African clergy as we have seen in this chapter and as shall be further examined and demonstrated in the following chapters.

186. Halpern, "Polarisation in Rhodesia," January 1971.

187. Linden, *Catholic Church and Struggle*, 115–16.

6

Concerted Efforts toward Bringing Independence

"One dead missionary is as good as one hundred dead terrorists."[1] These words by a Rhodesian soldier express and reflect how the church in Zimbabwe had come to be viewed as an anti-colonial symbol in the seventies. In this chapter I will seek to show how the concerted efforts of Christians, especially in the African church leadership, accelerated the process of ending colonialism in Zimbabwe. These efforts though expressed in varied ways, and at times in conflicting ways, were crucial in the broader liberation struggle by Africans and in the attaining of independence.

The Test of Acceptability

By the early seventies newspaper headlines such as that which appeared in the *Rhodesian Herald* of 9 March 1973, "Politics in African Clergy" were becoming a common feature of the country's news headlines.[2] It was becoming evident that, besides its settler section, the general liberal–African church leadership in Zimbabwe was making serious attempts to address the political problems facing Africans. The various changes that had gradually taken place in the past decade within the leadership were now reflected in its response to the political challenges of the seventies. 1972 was to prove a decisive year, in which political developments again tested approaches amongst the churches to fundamental political issues. This arose from a

1. Rhodesian soldier quoted in, McLaughlin, *Liberation War*, 96.
2. "Politics in African Clergy," 9 March 1973.

series of diplomatic efforts aimed at breaking the political impasse between the British government and the Rhodesian Front government that stretched back to the dissolution of the Federation of Central Africa.[3]

In 1971 Britain, still trying to find a solution to the Rhodesian crisis, tasked Sir Alec Douglas-Home, the Secretary of State for Foreign and Commonwealth Affairs, to conduct a consultation with Smith and other interested parties such as African nationalists and churches to present their opinions on the best way to settle the Rhodesian political crisis.[4] The outcome of the consultation was referred to as the Home-Smith Proposals[5] or, in some quarters, as the Anglo-Rhodesian Settlement Proposals.[6] In the final draft the opinions of Africans and liberals alike were ignored, but the British government, in order to ascertain and assure Rhodesians that the proposals forwarded by Douglas-Home were a true reflection of the broad spectrum of the Rhodesian community, had stipulated beforehand that a test of acceptability would be conducted.[7] A referendum was ruled out in favor of a public expression of opinions in open public meetings. According to Ian Smith, the Rhodesian Front's rationale for this approach was because: "[I]t would be impossible to obtain an honest assessment from our black people, since the vast majority of them had never exercised a vote in their lives, could neither read nor write, did not understand the meaning of the word constitution, and were completely bemused by all the talking and manoeuvring going around them."[8]

However, Africans were fearful of expressing their opinions openly in the face of intimidation by the government, who placed intense pressure on chiefs to have their subjects vote for the proposals. A letter written by Judith Todd highlights the fears that any demonstration of unrest would be seized on by the government for their own purposes: "He [Todd] said at the meeting called to discuss the proposals if anyone suggested violent action, the people present should make very sure who that person was "because he will be no friend of ours." There has been for a long time the fear that *agents provocateurs* would be used to stir up violence to discredit opposition to the proposals and at every subsequent meeting I attended there were always

3. Hutson, *Rhodesia Ending an Era*.

4. Muzorewa, *Rise Up and Walk*, 92.

5. Smith, *The Great Betrayal*, 154.

6. "Christian Council of Rhodesia," 30 December 1971.

7. Smith, *Great Betrayal*, 156.

8. Ibid., 153.

pleas from the platform that people should be quiet and peaceful, whatever the provocations."[9]

Within the meetings there was strong opposition to the proposals, but this was not the "official" version of events: "The meeting I was invited to later, where four Chiefs were present, at Mataruse Council (Belingwe area) was large and the people rejected the proposals . . . After this meeting I was sent a copy of a resolution passed rejecting the proposals and signed by chiefs. Chief Mataruse, who is a very unhappy and frightened man, is on the Chiefs Council which, a few days later was reported as having unanimously accepted the proposals."[10]

The meetings were to be held in what were defined as traditional meeting places.[11] In January 1972 the Pearce Commission[12] arrived in Rhodesia to conduct the test. The public had two only answers available to them, "Yes" and "No."

Before the Pearce Commission arrived on the 30th December 1971 the Christian Council of Rhodesia, which stood as the primary voice for the Protestant community on sociopolitical matters, held a meeting in which twenty-nine members out of a total of thirty-eight present voted against adopting the proposals.[13] Although the proposals promised an increase of African representation in the House of Assembly, a declaration of human rights by which new laws could be implemented in courts, and a review of legislation with regards to racial discrimination,[14] Africans were still left facing serious inequalities, and not properly represented in parliament. The perpetuation of A and B voters' rolls instead of a common voters' roll would have continued to perpetuate racial polarization.[15] The Christian Council did not think the proposals went far enough in addressing the racism and oppression of Africans which was still embedded in the constitutional out-

9. Todd, "Chikarubi," 18 February 1972.

10. Ibid.

11. Watyoka, 25 *Years*, 17.

12. The commission was made up of twenty members from Britain under Lord Pearce. Their task was to find out whether Zimbabweans, Africans, and settlers were in favor of the Smith-Home proposals

13. "Christian Council of Rhodesia," Emergency Meeting Held at the University of Rhodesia to deliberate on the Anglo-Rhodesian Proposals in light of the impending arrival of the Pearce Commission, Salisbury, 30 December 1971, NAZ, GEN-P/WOR.

14. Ibid.

15. "A" voters were mainly whites and "B" voters were Africans. The "A" voters roll elected more than two-thirds of members of parliament.

comes of the proposals.[16] It was pointed out that the Law and Order Maintenance Act (LOMA) and the Land Tenure Act had not been sufficiently reviewed in the proposed constitution. Hence with regard to the proposals the Christian Council of Rhodesia declared no settlement better than an unjust one, "While we hope for a settlement, our prayer is that there will be no sacrifice of justice and of human dignity and rights. Indeed we would prefer no settlement for an unjust one. In light of the serious defects in the proposals for a settlement it is our considered judgement that they should be rejected."[17] It was their belief that the settlement provided no solution to Rhodesia's basic problem, fear and tension between races.

The Executive of the Christian Council had galvanized institutions into rejection of the proposals before the arrival of the Pearce Commission. They published and distributed nationwide through churches a pamphlet entitled; "*Think Again: 'A Guide to the Proposals for a Settlement*,'"[18] advocating rejection of the proposals. They also used African university students to distribute the pamphlets and explain them to the families and communities throughout the country when they were on holidays. These pamphlets were translated into Shona and Ndebele to make their opposition to the proposals widely known.[19]

The Rhodesian Front Government sought to gain an advantage by having the tests of acceptability conducted in government controlled areas such as local councils, where it believed it could predetermine the outcome of the African results.[20] The Rhodesian Front Government had further managed to convince Douglas-Home to include what it defined as "traditional meeting places" as venues for the meetings. These were preferred by the Rhodesian Front[21] because, through their policy of installing chiefs who supported their policies and offering them benefits, the government was assured of their support.[22] It would remain to be seen whether most chiefs' general support for the government would translate into the local people's vote.

16. "Christian Council of Rhodesia, "30 December 1971.

17. Ibid.

18. Watyoka, 25 *Years*, 17.

19. Ibid.

20. Smith, *Great Betrayal*, 153ff.

21. Muzorewa, *Rise and Walk*, 90.

22. Daneel, "The Growth," 182.

However, mission stations were left out of the initial proposals,[23] and the Christian Council launched a campaign to persuade the Pearce Commission to include mission stations as traditional meeting places, which was eventually agreed to.[24] African Christian influence on the political process was beginning to be felt, ensuring African Christian voices would be heard in the process being established.

Compared to the sixties where the influence of traditional religious leaders had been minimal in nationalist politics, in the seventies they were to take prominence mainly within ZANU armed struggle initiatives in the Dande Valley[25] and later in its guerrilla camps in Mozambique.[26] David Lan gives a prominent place to the influence of traditional religious beliefs and *masvikiro* (spirit mediums) during this period;[27] and so does Fay Chung who was also involved in educating Zimbabweans in ZANU's refugee camps and briefly was part of ZANU's political leadership in 1974.[28]

Joshua Nkomo takes a position that acknowledges only minimal influence of traditional religious agents in the liberation struggle during this period.[29] Hence he offers a perspective that seems to be different from that of Lan and Chung. These seemingly different perspectives need further exploration. Chung recounts the role of mediums within ZANU guerrilla camps and demonstrates how the presence and use of spirit mediums had mixed responses especially among the guerrilla leadership and sections of the ZANU guerrillas that subscribed to Marxist-Leninist teachings.[30]

In what serves as evidence that the military leadership undermined the role of *masvikiro* Chung contended that there were tendencies among ZANU guerrilla leaders towards taking liberties with women. According to Chung women who had come to be generally referred to as "warm blankets" were usually forced to provide sexual services to their leaders.[31] Refusing to do so was equated with refusing to take orders from one's commander. The guerrillas without ranks were not allowed to have such liber-

23. Watyoka, 25 *Years*, 17.

24. Ibid.

25. Lan, *Guns and Rain*, xvii passim.

26. Chung, *Second Chimurenga*, 171.

27. Lan, *Guns and Rain*, 2, passim.

28. Chung, *Second Chimurenga*, 171ff.

29. Nkomo, *The Story of My Life*, 15.

30. Chung, *Second Chimurenga*, 197–202.

31. Ibid.

ties. One such leader identified by Chung as having taken such liberties was ZANU's most revered army commander Josiah Magama Tongogara.[32] In an interview with the author Sister Janice McLaughlin, a Maryknoll nun who helped in ZANU guerrilla camps in Mozambique from September 1978 after she had been deported by the Smith government for her support for nationalists[33]—though friends with Chung since the armed struggle days in ZANU camps in Mozambique—disagreed with her criticism of Tongogara: "Women threw themselves at Tongogara. I never saw him behave inappropriately towards women and never towards me, although some guerrillas tried to impress me. They still behaved appropriately."[34]

Tongogara was generally viewed as a decent and respectable commander even by his opponents such as Ian Smith.[35] If one was to take the common view that Tongogara was reasonable it raises the question as to why Chung offers such a different portrayal of Tongogara. Chung's view of Tongogara may have been coloured by events mentioned by Edgar Tekere in *A Lifetime of Struggle*.[36] Tekere believed that Tongogara wanted Rugare Gumbo dead, and although not successful in achieving this goal, he was later responsible for the imprisonment of Gumbo[37] until independence, for supporting Henry Hamadziripi's failed attempt to remove Mugabe and Tongogara from the leadership of ZANU in 1978.[38] Gumbo and Chung had a child together although the two later separated. Gumbo and others involved in the Hamadziripi attempted power grab were spared death as a result of Muzenda's intervention when Tongogara and Mugabe are said to have wanted them executed.[39]

32. Tongogara did his primary education at an Anglican mission school and had only two years of secondary education but was deemed very intelligent. He was the ZANU army commander and is credited for leading ZANU's successful armed struggle. He died in December 1979 in a car accident.

33. McLaughlin, "We did it for love," 127. She also was a member of ZANU's coordinating committee for relief and development efforts and worked with ZANU's department of Education and culture to establish the school of Administration and Ideology based in Maputo, Mozambique.

34. Janice McLaughlin.

35. Smith, *Great Betrayal*, 314.

36. Tekere, *Lifetime of Struggle*, 97.

37. Rugare Gumbo serves today as a ZANU PF member of parliament for Mberengwa west. He was later readmitted into ZANU.

38. Tekere, *Lifetime of Struggle*, 97.

39. Ibid., 101.

Chung further points out that even female guerrilla leaders were guilty of taking liberties with young males. Although equally liberal, Chung seems not to condemn them as fiercely as she does Tongogara. *Masvikiro* also seemed not to have equally condemned or criticized the female leadership for such liberties.[40] If such liberties continued to take place among the male guerrilla leadership even though *masvikiro* condemned them it begs the question whether their influence was really that significant?[41]

Chung further argued that among the leaders *masvikiro* were not respected. She wrote, "Among those that subscribed to communism and the leadership as well as among some veteran guerrillas faithful to Tongogara they were not accorded the same respect."[42] At times *masvikiro* were publicly reprimanded and even threatened with imprisonment if their utterances were not pleasing to the political leadership.

The influence of traditional religious tenets and spirit mediums in the seventies is indisputable but the impact of their role in relation to the wider nationalist efforts remains a contentious subject.[43] Even within ZANU, where they seemed to be an integral part of the system, their general impact and the extent of their influence remain uncertain. There are several issues that need further investigation and clarification if one is to ascertain a complete picture of their influence and impact. Therefore in this respect I will seek here to raise and briefly explore some questions that demand further investigation.

First and foremost, the lack of statistical data on the general number of the spirit mediums in ZANU camps and in Zimbabwe during the seventies makes it difficult for one to ascertain the impact and scope of their influence. Determining this figure will highlight the scope of their influence both regionally and nationally. At a national level significant differences were observed by Ncube and Ranger in terms of the involvement of spirit mediums within ZAPU in the South-West part of the country which is dominated by the Ndebele.[44] Ncube and Ranger argued that although religion was involved there were differences in terms of the role played by religion in Zimbabwe's war of liberation in the south-west compared with the north where the Dande Valley, the subject area of discussion in

40. Chung, *Second Chimurenga*, 200ff.

41. Ibid., 198.

42. Ibid.

43. Bhebhe and Ranger, "Volume Introduction," 10.

44. Ncube and Ranger, "Religion in the Guerrilla War," 35.

Lan's thesis, was located.[45] Could it be that the phenomenon described and examined by Lan in *Guns and Rain* was largely limited to the Dande Valley?

Another significant aspect that needs to be taken into consideration was the difference in political ideology embraced by ZANU and ZAPU.[46] ZAPU did not, as a party, seek to embrace or adopt traditional religious teachings or agents as part of its political or ideological system or network, although some ZAPU guerrillas at a personal level undoubtedly may have sought guidance from such sources.[47]

Furthermore, the relation between *masvikiro* and ZANU in Mozambique and in Dande should not be interpreted as the standard template on how *masvikiro* operated within the rest of the country, among the guerrilla movements or generally within the liberation struggle. Even within the operations of ZANU although there was a constant belief in the guidance of the ancestors among most involved in the liberation struggle, the developments that took place in the mid-seventies beg the questions, how much influence or power did *masvikiro* wield within ZANU's operations and were their influences really significant in the wider scope of ZANU's liberation activities?

The Nhari rebellion (1974),[48] Mgagao declaration (1975)[49] and the *Vashandi*[50] saga (1975–76) pose significant challenges for a position that asserts the significant influence of *masvikiro* or any other religious tradition during this period within ZANU. The formal adoption of Leninist-Marxist teachings by the dominantly educated young ZANU guerrillas represented by these groups and the declaration made at Mgagao in 1975 were to have a negative impact on the role of spirit mediums and religion in general,

45. Ibid., 57.

46. J. McLaughlin.

47. Ncube and Ranger, "Religion in the Guerrilla War," 35.

48. Thomas Nhari led a rebellion within ZANU. In his attempt to usurp power his group was defeated and he was executed with seventy other guerrillas who supported him. For further reading, consult Chung, *Second Chimurenga*, 170ff.

49. In the October 1975 Mgagao Declaration ZANU guerrillas agreed to be led by Mugabe on condition that he followed a Marxist-Leninist course and the liberation of Zimbabwe was to be achieved through an armed struggle; the declaration constitutes appendix I in Chung, *Second Chimurenga*.

50. Shona word for workers, the word was adopted by the educated guerrillas to refer to what Karl Marx referred as the working class. For further reading, consult Tekere, *Lifetime of Struggle*; and Chung, *Second Chimurenga*.

Christianity included, within ZANU.[51] About these generally young and educated guerrillas, Chung, who was sympathetic to them and also a leader in the ZANU camps during this period when *masvikiro* are said to have held a significant amount of influence, wrote: "While the Vashandi assiduously studied the works of Marx, Lenin and Mao Tse Tung, they had little time for the ideology of the peasants, which was dominated by ancestor worship and the power of the ancestral spirits, the midzimu, who controlled the day-to-day decision-making of the majority of the peasants and their veteran leaders. The Vashandi dismissed traditional religion as superstition, which had to be destroyed."[52]

After the fall of Vashandi in 1976 at the hands of Tongogara, African Traditional Religions just as communist ideology was viewed as divisive and there was from then an emphasis on focusing on national grievances.[53] This was spearheaded by Tongogara who had become suspicious of both the communist ideology and *masvikiro*.[54] In the later period of the War, as I shall later explore in this chapter, ZANU being the only nationalist movement that seemed to have incorporated *masvikiro* was to be dominantly led and supported by people of Roman Catholic tradition. It then also leaves one wondering how significant the influence traditional religious leaders would have on the movement. These factors may have undermined the role of *masvikiro*. It is therefore difficult to see how significant the role of *masvikiro* would have been in such an environment. Nkomo wrote, "In 1974 when I was released after more than ten years in prison, I was told that the voice of the shrine had issued a message. It had said farewell, and ceased speaking to the people, but their complaints and pleas would still be heard. Perhaps as people become more 'civilized,' God takes a step back."[55]

Nkomo paints a picture here of a sociopolitical Zimbabwean seventies that did not have a central role of traditional religious leaders or influence. What was significant was that during this period, critical to the struggle against colonialism, Christian influence, and especially African Christian protest was beginning to take a central role.

51. McLaughlin, "Avila Mission," 92.

52. Chung, *Second Chimurenga*, 171.

53. Ibid.

54. Ibid.

55. Nkomo, *The Story of my Life*, 15.

The African National Council

The Test of Acceptability spurred another significant social development in "Rhodesia." On the 16th December 1971 a group that became known as the African National Council was formed solely to lobby against the Anglo-Rhodesian proposals and further address the constitutional problems.[56] ZAPU claims that it was its leadership that hatched the idea of the National Council.[57] Since political parties had been banned and leading African nationalists were in prison the need for a distinct African voice to oppose the Home-Smith proposals had necessitated the formation of the National Council.[58] It was solely African in terms of its leadership composition but accepted whites if they wanted to be members.[59] Furthermore, according to Muzorewa it claimed to be guided by a Christian ethos, proclaiming: "We declare our solidarity with those international organisations dedicated to the peaceful creation and preservation of the basic universal human rights and the brotherhood of man under the Fatherhood of God."[60]

The National Council differed from the Christian Council in being simply a political lobby group, but it was one with a religious ethos.[61] It re-introduced a united voice of protest among Africans that had been missing since the split of the African nationalist camp in the early sixties.[62] Some semblance of unity and a single African voice had been viewed as necessary if the Pearce Commission was to take the African call for a "No" to the proposals seriously.[63] The ANC sought to be a non-partisan lobby group acceptable to both ZANU and ZAPU supporters and their leaderships.[64] Christian leaders were believed to be suitable for such a task and hence the National Council was formed in which they held a predominant position in its leadership.[65]

56. Chambati, "National Unity," 147–49.
57. ZAPU Publicity Bureau, "Z.A.P.U.," 16–19 June 1977.
58. Chambati, "National Unity,"148.
59. Banana, "African National Council," May 1973.
60. Muzorewa, "The Banner of Unity," 10 March 1972.
61. Ibid.
62. Chambati, "National Unity," 148.
63. ZAPU Publicity Bureau, "Z.A.P.U.," 16–19 June 1977.
64. Chambati, "National Unity," 147.
65. Ibid., 148.

According to Fay Chung in *Second Chimurenga*, the clergy were chosen to lead because they were weak and therefore ZANU and ZAPU assumed they could control them.[66] However, the evidence does not support this assertion, and in fact points to the contrary. Muzorewa had by then proved that he was both courageous and capable, not just by acquiring a Master's degree and being voted the Methodist church bishop, but also in that he was restricted and barred from entering Tribal Trust Lands by the Smith regime in 1970.[67] It would not have served the nationalists' goals to employ a weak caretaker leadership to protest against the proposed constitution reforms proposed in the Smith-Home agreement. These clergy were capable and trusted community leaders and it is this that also attracted the nationalists in prison to ask them to lead the struggle towards the restitution of Africans' political rights.[68]

On the other hand, it is also evident that nationalists had chosen Christian leaders to run the Council with the hope that that arrangement would serve their own interests.[69] The National Council was to be a temporary caretaker organization that would relinquish political power once successful in the "NO Campaign," although no termination date was set.[70] They seemed to believe that the clergy would have no political ambitions of their own.[71] Bishop Abel Muzorewa the first president of the National Council upon his appointment appeared to confirm this view, "I have no personal ambition. I seek no office, nor position for myself, only democratic rule for my country."[72] The same declaration was repeated in the following year, "I have no political ambition, I seek no office position or financial gain, only democratic rule for my country."[73] It would remain to be seen whether both Muzorewa's claims and the nationalists' assumptions proved correct.

Alongside Bishop Muzorewa, other African clergy selected in the leadership of the National Council[74] included Reverend Canaan Sodindo Banana, who became its vice-president, and later the first President of

66. Chung, *Second Chimurenga*, 88.
67. Muzorewa, *Rise and Walk*, 78ff.
68. Brand, "African Nationalists," 78.
69. ZAPU Publicity Bureau, "Z.A.P.U.," 16–19 June 1977.
70. Ibid.
71. Chambati, "National Unity," 147.
72. Muzorewa, "Return to Legality," 20 July 1972.
73. Muzorewa, "Speech," 29 May 1973.
74. Muzorewa, "Address to the UANC," 9 September 1977.

Zimbabwe.[75] Rev Henry Kachidza, who was the General Secretary of the Bible Society in Rhodesia,[76] was appointed the deputy treasurer and was later promoted to be the treasurer.[77] Muzorewa and Banana who held the Council's top leadership roles had not been formally involved in nationalist politics before then,[78] although in 1970 Muzorewa had protested against the Land Tenure Act which led to his prohibition by government from entering Tribal Trust Lands (TTLs).[79] Even Ian Smith recognized the capabilities of the National Council's leadership.[80]

The influence of African Christian leaders in the final struggle against colonialism was consolidated as the National Council began to work closely with the Christian Council and various churches in the campaign to reject the Home-Smith proposals. The two bodies became closely identified, and it was only in 1979 that members were required to officially resign from their Christian Council duties if they held offices in the National Council.[81] The clergy chosen to lead the National Council were already part of the Christian Council. Muzorewa worked tirelessly campaigning for a refusal of the proposals and his efforts were further complemented by various Church groups in general and by the Christian Council in particular.[82] On January 11 1972 when the Pearce Commission arrived to conduct the test of acceptability the efforts of these two groups had effectively shaped African opinion.[83] The secretary general of the Christian Council of Rhodesia during this period, CD Watyoka noted, "By the time the acceptability of the Anglo-Rhodesian proposals was tested, the country was literally shouting, NO! NO! NO!, at each meeting place."[84]

75. Banana, "The Role of the Church," 206.

76. Muzorewa, *Rise and Walk*, 91. Kawadza was also known for his evangelical conviction.

77. Muzorewa, "Return to Legality," 20 July 1972.

78. Muzorewa, *Rise and Walk*, 94.

79. Ibid. 78ff.

80. Smith, *Great Betrayal*, 154.

81. Watyoka, 25 *Years*, 19; the Christian Council argued that the demands of political office in the Internal Settlement government would not allow those that had been elected into parliament to effectively undertake their duties in the council.

82. Muzorewa, *Rise and Walk*, 92ff.

83. Smith, *Great Betrayal*, 155.

84. Watyoka, 25 *Years*, 17.

Fig. 6 African workers in opposition to the Home-Smith Proposals in 1972
Courtesy of the NAZ

Within a few days of the start of the Pearce Commission, as the popularity of the NO protest was becoming clear, the Rhodesian Front arrested and restricted some of the leading figures in the campaign. On the 18th January 1972 Todd and his daughter Judith were arrested on the grounds that they were inciting violence.[85] Neither father nor daughter had advocated violence, and Judith Todd was clear that the reason was "their opposition to the settlement."[86] Other members of the National Council and Christian Council were detained or restricted in their movements, including Percy M'kudu (leader of the opposition in Parliament, and one-time President of the Christian Council), and Rev. Henry Kachidza.[87]

The African population was subjected to a further excessive use of force by government security agents.[88] The African Registration Act was amended and consequently made it compulsory for all Africans to carry registration certificates at all times.[89] The government introduced "collective fines" for rural communities suspected of harboring guerrillas especially in the northern parts of the country where there were increased guerrilla attacks,[90] and livestock could be confiscated.[91] A drinking regulation was also

85. Todd, "Chikarubi," 18 February 1972.

86. Ibid.

87. Watyoka, *25 Years*, 18.

88. Banana, "The African National Council," May 1973.

89. Ibid.

90. Windrich, *The Rhodesian Problem*, 292.

91. Banana, "The African National Council," May 1973.

Fig. 7 Banners expressing the National Council's position to the Pearce Commission Courtesy of NAZ (The smaller banner reads *Sonke Sithi* No!)[92]

92. Sonke Sithi No! is Ndebele for "We all say No!"

introduced which barred Africans from drinking alcohol in areas registered as white areas after 7pm during week days and after 1pm on Saturdays. On Sundays Africans residing in white areas were prohibited from drinking alcohol.[93] To some in the churches these regulations were simply viewed as promoting morality, and were not opposed, but to most Africans the laws re-enforced their inferior social status,[94] To Banana the actions were: "Purely a product of the racial policies of the Rhodesian Front, that breed contempt and resentment and deliberately seek to creat [*sic*] conditions and platforms of bitter racial conflicts."[95]

The Pearce Commission finished its task on the 12th March and the results were officially published on the 23rd May 1972. The "No" response had carried the day.[96] The Christian Council and the National Council through a vigorous campaign chiefly based on the dissemination of information on a national scale had played a key role in ensuring one inequitable solution to ending colonial power was defeated. It would remain to be seen if this success could be repeated in relation to other political problems that faced the Rhodesian community.[97]

Perhaps it was the respect the National Council's leadership won through the successful "No" campaign, that propelled the succession of events that followed in the National Council after the Test of Acceptability.[98] When a council seeking to represent all Africans was established, its ultimate purpose was not clearly established, leaving the potential for it to take a life form of its own or a different life form from that desired by the ZAPU and ZANU nationalists.[99]

On the 10th March 1972 the National Council was transformed from being a lobby group into a political party. Muzorewa declared, "This organisation, like the old ones, will be referred to, by outsiders, as an African Nationalist Organization . . . heirs to the People's struggle which has ceaselessly been waged since the imposition of alien rule in 1890, in the name of Almighty God, who, in His love and mercy, created all people and races

93. Ibid.

94. Ibid.

95. Banana, "Racialism," 29 August 1972.

96. Smith, *Great Betrayal*, 155.

97. Muzorewa, *Rise and Walk*, 106.

98. Smith, *Great Betrayal*, 154.

99. ZAPU Publicity Bureau, "Z.A.P.U.," 16–19 June 1977.

in His image.[100] It then went on to boldly claim, "[W]e here now summon every African in this land, young or old, rich or poor educated or uneducated, chief or subject, and those members of other races dedicated to the establishment of human brotherhood, to recognise the trumpet we here sound and to rally around us, so that together, we continue our arduous journey to Zimbabwe in a Christian and non-violent manner."[101]

The African National Council believed that its success nationally in orchestrating the "NO" response gave it a clear mandate from the African masses to turn into a political party.[102] Muzorewa accepted his nomination as the African National Council's (ANC) president. Notable was the dominant role played by African Protestant Christian leaders and their continued presence at different points throughout its life, including Rev Banana (who later resigned and rejoined ZANU), and Rev Max Chigwida of the Presbyterian Church who later became its secretary general. Rev. A.T. Kanodereka and Rev. Henry H. Kachidza were other clergy who held leading roles in the ANC.[103]

The Programme to Combat Racism

In the 1970s a decision was made, and executed not just in "Rhodesia" but worldwide. This was the controversial program known as the "Programme to Combat Racism," initiated by the ecumenical world mother body, the World Council of Churches (WCC).[104] After years of press statements and drawing up policies against racism in the years after 1948 when the WCC was formed, little had been achieved by way of decisive political change. Rhetoric prevailed over action.[105] This state of affairs was to change after 1969.[106] Garfield Todd and Nathan Shamuyarira were delegates at the Octo-

100. Muzorewa, "The Banner of Unity," 10 March 1972.

101. Ibid.

102. Muzorewa, "Speech," 29 May 1973.

103. List of ANC / Muzorewa Central Committee Members, n.d., NAZ, Acc: MS 771/1–3.

104. Bent, *Breaking Down the Walls*, 10.

105. Ibid. In 1954 statements against racism were made at the "Second Assembly of the World Council of Churches Evanston" and in 1960 at the consultation of WCC members in South Africa (Cottesloe).

106. Vincent, *The Race*. In the 1969 Consultation on Racism held from the 19th to the 24th May, members called upon member churches of the WCC to begin to apply economic sanctions against corporations and institutions that practice blatant racism,

ber 1969 Notting Hill conference which adopted the resolution to provide financial support to movements combating oppression.[107] Previously, Todd had been detained by the Rhodesian Government, and Shamuyarira exiled to Tanzania where he both lecture and was involved in the nationalist struggle.[108]

The decisions reached at the Notting Hill Consultation came as a follow-up to discussions in August of the same year at the Canterbury Consultation. In a bold decision, the WCC announced it would provide finances to liberation movements.[109] In accordance with the Notting Hill and Canterbury decisions of 1969, at a meeting held from the 31st August to the 4th September 1970 in Arnoldshain, the WCC Executive Committee allocated the first financial grants to liberation movements.[110] US$200 000 was allocated for what was termed "anti-racist organisations"; this included liberation movements, even those involved in the armed struggle, and pressure groups worldwide that were fighting against racism. In southern Africa, alongside Mozambique, Zambia, Angola and South Africa, Rhodesian movements were also beneficiaries of the funds of this program. These were the Zimbabwe African National Union (ZANU), the Zimbabwe African People's Union (ZAPU) and, later, the African National Council (ANC).[111]

The WCC insisted that its grants were not for buying weapons but they were to be used for humanitarian purposes by the movements, but it also made it clear in its statements that, "action accompanied by mistrust was hardly likely to create trust"[112] hence they would not supervise or call beneficiaries to account on how they administered the grants. Critics of the WCC were quick to realize that since the program would not hold accountable liberationists on how they used the grants it was inevitable that some funds would be used for the purchase of ammunition.

---

and to support resistance movements. At the 23rd meeting of the WCC's central committee from the 12th to the 22nd August 1969 at Canterbury, the Notting Hill, conclusions were confirmed and provided guidelines for a creation of a department within the WCC that would pursue these decisions.

107. Banana, *Repression and Resistance*, 169.

108. *The Christian Century*, 23 September 1970.

109. Statement of the General secretary of the World Council of Churches in Response to the statement of the council of the Evangelical Church in Germany, 24 September 1970, NAZ, GEN-P/WOR.

110. Ibid.

111. Ibid.

112. Ibid.

In Southern Africa the debate was intense. South Africa's Prime Minister B.J. Vorster responded to the decision by demanding the withdrawal of South African churches' membership from the WCC.[113] Vorster viewed the decision by the WCC as blatant support for what he viewed to be terrorism. The Dutch Reformed Church responded in accordance with Vorster's demands, but the University Church Movement (UCM) in South Africa refused to condemn the WCC. Instead they released a press statement in which they criticized their own South African sociopolitical policies: "The churches need to explain their ambiguous attitude to the use of violence. While the churches condemn the WCC's decision, they keep quiet about the use of violence by white regimes in Southern Africa, and also keep quiet when South Africa continues to invest in military equipment used against its own citizens."[114]

They questioned the sincerity of fellow South African Christians who objected to violence whilst at the same time paying taxes to the apartheid government which were used to buy arms. These same arms were being used for military training for pro-apartheid youths.[115] The UCM further argued that the fact that South Africa was sending food and other services, from taxes also paid by Christians, to Rhodesian and Mozambican soldiers who were being used as oppressive agents, meant that their own government deserved to be equally condemned by Christians. To the UCM, liberation movements were not terrorists who did not deserve Christian support, but liberators who deserved to be helped.[116]

However, the South African Council of Churches (SACC) refused to support the WCC decision,[117] and declared: "[W]e dissociate ourselves from this action and its implied support of violence. Any practical assistance to liberation movements prepared to achieve their means through violence, would only condone and inflame violence which was to be avoided at all costs."[118] When Desmond Tutu became its Secretary General from 1978, the SACC's attitude on sociopolitical matters changed considerably.[119]

113. "British Priests," 26 September 1970

114. "Response of the SA Church Leaders," 12 September 1970.

115. Ibid. The statement was issued by the UMC head office.

116. Ibid.

117. "Statement of South African Member Churches," 11 September 1970.

118. "South African Church Council," 25 September 1970. Although insisting to be dissociated with the WCC the South African Council of Churches refused to leave the WCC as commanded by BJ Vorster, then South African president.

119. Tutu, *Hope and Suffering*, 17.

The program to combat racism was equally contentious on the wider international scene. Some Protestants found the decision incompatible with their Christian faith. The governing body of the United Evangelical Lutheran Church in Germany (VELKD) rejected the principle that financial support be given to liberation fighters.[120] Some Swiss Protestants also thought that the decision made by the WCC to sponsor liberation movements was irreconcilable with Christianity, and viewed their continued affiliation with the now "more politically engaged" WCC as problematic.[121]

In Germany the Lutheran churches, which had ties with the Evangelical Lutheran Church of Rhodesia, joined in the debate. The Council of the German Evangelical Churches raised a number of questions: "The New Delhi Assembly in 1961 recommended that where measures were to be taken in the field of race relations, cooperation with the churches directly involved was desirable . . . How can liberation movements be influenced to strive for the peaceful achievement of their objectives? White racism provokes an opposing 'coloured' racism, sometimes bound up with nationalism. What can Christendom do to combat effectively all forms of racism?"[122]

The WCC had wrestled with similar questions at two consultations held in 1969 at which its Executive Committee had reached this decision.[123] They had concluded that merely rhetorical initiatives had been ineffective and a more resolute approach was necessary.[124]

Other bodies had fewer questions. The Lutheran World Federation that had influence in the Evangelical Lutheran Church of Rhodesia unequivocally declared the sinfulness of the Rhodesian situation and agreed with the WCC on this matter: "The decision of the WCC has to be interpreted as an effort to demonstrate that the churches mean business when they condemn racism. Race discrimination is sin. Sin has to be opposed."[125] The Swiss, *La Vie Protestante*, believed that the decision would shock some,

120. "United Evangelical Lutheran Church in Germany Against Race Programme," 28 September 1970.

121. "Statement by the Swiss Evangelische Landeskirchen," 27 September 1970.

122. "Programme to Combat Racism," 24 September 1970.

123. The Evanston Assembly of 1954, the New Delhi Assembly of 1961, the Mindolo Consultation on 1964 and the Uppsala Assembly of 1968 were efforts by the WCC to address the race issue.

124. "Church Call," 6 February 1973.

125. Prof. Mikko Juva of Helsinki, President of the Lutheran World Federation, in *Kotimaa*, September-October 1970, NAZ, GEN-P/WOR.

but strengthen the faith of others: "The World Council of Churches is congratulated for its courageous initiative. It has by its decision to support groups combating racism left the domaine [sic] of ideas and engaged itself into practical action . . . if some churches are shocked by this, many others on the contrary will feel strengthened in their faith."[126]

The British Council of Churches[127] which had close ties with the Christian Council of Rhodesia responded, "Christians may differ about method, but they cannot evade the responsibility laid upon them by their faith to relieve the oppressed and to strive for justice for all men."[128] They justified their position by appeal to the use of force to rid Europe of the racist Nazi regime in the Second World War: "In 1939 the majority of Christians in Britain believed it right to resist by force a racist regime in Germany, pursuing its policies by overt and covert violence. It cannot be doubted that violence, implicit or explicit, exists also in regimes whose avowed aim is to maintain indefinitely the dominance of a minority race over the great majority of the population."[129]

In the view of the British Council of Churches, the WCC Executive had little alternative, and it was important that something be done. They identified liberation movements as freedom fighters who deserved to be supported by Christians on the basis of the traditional Christian theology of "a just war."[130] They believed that urging subjects of oppressive governments to avoid violence when seeking freedom was only furthering the ends of the oppressive governments.[131] Those committed to non-violence were not to be condemned, nor were those who wanted to raise funds or join the liberation movements, only the indifferent were to be censured.[132] To the BCC, biblical teachings on humanity and justice demanded a strong line. It concluded, "It is too late to insist that our support should be confined to those pledged to non-violence . . . The time has come to show our solidarity with those seeking radical change and struggling for freedom in southern Africa"[133]

126. "200,000 Dollars Qui Font," 18 September 1970.

127. British Council of Churches, *Violence in Southern Rhodesia*, x.

128. "Combating Racism," 30 September 1970.

129. Ibid.

130. British Council of Churches, *Violence in Southern Africa*, 77.

131. Ibid.

132. Ibid., 78.

133. Ibid., 77.

In most independent African countries in the seventies there was a general agreement that both churches and governments had to do something about the oppression of people in "Rhodesia" and the rest of Southern Africa that still faced various forms of sociopolitical oppression. Kenneth Kaunda, the then Zambian president, who was also a Presbyterian, summarized the welcome among African leaders of the WCC program to combat racism, "[I] could not understand how anyone calling himself a Christian could object to the churches helping those who are oppressed and fighting for their rights."[134]

The Tanzanian Christian Council openly declared their support for the WCC's decision, and for liberation fighters.[135] The Executive of the All Africa Conference of Churches also welcomed the decision to "trust people who are taking radical action against racism," alongside its hope that "all churches will continue to work to reconcile those divided by barriers of race and justice."[136]

Garfield Todd was one of the chief architects[137] of the "Programme to Combat Racism" and wielded influence in both the Rhodesian church and nationalist movements:[138] "The decision has the support of the majority of Christian churches, including I believe, the majority of Christians in Rhodesia. However, as the majority in this country are Africans they have no adequate means of expressing themselves. Africans also have good reasons to fear an expression of opinion so unpopular with Government."[139]

To Todd, the WCC had become the international voice for the African Christian majority, and he described its position on the matter as a "brotherly practical measure of love." He also insisted that the WCC grants were for humanitarian work, but furthermore he contended that liberation movements had to be supported in cash or kind. The Rhodesian constitution and legislation adopted in 1970 were drafted to ensure permanent domination of whites and further intensified racial discrimination.[140] This justified

134. "World Council of Churches," *Oikoumene.*

135. Ibid.

136. "The Executive Committee of the all Africa Conference of Churches," September 21–23 1970.

137. Banana, *The Church and the Struggle*, 208.

138. Todd, "World Council's Object," 27 September 1970.

139. Ibid.

140. Ibid.

support for liberationists by the church in and outside "Rhodesia."[141] Todd argued that the WCC's grants in "Rhodesia" were intended to support not terrorism, but the attainment of justice, equality, human dignity and freedom for all people, in the face of the imprisonment of people without trial, deportation of church leaders and the restriction of Christian leaders into Tribal Trust Lands (TTLs).[142] To Todd, failure to act would be a betrayal of the people by the church.[143]

This radical stance by a former missionary and Prime Minister of "Rhodesia" may seem surprising, but Todd had been imprisoned by the Smith regime in 1966. He may also have been seeking to affirm his credentials as a nationalist to Africans bearing in mind that he faced criticism from some radical African nationalists who did not believe that any white person could be totally committed to the African nationalist cause, as indicated in a letter by the nationalist, Edison Zvobgo, sent to Todd's daughter Judith, "You will face a question [from Africans] which has been put to me . . ..Being a white person, can you be sincere in wanting Africans to rule Zimbabwe? Why did your Dad, when he was Prime Minister not bring about majority rule? It has been said that your family own an estate too vast to be explained in terms of need—how do you reconcile your family's commitment to African liberation and all this?"[144] Zvobgo in Todd's defense went on to note Todd's ability to empathize with the cause of Africans as a result of his own arrest and ill-treatment, and his resulting ostracism by most whites.[145]

Why Todd and other Christians who were keen to stage an armed struggle, especially in the case of Zimbabwe, did not seek first to pursue the route of organizing the masses for a non-violent revolution before pursuing the route of war is unclear. In previous decades people had witnessed in America and India that non-violent protest could be a potent route to sociopolitical transformation.

The grants from the WCC certainly helped to boost morale among nationalists and especially those involved in the armed struggle since there was acute shortage of resources among them including food.[146] ZAPU and

141. Ibid.

142. Ibid.

143. Ibid.

144. Zvobgo, A letter to Judy (Judith Todd), 21 January 1973.

145. Ibid.

146. Todd, "World Council's Object," 27 September 1970.

ZANU cadres by 1970 were based in Zambia and Tanzania, and were waging a guerrilla-warfare against the regime, but beset by shortages of food, medication and ammunition. What the Chinese and Soviet Union governments offered was of limited value in the armed struggle.[147] Although the WCC had insisted that the money was mainly for humanitarian purposes, the grants were not monitored by the WCC, and some of the £10,000 grants received by ZANU and ZAPU in 1970 could have been used to purchase arms. Unmonitored grant allocations of varying amounts continued to be disbursed throughout the seventies.[148]

The "Programme to Combat Racism" further highlighted the polarization in the Rhodesian church. Amongst the mainline denominations there was either outright opposition, or a marked internal friction between the largely white opponents of the policy, and the largely black supporters. The Anglican dean of Bulawayo Cathedral, Rev. Allan Shaw, declared "It is not the function of the Christian world body to advocate force and terrorism."[149] Most of the African clergy and radical liberals disagreed. According to Bishop Abel Muzorewa the unanimity of opposition from white Christians to the "Programme," was equaled by African appreciation for it.[150]

On November 11th 1970 thirty-four members of the Christian Council of Rhodesia met to deliberate on the acceptability of the "Programme," with some white members arguing that financing nationalists was in fact advocating violence. Thirty members voted in favor of the "Programme," and in consequence the Salvation Army–known world-wide for its opposition to violence–resigned from the Council and the Presbyterian Church of Southern Africa threatened to resign. The Anglican Bishop of Mashonaland, Paul Burrough, who had replaced Cecil Alderson, proposed that the Mashonaland diocesan standing committee withdraw from the Christian Council. This was challenged by an African lay Anglican representative in the Christian Council, Percy M'kudu, who was also a member of the opposition in the Rhodesian Parliament, warned that the African membership of the Anglican Church would not resign from the council, and that withdrawal would split the Anglican denomination on racial lines.[151] Burrough

147. Chung, *Second Chimurenga*, 89.

148. "WCC Actions," NAZ, GEN-P/WOR.

149. Muzorewa, *Rise up and Walk*, 87.

150. Ibid., 88.

151. Ibid.

withdrew his proposal, and an uneasy unity was retained amongst Anglicans. The clash revealed the huge tensions in the mainline denominations between a white leadership, and an African majority membership whose interests were not seen as primary or fully understood.

In the Methodist Church in Rhodesia the World Council of Churches' program to combat racism also caused tension between its African and white clergy.[152] Even some liberals like Rev. Fred Rea who had in the past condemned the Rhodesian Government policies and taken sides with Africans,[153] opposed the "Programme to Combat Racism" on the grounds that it encouraged violence. Rea was "distressed" by the decision: "I do not believe that in Rhodesia the interests of freedom will be served by a policy of violence, nor am I able to reconcile its advocacy with the way of Christ . . . this must not be our way in Rhodesia. Here we shall overcome evil with good."[154]

Its governing body, dominated by white missionaries, also released a press statement distancing itself from the policy: "The Synod of the Methodist Church in Rhodesia believes that Christians ought not to support violence in any form. Violence will only create further mistrust between races and amongst people."[155]

Some believed that the position taken by the Methodist Church in Rhodesia had been tailored to assuage its white membership.[156] Rev. Canaan Banana in protest against his denomination's position resigned from the Methodist ministry, declaring: "I now find myself unable to reconcile the gospel of Christ . . . with the pronouncement of my church. I find it impossible to exercise my special ministry with a church that has, to my concepts, denied its Christ . . . stop pretending that we are a Church or a nation of Christian pacifists."[157]

Four months later Banana rescinded his resignation after being persuaded by fellow Methodist ministers and missionaries to reconsider his position. In the light of his resignation some within Methodism had questioned "the authenticity and meaning" of it. Other Methodists, Banana recognized, had become inured against analyzing closely questions of political

152. Banana, *Church and Struggle*, 213.

153. Rea, "The Impact of Habit and Custom," 106.

154. *Rhodesia Herald*, 5 November 1970.

155. Quoted in, Banana, *Church and Struggle*, 218.

156. Muzorewa, *Rise and Walk*, 88.

157. Methodist Connexional Archives, CS Banana's file, 7 January 1971.

importance. He asserted, “There are those among the perceptive who would find it in themselves to question the rationality of my resignation only to rescind my position without necessarily managing to effect a reconsideration of the church’s stance. In my defence I would stolidly maintain that I had made the point.”[158]

On the other hand the Rhodesian Reformed Church, born out of the South African Dutch Reformed Church, condemned the “Programme” and pleaded with fellow denominations of reformed tradition to renounce their membership of the Christian Council of Rhodesia in protest.[159] Those that did not want to leave the body were advised by the Reformed Church to use their presence in the Christian Council to stifle any initiatives by the Christian Council to aid what it termed terrorists.[160]

The Christian Council itself took a different line, at first resolving to “suspend judgement on the WCC grants for welfare and propaganda until such dialogue has taken place,”[161] but then on the 11th of November 1970 openly expressed its support for the grants to liberation movements.[162] In a press statement they said, “We recognise that the help we have received has come from the free will gifts of our brethren in churches throughout the world and for this Christian concern we record our thanks.”[163]

The WCC action demonstrated to the world that some members of the church had lost confidence in the fact that sociopolitical justice could be achieved globally only through non-violent channels. Other alternatives to non-violence had to be tried. Although the grants were small in scale, the churches associated with the WCC had moved away from simply preserving the political status quo to, by words and deeds, prove that the churches were an agent of sociopolitical change.

The “Programme to Combat Racism” polarized the worldwide Christian community, and added to the tensions in the already polarized Rhodesian Christian community. For those that wanted political change its efforts were welcome, bringing a sense of support from other Christians in the worldwide community. Those that had adopted violence as a method of protest were further encouraged in their efforts at political

158. Banana, *Church and Struggle*, 221.

159. “Church Call,” 6 February 1973.

160. Ibid.

161. “WCC Invited to Rhodesia,” 16 February 1973.

162. Banana, *Repression and Resistance*, 172.

163. Watyoka, 25 *Years*, 16.

protest. Beneficiaries, such as the African National Council (ANC), had a strong Christian affiliation and composition in its leadership, and were further spurred into vibrant social action.[164] However, the grants had more symbolic than practical value in sustaining the war. Fay Chung observed conditions in ZANU guerrilla camps around 1974: "[N]ew recruits faced a severe shortage of food . . . There was also a short supply of plates—recruits had to receive what little food there was on leaves or in their bare hands . . . there was also a serious shortage of guns and ammunition."[165]

164. "WCC Actions," August 1978.

165. Chung, *Second Chimurenga*, 89.

7

The Coming of Independence

"The last and bitterest stages of the Zimbabwean liberation war were entirely unnecessary."[1] These words by Joshua Nkomo, aptly sum up the efforts of those involved in the armed struggle against colonialism during in the late seventies. Diplomatic efforts from the international community as well as protest and various peace initiatives from Christians and Christian institutions by 1974 which also saw the release of nationalist leaders after ten years or more of incarceration had brought the end of colonial rule within sight.

The War within the War[2]

The transformation of the Christian dominated ANC into a political body had gradual significant impact on Rhodesia's political developments in the nineteen seventies. This impact was also significantly felt among the leadership of ZANU and ZAPU.[3] The ZAPU publicity bureau began a systematic attempt to discredit Muzorewa: "Bishop Muzorewa rode on the crest of his wave and found himself suddenly looking at the world from its horizons as caretaker of the African National Council. He mistook the storm of enthusiasm over the surface revival of ZAPU (under the cover name ANC)

1. Nkomo, *Story of My Life*, 187.

2. Some portions of this section have been published in a journal article, "The Struggle within the Struggle" in the August 2012 issue of *Studia Historiae Ecclesiasticae*.

3. ZAPU Publicity Bureau, "Z.A.P.U.," 16–19 June 1977.

for personal support. This had an accidental effect on his mind. He was tempted to change the course of history and seize the moment for himself and the opportunists."[4] The political presence of the ANC now left the claim of ZANU and ZAPU to the political leadership of the country in jeopardy.[5] The ANC stepped into the gap created by the banning of other nationalist parties and the imprisonment of their leaders, and offered a vehicle of protest markedly different from ZAPU/ZANU with its commitment to violent means, not just against the Rhodesian Front government, but against fellow Africans. Muzorewa believed that even some Christians who did not want to join partisan politics were swayed by the new party's initial dedication to non-violence,[6] and motivated some Africans to seek the transformation of the ANC into a political party despite the consequences.[7]

With ZANU and ZAPU in detention, the future direction of the ANC was in the determination of the new ANC leadership.[8] Although Muzorewa did not disown the other nationalist leaders in the first few years of the ANC becoming political, it was clear that the ANC was no longer their political baby or junior. Muzorewa believed that it had superseded ZANU or ZAPU: "We of the ANC Executive saw the verdict as a clear-cut summons for black Zimbabweans to realise the essential power of unity. This was a victory which outshone the achievements of all the other previous black organisations."[9]

There was failure to realize how threatening this was to the other nationalist leaders.[10] Despite the common enemy of the Rhodesian government, ZANU and ZAPU still contested with each other for political power, and now with the ANC.[11] Their war within the war, was as equally brutal as the armed struggle.[12] Political contestation within the struggle for national liberation, was far from being resolved, but rather increased.[13]

4. Ibid.
5. Muzorewa, "Address to the UANC."
6. Muzorewa, *Rise and Walk*, 119.
7. Ibid.
8. ZAPU Publicity Bureau, "Z.A.P.U.," 16–19 June 1977.
9. Muzorewa, *Rise and Walk*, 118.
10. ZAPU Publicity Bureau, "Z.A.P.U.," 16–19 June 1977.
11. Chambati, "National Unity," 148.
12. ZAPU Publicity Bureau, "Z.A.P.U.," 16–19 June 1977.
13. Bhebhe, *Simon Muzenda*, 166.

Towards the end of 1973 divisions between ZANU, ZAPU and the ANC brought negative reaction against Christians, churches and her institutions that were viewed as supporting the ANC. Some prominent nationalist members who had become part of the ANC leadership during its non-partisan period began to shift their allegiance to their old parties. The resignation of Edison Zvobgo[14] who was the principal overseas representative of the ANC, and his subsequent identification with ZANU, illustrates the tensions: "I admire the bishop. I believe he is a man of great courage and sincerity. But I am convinced that he is not an experienced negotiator. Remember that he has not been schooled in the crucible of real nationalist politics. He is not able to speak with more than one voice. Whites must be led down the garden path of slaughter. Morality does not come into it. What frightens me and other nationalists abroad is that the bishop might not be able to demonstrate this versatility. This may result in the wholesale sale of the people."[15]

Zvobgo ignored Muzorewa's success in opposing the Land Tenure Act and a successful "No" campaign,[16] Zvobgo and others began to be enticed back to their former nationalist political loyalties when it had become clear that Muzorewa would not settle for the position of titular leader of the joint nationalist movement.[17]

Efforts were made by the Frontline states in 1974 to unite nationalists and consider a settlement with the Rhodesian government in a political deal,[18] negotiated by the American Secretary of State Henry Kissinger in consultation with John Vorster of South Africa.[19] Part of the ZANU leadership still in prison from the early sixties, including Edgar Tekere, Enos Nkala and Maurice Nyagumbo removed their party leader Rev Ndabaningi Sithole in favor of Mugabe, who was also in prison, on the grounds of jeopardizing the liberation struggle.[20] The jail leadership coup had been orchestrated, among other reasons, because of Sithole's refusal to admit in court

14. Zvobgo was appointed Minister of Local Government and Housing in the first cabinet of the postcolonial era.

15. Edison Zvobgo quoted in, "Guerrilla leader resigns," 27 September 1973.

16. Bhebhe, *Simon Muzenda*, 163.

17. Ibid.

18. For a further reading on these Kissinger proposals consult, Chung, *Second Chimurenga*, 81–88; Smith, *The Great Betrayal*; Verrier, *The Road to Zimbabwe*.

19. ZAPU Publicity Bureau, "Z.A.P.U.," 16–19 June 1977.

20. Tekere, *A Lifetime of Struggle*, 68–69.

that he had committed sabotage[21]–a crime punishable by hanging. This was viewed as an ethical predilection towards non-violence, which was despised by ZANU leadership hardliners in prison.[22] According to Bhebhe these actions created "confusion" in the party, and were denounced by Frontline leaders, Herbert Chitepo and Josiah Tongogara, a member of the executive of the external wing of ZANU and the party's Chief of defense, as "an illegal coup."[23] Frontline leaders forced the reinstatement of Sithole, compelled the leaders of ZANU, ZAPU, ANC and FROLIZI[24] to unite, and then later used their diplomatic influence on the OAU to withdraw recognition of ZAPU and ZANU as a means of putting pressure on the parties to unite.[25]

These efforts saw the three main African nationalist movements briefly reconstitute under the ANC and under the leadership of Muzorewa.[26] In the process the ANC changed its name to United African National Council (UANC) to reflect this new found, if not imposed, unity among nationalists and also in order to differentiate it from the old ANC.[27] It was not long before internal power struggles resurfaced. Muzorewa at one point suspended Joshua Nkomo from leadership of the ANC, but when he also tried to bring the ZANU leadership in Mozambique under his control he was rejected.[28] A ZAPU publicity attributed Muzorewa's growing influence between 1974 and 1977 as a product of "imperialist forces" and their "propaganda media" who "used an immature and inept leader with which to forge a reactionary neo-colonial deal for Zimbabwe," and preserve their own interests. Muzorewa, as a bishop, was dismissed for convincing himself that he had a "messianic role," but was also perceived as being naïve. They believed that Muzorewa could not understand that he was being used as a front for the vicious Rhodesian regime. To his surprise, on the 2nd June 1974 some members of the ANC executive who had shifted their loyalty

21. Bhebhe, *Simon Muzenda*, 169.

22. Chung, *Second Chimurenga*, 86.

23. Bhebhe, *Simon Muzenda*, 169.

24. Front for the Liberation of Zimbabwe (FROLIZI) was made of up disgruntled former members of ZANU and ZAPU. The movement was led by James Chikerema. It merged into the ANC on 6 December 1974.

25. Bhebhe, *Simon Muzenda*, 170.

26. ZAPU Publicity Bureau, "Z.A.P.U.," 16–19 June 1977.

27. For a further reading on the causes and nature of these splits, consult Bhebhe, *Simon Muzenda*; Banana, *Turmoil and Tenacity*; and Nyangoni and Nyandoro, *Zimbabwe Independent Movements*.

28. Ibid.

to ZAPU rejected the deal he had made with Ian Smith when he had accepted a constitution rejected by the masses as a basis for independence. When the leaders of ZANU and ZAPU were released from prison on the 3rd December to discuss the possibilities of a constitutional solution, the need to present a united African front became also a priority. ZAPU believed that, ignoring the powerful influence of the other organizations on the African National Council, Muzorewa "took an opportunistic posture," which precipitated a series of regroupings, and factions. He failed to call the planned congress, fearing he would lose to comrade Nkomo. His chances to become one of the established leaders slipped away. ZAPU believed that Muzorewa had mistaken the rejection of the Pearce Commission proposals as support for himself.[29] It seems that any attempt at a political settlement initiated by Muzorewa and including ZANU and ZAPU was bound to fail.[30] A UANC settlement would have spelt disaster for ZANU and ZAPU nationalist leaderships.

ZANU and ZAPU leaders took every opportunity to reassert themselves in order not to lose out to the UANC.[31] From 1974 onwards, with Kissinger and South Africa pushing for a settlement and Mozambique becoming independent (leaving Rhodesia's eastern border accessible to guerrilla incursions), the liberation of Rhodesia from its colonial past appeared within sight, but there was still one war which was far from being over; and in fact that was beginning to escalate as a result of the confidence that independence was imminent. Dzinashe Machingura[32] a member of the Zimbabwe People's Army (ZIPA) which was a joint military wing for ZANU and ZAPU commented, "[T]he traditional political leadership of Zimbabwe . . . divided the people . . . it became quite clear to us that if we were ever going to be able to prosecute a successful armed struggle we could not be either part of the two rival ANC factions, the Muzorewa faction or the Nkomo faction. We realized the time of personality politics had long passed. It was this approach to politics which had divided the people of Zimbabwe."[33]

29. Ibid.

30. Dzinashe Machingura, interview by Mozambican Information Agency, Maputo, September 22, 1976.

31. ZAPU Publicity Bureau, "Z.A.P.U.," 16–19 June 1977.

32. Whose real life name was Wilfred Mhanda, guerrillas used pseudonyms as a way of safeguarding their anonymity, hence protecting their families still in the country from retribution from the settler forces for having joined the armed struggle.

33. Dzinashe Machingura.

ZANU saw its access to power as primarily through the barrel of the gun,[34] called for the intensification of the war, downplayed attempts to settle the Rhodesian problem at the table.[35] ZANU thought talks would "rob it of a military victory."[36] ZAPU policy alternated negotiation and a continuation of the armed struggle in line with ZANU.[37] After 1976, with the parties now maintaining separate identities, Muzorewa's UANC, looked to continue talks to secure restitution of African rights and negotiate a political settlement with the Smith regime.[38] Sithole who had been deposed in jail as ZANU leader and choosing also to keep the name ZANU for his newly formed party, also distanced himself from those still bent on prosecuting the armed struggle and concentrated on talks.

As the nationalists fought for political control, tribal animosities were stirred up, and many died.[39] To Mugabe, Muzorewa and Sithole were "idiotic characters"[40] and also "irreligious," who valued personal glory more than the freedom for the masses. He dismissed them as praying to "the white man as their only god," and for being "pledged to sacrifice the whole black race to appease their monstrous deity . . . those whom the gods wish to destroy."[41]

Sithole's ZANU reminded people that contrary to press coverage, "The father of the armed struggle in Zimbabwe Rev. Sithole is militarily and politically very strong inside Zimbabwe, but our pronouncements have often fallen on deaf ears."[42] Those advocating the non-violent approach were dismissed by ZANU and ZAPU for being "black puppets" of the state. ZAPU claimed to expose the "lies" of the Christian leaders, "The Bishop told Mr. Smith that as soon as they enter into some agreement he, as a cleric, will be able to lift up both his hands and order all the young men to come home and they will do it overnight. Another Rev. Ndabaningi Sithole, told Mr. Smith, 'You know Mr. Smith, Mr. Mugabe does not command the ZANLA

34. Chung, *Second Chimurenga*, 83.

35. Tekere, *Lifetime of Struggle*, 83.

36. Chung, *Second Chimurenga*, 83.

37. ZAPU Publicity Bureau, "Z.A.P.U.," 16–19 June 1977.

38. Ibid.

39. Bhebhe, *Simon Muzenda*, 181.

40. Mugabe, "Speech on Chitepo Day," 141.

41. Ibid.

42. Dzvova, (Chief ZANU representative in UK & Europe and ZANU's Publicity Secretary), letter addressed to Mrs. P. Altman, 26 September 1978.

guerrillas but I do it.' Now these two Rev, gentlemen have been telling lie after lie . . . I say to the Black Silent Majority, it is high time you called a lie a lie."[43] The UANC still claimed that the masses "remained solidly ranged behind" it, and bitterly dismissed "as naked hypocrisy" Sithole's attempt to pose as a champion of unity when he had broken away from the UANC in September 1976.

ZANU and ZAPU focused their attacks on discrediting Muzorewa and the UANC for its political philosophies of gradualism or political evolution,[44] and non-violence. This included an attack on its Christian stance, since the UANC was generally believed to be Christian-friendly and supported by the Protestant leadership.[45] Josiah Chinamano, vice-president of ZAPU, dismissed claims of assassination plots against Muzorewa, and attacked his integrity as a leading cleric: "I say to the Bishop, please preach what you do or do what you preach. Do not continue to cheat people. Do not continue to cheat the masses of people pretending to be a nationalist and yet in fact you are being used as an agent of oppressors and imperialists."[46] Chinamano noted that some were calling, "Down with *VAFUNDISI*."[47] While he distanced himself from this, he asserted, "You know there are some who put on sheep's skin and yet they are wolves. Some people put on clerical uniform and yet they are crooks," and added a warning which sought to undermine his clerical opponents: "I say to all Christians, all church-goers, the silent majority, please draw a line between crook *vafundisis*[48] and genuine *vafundisis*. And when you do that then you must be brave to say *pasi nema*[49] crook *vafundisi pamberi nevafundisi vakanaka*.[50] In the

43. Chinamano, Speech, 10 June 1978, NAZ, GEN-P/CHI.

44. Max Chigwida, personal interview, Harare, March 2, 2006

45. Janice McLaughlin.

46. Chinamano, Speech, 10 June 1978, NAZ, GEN-P/CHI.

47. *Vafundisi* is a Shona word which means ministers or pastors and its singular is *mufundisi*.

48. "*Vafundisis*" is another colloquial Shona anglicized version for ministers or pastors.

49. "*Pasi nema*" is Shona for "down with." It was a term very popular and still popular among nationalists for denouncing their opponents.

50. "*Pamberi*" is another Shona term that was popular and still popular as part of nationalist slogans. It means "forward" hence in this case forward with "*vafundisi*" (ministers) that are "*vakanaka*" (good).

same way there are certain white leaders who have led people astray and brought about the bloodshed. They are not all white leaders who do that."[51]

ZANU and ZAPU, from the time that the ANC became formally political, began to redefine some major aspects of their identity, stressing the need for an intensification of the armed struggle.[52] In order for ZANU to be distinguished from the UANC and other nationalist parties in "Rhodesia" it officially adopted Marxist Leninism in 1973, although this move was later challenged by some within the party.[53] An adoption of communism in general even without its atheist component, was a deliberate distancing itself from the UANC which openly declared its commitment to Judaeo-Christian beliefs in its manifesto, "We here declare that we are simply creatures made in the image of God . . . Only as we are fully liberated can we fulfil the purpose for which we are created . . . we shall strive to create a nation where black and white can live as children of the One Almighty God."[54]

In 1974 ZANU was advised by the Chinese government in 1974 to retain its identity, even if it chose to unite with other nationalist forces in Zimbabwe as demanded by the Frontline States.[55] ZANU's strategy was to place Muzorewa and the ANC in a situation where they would either choose to stand alone or declare a communist allegiance. Muzorewa as expected rejected to partner with a movement he believed to be driven by a communist agenda, and that he perceived to have believed that violence was the primary solution to the Rhodesian crisis; "I do not subscribe to the romantic and unhistoric view that the liberation struggle is won by armed clashes between the forces of liberation and the colonial army. Important as they are, such acts of war form only sporadic episodes in the total process of liberation."[56] Muzorewa continued to assert that only his Christian approach was sufficiently rounded to bring an end to colonial oppression, "Liberation embraces the whole process of opposition to all forms of the colonial oppression. This opposition is at various times moral, spiritual, mental, economic, political and physical as appropriate. The church's contributions

51. Ibid.

52. Dzinashe Machingura.

53. Mugabe, *Our War of liberation*, 153ff.

54. Muzorewa, "Under the Banner of Unity," 10 March 1972, NAZ, GEN-P/MUZ. About six times the word God is repeated in the manifesto.

55. Bhebhe, *Simon Muzenda*, 179.

56. Muzorewa, *Rise and Walk*, 91.

are manifold including its attack on the very rationale and philosophy of racism."[57] Once each nationalist group had redefined its identity and stood alone there was then need to compete for support and recognition both inside and outside Zimbabwe. Major criticism was directed at Muzorewa by ZANU and ZAPU. They felt Muzorewa had broken Zimbabwean traditional ethical code as taught by the Shona idiom: *Kunzi dzipakate handi kunzi dziridze* (When you are given a drum[58] to carry it does not mean you should play it.)[59] In other words, if one is asked to carry something it does not mean they should use it as they please. ZANU and ZAPU viewed Muzorewa as an opportunist who should have not turned his role as caretaker leader into a permanent nationalist leader's role although no nationalist group ever communicated to Muzorewa that he was a caretaker leader.

In Malawi when Orton Chirwa was placed in a similar position after the arrest of Hastings Kamuzu Banda, it was clearly communicated to him before assuming the MCP leadership that as soon as Banda was released he would hand over to Banda.[60] In Muzorewa's case the situation was different. When he was appointed as leader of the ANC the nationalist movement was divided, with power struggles between ZAPU under Nkomo and ZANU under Sithole—as well as internal divisions within ZANU which led to the jail leadership coup that saw Mugabe temporarily being thrust into leading ZANU. Therefore when Muzorewa accepted the position of nationalist leader he did not perceive himself as breaking any moral code, but saw himself as taking a step forward towards bringing unity to Zimbabwe's nationalist movement and the nationalist cause to end colonialism.[61]

Among Christians the ANC found considerable support since it was viewed as a moderate voice.[62] Its message of non-violence and claims to be guided by Christian principles resonated well with most members of the church leadership, especially among those who believed violence could not be adopted as a viable Christian stand against oppression.[63] Some nationalists in ZAPU and ZANU began to speak openly against Christianity whose

57. Ibid.

58. *Mbira* is the instrument referred to in Shona because of a lack of similar word in English a dynamic equivalence has been employed.

59. Translation from Hamutyinei and Plagger, *Tsumo—Shumo*, 364.

60. Short, *Banda*, 131.

61. Janice McLaughlin.

62. Henry J. Mugabe.

63. Ibid.

adherents were viewed to be in league with and sustaining the ANC.[64] In 1976, Dzinashe Machingura of the Zimbabwe People's Army, which was the ZANU military wing, included Muzorewa among the enemies of the guerrillas: "These comprise the Smith racist regime and the imperialist powers that back it, puppet Africans serving the Smith regime, and all those opposed to the independence of the Zimbabwean people."[65] Hence when the armed struggle intensified in the mid to late seventies some guerrillas, not just because of their communist beliefs but also because of anti-Christian sentiments as a result of their loathing of what they viewed as an attempt to grab power by a Christian dominated and supported movement, burnt bibles and discouraged locals from attending services.[66]

Sithole and Muzorewa's efforts to find a form of non-violent settlement were portrayed by fellow nationalists as selling out to the interests of the Smith regime,[67] and such suspicions grew as Muzorewa dropped demands for "one man one vote"[68] and for immediate parity between Africans and whites in Parliament, arguing that parity would eventually come.[69] Willingness to compromise was attributed to his desire to gain political office. The same charge was levelled at Nkomo by both Muzorewa[70] and ZANU. Sister Janice McLaughlin commented: "ZANU (under Mugabe) felt that Nkomo was ready to make a deal with Smith. They felt, they couldn't trust the guy. They always felt he was ready to make a deal behind their back."[71] This was a powerful charge to level at opponents, and created a barrier to political negotiation with its need for the dimension of give and take.[72] Sister McLaughlin did not feel the charges were justified, "I don't think Muzorewa agreed to the Internal Settlement because he was power hungry, but I think he honestly thought it was a way of ending the war. A lot of people had and were dying so he thought he had an opportunity to end the war."[73] Muzorewa was convinced that once the Internal Settlement was

64. Kudakwashe Gwemende.
65. Ibid.
66. Ibid.
67. Dzinashe Machingura.
68. "Settlement Bishop to Knight," 13 July 1973.
69. Ibid.
70. Muzorewa, *Rise and Walk*, 57ff.
71. Janice McLaughlin.
72. "Settlement Bishop to Knight," 13 July 1973.
73. Janice McLaughlin.

signed, the need for bloodshed was over. He appealed to the United Nations and the Frontline States in strongly Christian terms: "[I]n the name of humanity and in the name of God, the Father of us all and the giver of all life to now stop urging those of our brothers you call the Patriotic Front to continue to send our youths to their deaths. Why should they now die? The rule of the majority for which they have so nobly and gallantly fought is now in sight."[74]

Mugabe and ZANU had little time for negotiation. One of those who knew Mugabe personally was Rugare Gumbo[75] who commented, "Mugabe could afford to be brutally tough and to crack the whip."[76] The armed struggle made nationalists tougher and more radical. Gumbo observed, "I was strongly persuaded that I wanted Mugabe because I had spent a lot of time with him in Salisbury Maximum prison. I found him eloquent, forthright, dynamic and radical."[77]

Under Mugabe, ZANU adopted a hard-line position, unwilling to negotiate with either nationalists or settlers.[78] To his critics, "he would have wanted to shoot his way into Salisbury," to get it all.[79] The policy of his future presidency was being forged. Negotiation meant compromise and weakness.

The transformation of the ANC affected both African nationalist politics and the religious complexion of the struggle. As a result of its significant Protestant representation in its Executive Committee,[80] and with strong support from the Protestant mother body, the Christian Council, the ANC appeared to mainly represent Protestant interests in the political crisis. The Internal Settlement was seen as a Protestant solution, as Sister Janice McLaughlin noted, "The Anglican Church leadership was well known for

74. Abel Tendekai Muzorewa, "Memorandum," to J. Callaghan, Jimmy Carter, Julius Nyerere, K. D. Kaunda, Samora Machel, and Sir Seretse Khama, with copies sent to leaders of the opposition USA and UK, J. Nkomo and R. Mugabe, 1 August 1978, NAZ, GEN-P/MUZ.

75. Rugare Gumbo still serves as a ZANU PF Member of Parliament. At independence he contested as a candidate for Sithole's ZANU having defected from ZANU under Mugabe

76. Rugare Gumbo quoted in, Bhebhe, *Simon Muzenda*, 211.

77. Ibid., 206.

78. Ibid., also confirmed by Janice McLaughlin.

79. Holland, *Dinner with Mugabe*, 134.

80. List of ANC/ Muzorewa Central Committee Members, n.d., NAZ, Acc: MS 771/1–3.

its backing of the Smith government. Watyoka who was then leader of the Christian Council also openly supported the Internal Settlement."[81]

The ANC continued to interact with the Protestant ecumenical body as if it was its sister organization.[82] One notable aspect of the ANC or later the UANC leadership was the absence of the Roman Catholic clergy, although they stood as the single largest denomination in the country. The formation of the Catholic Commission for Justice and Peace in 1972, which became their internal organ of protest within Rhodesia, and the liberation of Mozambique, a dominantly Roman Catholic state, in 1975, gave the Roman Catholics closer contact with ZANU specifically.[83] From around 1978 onwards ZANU was largely controlled by those from a Roman Catholic religious background,[84] giving Catholicism significant influence in African nationalist politics and the armed struggle.[85]

With a leadership dominated by people professing Roman Catholicism, or educated at Roman Catholic schools or colleges, the Roman Catholic Church leadership became comfortable in working with ZANU, and bred a sense of loyalty and commitment amongst some Roman Catholics to ZANU. As Sister McLaughlin observed, "There were a significant number of people who were part of the church in the ZANU leadership in 1978. Simbi Mubako, Dzingai Mtumbuka, Walter Kamba, Stanley Mudenge and many more, these were all close to the church.[86] Father Michael Traber, working in the Gweru diocese also knew Mugabe, Muzenda and Takawira personally, who were members of the Roman Catholic Church."[87]

Political divisions began also to take a Roman Catholic-Protestant complexion between the UANC under the Methodist bishop Muzorewa and ZANU under Mugabe a Roman Catholic convert, who had replaced Sithole who was a Protestant minister. Catholics feared a repeat of what had happened in Malawi in the early sixties where the Presbyterian dominated Malawi Congress Party had assumed political control with negative consequences to the Roman Catholic community after a political contest which

81. Janice McLaughlin.

82. Herbert Chikomo.

83. Banana, *Repression and Resistance*, 306.

84. Auret, *Reaching for Justice*, 120ff.

85. Ibid.

86. Janice McLaughlin. All the names provided were also part of the of successive postcolonial ZANU PF governments.

87. Ibid.

had seen the Christian Democratic Party partly founded by some Roman Catholic clergy lose in the elections.[88]

In two other former Portuguese colonies, Angola and Mozambique, the Roman Catholic Church being the dominant church had been close to the colonial governments. This had left the Roman Catholic Church in these countries in a bad light in terms of the Africans' fight against colonialism.[89] In Angola nationalists often destroyed church institutions related to Roman Catholics which were identified with colonial Portuguese rule, whereas the Methodist and Baptist Churches were not. Protestant missions were left untouched.[90]

In Mozambique the White Fathers in 1971 withdrew their personnel to avoid being identified by nationalists as part of the Roman Catholic church-state oppressive coalition.[91] In Rhodesia they did not have such an association with the Rhodesian government, whereas Protestant churches did. Although Roman Catholic missions became famous for supporting nationalists, they were not entirely exempt from being targeted by guerrillas. Sister McLaughlin attributed the killing of missionaries[92] in general in Rhodesia by ZAPU guerrillas in the seventies to their Russian atheist ideological training.[93] However, the ZAPU leader Nkomo did not see his forces as antagonistic to the church in general, and rejected any thought that killing missionaries was their policy. He commented in 1978: "Under no circumstances have any orders been given by the Patriotic Front leadership for the murder or harassment of missionaries; in fact quite the reverse, but if the Patriotic Front have been guilty of this, blame the system, the war, frustrations, ill-discipline and possibly the fact that the church in the past has supported or accepted the system."[94] Nkomo continued, "The Church should simply work as the people within the state. Missionaries should not leave the country, they will be needed."[95]

88. Schoffeleers, *In Search of Truth and Justice*, 27.

89. Hastings, *A History of African Christianity*, 143.

90. Ibid.

91. Soderstrom, *God Gave Growth*, 171.

92. Forty missionaries were killed during the liberation struggle compared to more than 30,000 Africans.

93. Janice McLaughlin.

94. Nkomo quoted in *State and Church*, 140.

95. Ibid.

ZANU, with strong ties to the Roman Catholic Church,[96] rarely attacked Roman Catholic institutions. When they occasionally did, as in the case of the Saint Francis of Assisi Mission in 1977, the institution was operating counter to ZANU political objectives. Some priests there were thought to be collaborating with government forces.[97] At the end of the armed struggle Mugabe visited Roman Catholic missions that had continued to operate during the war such as Matibi Mission to personally thank Roman Catholic staff for the help they offered in the liberation struggle, or specifically the help they had offered to ZANU.[98] The largest massacre of missionaries attributed to ZANU was at the Elim Mission which was a Protestant, and specifically Pentecostal mission, in 1978. Ironically this mission was located close to the Roman Catholic Avila Mission, a bastion of ZANU guerrilla support, and whose priest and staff had been arrested and tortured by government forces in 1976.[99] It is possible that ZANU's massacre of Elim missionaries was partly a response to what had happened at Avila.

These often ignored Roman Catholic and Protestant dynamics within the nationalist struggle by Zimbabwean Church historians such as Canaan Banana[100] and Ian Linden[101], were to prove significant in the events that finally led to the independence of Zimbabwe from 1978. Even Rhodesian soldiers had come to acknowledge the role of the church[102] in the liberation struggle and were changing Rhodes' dictum in a play of words to, "One dead missionary is as good as one hundred dead terrorists."[103]

The Internal Settlement

When the Rhodesian government finally realized that the war was unwinnable,[104] and that African rule was inevitable they sought to find a

96. McLaughlin, "Avila Mission," 97ff.

97. Bourdillon and Gundani, "Rural Christians," 151–53.

98. Holland, *Dinner With Mugabe*, 148ff.

99. McLaughlin, "Avila Mission," 75.

100. Banana, *Repression and Resistance*, 1ff.

101. Linden, *Catholic Church and Struggle*, 1ff.

102. What should also be noted is that the Rhodesian churches' protest was not based on liberation theology.

103. Rhodesian soldier quoted in McLaughlin, *Liberation War*, 96.

104. Herbert Chikomo; for a further reading on this matter consult; Verrier, *Road to*

nationalist party that was willing to enter into dialogue and government, but from whom they could extract maximum concessions.[105] After the first failed talks with Nkomo,[106] in November 1977 Smith initiated dialogue with Muzorewa, Sithole and chief Jeremiah Chirau to form a broad-based government. This initiative came after the failure of the Geneva Conference[107] from October 1976 to January 1977, which had only served to further highlight the divisions among nationalists and between nationalists and the Smith government. It was adjourned with no meaningful agreement made. The failure of the Frontline states to unite the nationalist parties in Tanzania before the Geneva Conference was significant. Personal and individual parties' ambitions had undermined the need for unity.[108] Rev. Canaan Banana who had come as part of the ANC delegation crossed the floor and joined Mugabe's ZANU.[109]

Hence the Internal Settlement of 1978 was reached under conditions of disunity and self-interest, from both the Rhodesian Front perspective, and also from the internal nationalists' perspective.[110] The ANC, the United African National Council (UANC) from 1974, were by 1977 operating within Rhodesia, having taken advantage of Henry Kissinger's "Package Deal" which gave immunity to nationalists and provided for their safe return to Zimbabwe awaiting talks towards independence.[111] Mugabe's ZANU and ZAPU refused to disband and opted to continue the armed struggle.

Dzinashe Machingura highlighted the roles of ambition and desire for power as some of the main sources of disunity among the leaders of the nationalist organizations,[112] and further noted ethnic divisions as another major source of conflict: "[T]hey seek to place people belonging to their own ethnic group in key positions, in strategic positions, so as to prepare secure power base which serves as a spring board to gain political ascen-

---

Zimbabwe; Gann and Thomas, *The Struggle for Zimbabwe*; Chung, *Second Chimurenga.*

105. Banana, *Repression and Resistance*, 195.

106. Gann and Henriksen, *Struggle for Zimbabwe*, 55.

107. For further reading, consult Nzombe, "Negotiations with the British," 170–79; Muzorewa, *Rise and Walk*; Smith, *Great Betrayal.*

108. Hallencreutz & Moyo, *Church and State*, 85.

109. Ibid. 84.

110. Banana, *Repression and Resistance*, 195.

111. Nzombe, "Negotiations with the British," 170–79.

112. Dzinashe Machingura.

dance . . . we should emphasize that their differences are essentially not ideological at all. Ideologically they belong to the same camp."[113]

On March 3rd 1978 the UANC, Sithole's ZANU and chief Chirau signed the Internal Settlement agreeing to usher in a new era of majority rule.[114] In April 1979 elections were held, despite both ZAPU and ZANU opposing both the Internal Settlement and the elections. 64% of the eligible African populace went to vote. Muzorewa won 52 of the 70 parliamentary seats allocated to Africans under the new constitution. About the election Gann and Henriksen wrote, "(it) was one of the fairest elections held during the decade on the African continent."[115]

All Bishop Muzorewa and the UANC needed to stay in power was international acceptance and support, but this was not forthcoming. The west and some local institutions, such as the Roman Catholic Church, insisted that the Internal Settlement was a facade to preserve "white interests."[116] In May 1979 when the Protestant-led Christian Council of Rhodesia urged everyone to give the Internal Settlement a "try,"[117] the Roman Catholic Committee for Peace and Justice condemned the Muzorewa government as a puppet regime, and lobbied at the Lusaka Commonwealth Heads of Government meetings not to recognize the regime.[118] ZAPU and ZANU intensified their war.[119]

The UANC strategy, of changing the system gradually, was workable, but it would have taken a long time to achieve its goal.[120] The desire to get quickly into power led to concessions on important aspects of the nationalist struggle, including the call for parity and majority adult suffrage.[121] This was a different policy to that adopted by the Christian Council during the Test of Acceptability debates: "While we hope for a settlement, our prayer

113. Ibid.

114. Muzorewa, *Rise and Walk*, Appendix D.

115. Gann & Henriksen, *Struggle for Zimbabwe*, 57.

116. Ibid.

117. Hallencreutz & Moyo, *Church and State*, 92.

118. Gundani, *Changing Patterns*, 89.

119. Chung, *Second Chimurenga*, 86–87.

120. Max Chigwida.

121. Publicity Bureau of ZAPU-Patriotic, "Z.A.P.U.," 16–19 June 1977, NAZ, GEN-P/WOR.

is that there will be no sacrifice of justice and of human dignity and rights. Indeed we would prefer no settlement to an unjust one."[122]

Protestant leaders were supportive of the Internal Settlement, but cautious, summed up in Bishop Burrough's words who said, "It needed to be given a chance."[123] Even some African Executive members of the Christian Council like CD Watyoka who had in the past strongly denounced the Rhodesian Front Government are said to have supported the Internal Settlement.[124] There was no Christian consensus on the internal settlement, but rather sharp division. Some within the Christian Council, such as Todd, opposed the Settlement, especially as it became clear that it had failed to end the war, further talks which included ZANU and ZAPU were needed.[125]

As a transitional arrangement, had it been given a chance, the settlement might have worked. The fact that 64% of the Rhodesian electorate constituting 1.8 million of the African population went to vote in April of 1979 when ZANU and ZAPU were urging voters not to vote meant the people intended to give it a chance, with the hope that it would end the war, and probably the UANC was more popular than their critics were willing to admit.[126] Such a large voter turnout cannot be simply attributed to intimidation as argued by Banana.[127]

Todd's stand on the Internal Settlement could have been driven by self-interest, because as a representative of ZAPU he was excluded from the Settlement. Todd had kept in close touch with Joshua Nkomo, the more moderate Africa revolutionary.[128] Rev Ndabaningi Sithole and Chief Chirau both agreed with the Internal Settlement. Judith Todd believed Sithole's motives were mixed,[129] "I think he has convinced himself that he is doing the right thing . . . he feels he must get power to protect himself, and that he translates this as getting power for the good of the country . . . He said

122. NAZ, GEN-P/WOR, Christian Council of Rhodesia, Minutes of emergency Council meeting held at the University of Rhodesia, 30 December 1971.

123. *The Link*, April 1978.

124. Janice McLaughlin.

125. Hallencreutz & Moyo, *State and Church*, 92–96.

126. Chambati, "National Unity," 154.

127. Banana, *Repression and Resistance*, 195.

128. Associated Press, "Rhodesia Foes," 7 October 1978.

129. At this stage Judith was now married to Lord Acton hence the name change to Judith Acton in the following letter.

the guerrillas at home had been instructed to go on fighting so that with their pressure as much as possible could be extracted from Smith, but that eventually he, Sithole, could arrange the peace."[130]

Although in the *Great Betrayal* Smith portrays Muzorewa as under his control, giving grounds for the ZAPU and ZANU label that he was his puppet, he also acknowledged him as being astute.[131] He noted the difficulties he went through to get Muzorewa to agree to the Internal Settlement, and attributed his agreement to pressure from the South African government, his American financial backers and liberal advisers.[132] The British Foreign and Commonwealth Office observed, "We are not so blind that we cannot recognise that the Patriotic Front want power. The Anglo-American proposals recognised that something had to be done in recognition of their fighting strength but would allow them to come to power only through the ballot box and on the same basis as everyone."[133]

Muzorewa's primary aim in accepting the Internal Settlement appears to have been his desire to have peace, as Sister McLaughlin observed, "Maybe he thought it was his own way of ending the war and bringing peace."[134] Chung agreed "Muzorewa was a peace-loving and obedient cleric."[135] In his autobiography Muzorewa wrote: "[T]here did not appear to be alternatives. The war was raging, taking scores of lives every week . . . What frightened me most and worried me sick was that the black population looked to me to do something about the situation."[136] Muzorewa was convinced that the essence of the March 3rd Agreement was that Smith conceded to majority rule, with "peace having been achieved."[137] The fact that at the Lancaster House Conference Muzorewa accepted the terms of the agreement when Smith had refused, even though the Bishop was attending the conference as part of Smith's delegation, raises further doubts over the charge he was "a puppet of the whites."[138] As the former ZANU nationalist and Minister

130. Acton, "Recollections," 18 February 1978, NAZ, GEN-P/TOD.

131. Smith, *Great Betrayal*, 154.

132. Ibid., 223–96.

133. Newman, "Foreign and Commonwealth Office," 3 August 1978, NAZ, GEN-P/TRE.

134. Janice McLaughlin.

135. Chung, *Second Chimurenga*, 230.

136. Muzorewa, *Rise and Walk*, 226.

137. Muzorewa quoted in Banana, *Repression and Resistance*, 197.

138. Herbert Chikomo.

of Mines in the first nationalist government, Maurice Nyagumbo admitted to Rev. Herbert Chikomo: "'You know Rev. Chikomo, if Muzorewa had not gone to Lancaster House we would be still in the bush. He played his role by agreeing to go to Lancaster, although he was finishing himself somehow.'[139] Smith wanted himself and Muzorewa to walk out of the talks but Muzorewa refused."[140] The evidence suggests that he was a peace-lover, and this lay behind the major concessions he made.[141] However, the failure to successfully sell the Internal Settlement, and win the support of Roman Catholics and other Christian leaders like Todd, sealed its failure. Muzorewa appealed as a Christian and a peace-lover to heads of states and leaders of the Patriotic Front to end the bloodshed: "The petition comes from the very depth of my heart and soul and is motivated by my status as a nationalist leader, a committed and practising Christian . . . The supreme sacrifice of life made by the youth of Zimbabwe was a regrettable necessity for the liberation of our country from oppression. But the spillage of our children's blood is now no longer necessary. Majority rule, the original objective of our war of liberation, has been won."[142] The clergyman Ndabaningi Sithole emphasized the democratic implications of what was happening, "The concession of majority rule based on one man, one vote and the coming of independence on the 31st December, 1978 are both events which effectively de-colonize Rhodesia/Zimbabwe and the OAU as such must have every reason to feel happy about the two events . . . it is truly of the people, by the people and for the people of Rhodesia/Zimbabwe."[143]

The British government remained opposed to the Internal Settlement, arguing in 1978 that Smith had "negotiated too successfully in his own interests and not enough in those of the country as a whole,"[144] and that Muzorewa and Sithole had subsequently accepted that they had "conceded more than they should."[145] Their fear was that Africans seeing that the

139. Bringing his own political career to an end.

140. Herbert Chikomo.

141. Chung, *Second Chimurenga*, 230.

142. NAZ, GEN-P/MUZ, "Memorandum,"1 August 1978.

143. NAZ, GEN-P/SIT, "The Anglo-American All-Party Conference."

144. Newman, "Foreign and Commonwealth Office," 3 August 1978, NAZ, GEN-P/TRE.

145. Ibid.

internal agreement had not brought meaningful transfer of power would increasingly turn to more drastic solutions.[146]

To liberals in Rhodesia and radical Christian leaders like Todd, a settlement that left Smith with a significant amount of power was anathema, and their voices weighed heavily on the international scene. Muzorewa accepted that the deal was "not perfect," but cited African precedent: "In 1958, Dr Julius Nyerere, for example was forced to accept not less than three separate and racial voters rolls in the face of intense domestic and international criticism."[147] But the world, and African events, had moved on twenty years.

Despite its weaknesses the Internal Settlement was a step forward. Smith had all along declared that neither in his "life time,"[148] nor "a thousand years" would Rhodesia succumb to majority rule nor have an African premier,[149] and to get a concession on this from a hardliner such as Smith in the prime of his life was an achievement. It signaled that the days of colonial rule were coming to an end. Criticism came from churches both close to, and more distant from, the regime. Barbara Tredgold,[150] an Anglican Church worker, wrote to Ian Smith urging him to hold a less dominant role than he intended to take, and which was weakening African support for the Settlement: "You are on a level with the three other members. Once you are named as Prime Minister you cease to be on that level and it looks to ordinary people as though you are the leader of the Executive Council and that the other members are doing what you say. This criticism is very strong at the moment and is one of the reasons for the immense amount of support that is falling away from Bishop Muzorewa and the Reverend Sithole."[151]

The sternest criticism of the Internal Settlement from the church constituency came from the Roman Catholic leadership. They refused to accept the agreement on the grounds that it simply offered Africans "half a loaf" when the rest of the "loaf" remained in the settlers' possession.[152]

146. Ibid.

147. *Africa News*, 24 July 1978, quoted in Memorandum 1 August 1978 NAZ, GEN-P/MUZ.

148. Banana, *Turmoil and Tenacity*, back cover page.

149. Dodge, *Revolutionary Bishop*, 153.

150. Barbara Tredgold was related to judge Sir Robert Tredgold who resigned in protest at the 1969 Land Tenure Act. Barbara held liberal views.

151. Barbara Tredgold, A letter to Ian Douglas Smith, 13 January 1979, NAZ, GEN-P/TRE .

152. McLaughlin, *The Catholic Church*, 143.

Church historian, Paul Gundani, stated that by 1978 the Roman Catholic Church had reached a conclusion that the Patriotic Front was "the government-in-waiting."[153] If this decision had been reached then any efforts or initiatives that would leave the UANC with political power would not have been on the agenda of the Roman Catholic leadership. Furthermore although they understood "the future of the church and the country to lie in the Front"[154] the hostility between Mugabe and Nkomo, and between ZANU and ZAPU the parties they represented that made the Patriotic Front, was well known. Therefore this state of affairs begged the question–which part of the "Front" did they envisage to be the "government-in-waiting"?[155] The answer to the question which side of the Patriotic Front did they prefer to take over government from the colonialists lay tellingly in the words of Sister McLaughlin: "During the war the Catholics learnt, 'we can cooperate with those people (ZANU) we are on the same wave length with these people we understand each other and we want development for the people.'"[156] To a similar effect Gundani wrote, "From the Lusaka meeting of August 1978 began a working relationship between General Josiah Tongogara and Brother Fidelis Mukonori who was assigned by the JPC[157] to cover 'complaints' regarding the guerrilla forces' behaviour in the war zones. 'He would carry out on-the-spot investigations of any negative reports about the guerrillas and feed them back to the senior ZANLA Commander.'"[158] Although a delegation of the Roman Catholic Church from Zimbabwe had paid a visit to ZAPU leaders in Lusaka in 1978 no such arrangement of a working relationship was established with ZAPU.[159]

Heidi Holland in *Dinner with Mugabe* tells how Roman Catholic bishops and even the Vatican were involved in lobbying against the Internal Settlement and further lobbied for an all-parties conference that resulted in

153. Gundani, *Changing Patterns*, 88.

154. Ibid.

155. For further reading on conflicts within the Patriotic Front, consult Bhebhe, *Simon*; Banana, *Turmoil and Tenacity*.

156. Janice McLaughlin.

157. Justice and Peace Commission.

158. Gundani, *Authority and Leadership*, 88–89.

159. Ibid.

the Lancaster House Conference[160] of September 1979 and eventually the democratic elections of 1980.[161]

Father Fidelis Mukonori who confessed to counseling and encouraging youths to join the liberation struggle and was also Mugabe's adviser claimed that Roman Catholic leaders took a key role in the negotiations that led to the all-parties conference at Lancaster House in 1979: "After acting as researcher and adviser to the nationalists during various failed Anglo-American initiatives, I knew exactly where everyone's weaknesses and problems were. We drew up a plan and spent five weeks shuttling between the two leaders of the Patriotic Front. Nkomo thought it an excellent document and Mugabe did too. We asked them, 'Are you willing to attend an all-party conference?' Both said yes—anywhere, anytime."[162] Sister Janice McLaughlin made a similar claim, "The church [Roman Catholic] indirectly influenced the outcome, maybe it is better for me to say the church was happy with the outcome [of the Lancaster House Conference]. . . The church played a big role in negotiations behind the scenes to make the Lancaster House Conference happen and to get everybody at the conference table. I was also involved behind the scenes."[163]

With Roman Catholics negotiating between Mugabe, a devout Roman Catholic,[164] and Nkomo, a former Methodist lay-preacher, the final product of their concoction would certainly tilt in favor of their religious loyalties as events were about to prove.

On the African political front Christianity continued to play a pervasive role in the efforts to bring colonialism to an end in Zimbabwe. The Frontline States leaders' support for the two main guerrilla leaders also resonated of sectarian bias. Kenneth Kaunda supported Joshua Nkomo with whom he shared a Protestant background. Samora Machel, then President of Mozambique, whose *Frente de Libertacao de Mocambique* (FRELIMO) had once fought alongside ZANU guerrillas against the Portuguese, and Julius Nyerere were solidly behind ZANU.[165] These two leaders shared a Roman Catholic background with Mugabe and many in the ZANU leader-

160. For further reading on the Lancaster House talks and agreement consult; Chung, *Second Chimurenga*; Banana, *Turmoil and Tenacity.*

161. Nzombe, "Negotiations with the British," 181.

162. Mukonori quoted in *Dinner with Mugabe*, 127.

163. Janice McLaughlin.

164. Ibid.

165. Nkomo, *Story of My Life*, 189.

ship. The three Frontline states leaders were critical in the overall struggle for Zimbabwean independence as well as wielding influence on who would eventually become the first postcolonial leader of Zimbabwe. With Nyerere and Machel behind, a fellow Roman Catholic, Mugabe, Kaunda was outnumbered in his push for Nkomo, a fellow Protestant, for a postcolonial control of Zimbabwe.

Nyerere was certainly known for being driven not just by his philosophy of *Ujamaa*[166] but also his Christian convictions.[167] Those that knew him personally described him as "a devout Roman Catholic who showed distinctive Christian virtues and vices."[168] It is likely that his religious convictions influenced his position on the question of Zimbabwe's postcolonial leadership. Reflecting on his relationship with Nyerere, Nkomo wrote; "Nyerere had a special problem with me."[169]

With both the Internal Settlement, and Lancaster House, the churches, especially Roman Catholics, were significantly involved in the quest for majority rule. Their influence, together with that of some liberals, the Frontline states leaders and, eventually with the Christian Council's call for an all-parties-conference, led to the Lancaster House Conference which started on 10 September 1979.[170] The Lancaster House Conference finally brought the end of rule by colonists, but the Agreement, like the Internal Settlement, had its own weaknesses, including the protection of settler political and economic interests.[171]

The Lancaster House arrangement offered 20% white parliamentary representation compared to the 50% that had been offered in the internal agreement, therefore retaining some racial element within the political process, which the nationalists had sought so determinedly to remove.[172] The land issue was basically left unresolved by saying farms could only be acquired on a willing seller willing buyer basis.[173] The evolutionary political

166. A Swahili word that could mean extended family or community which was adopted by Nyerere to espouse his socio-economic philosophy of villagization/communalism.

167. Listowel, *The Making of Tanganyika*, 168.

168. Osborne, "Obituary," December 1999.

169. Nkomo, *Story of My Life*, 110.

170. Chung, *Second Chimurenga*, 242–47. For further reading on the Lancaster House deliberations, consult also Smith, *Great Betrayal*; and Banana, *Turmoil and Tenacity*.

171. Nzombe, "Negotiations with British," 186.

172. Ibid., 184.

173. Ibid.

process, for adherence to which Muzorewa had been so criticized, led the postcolonial government to remove gradually the aspects of the Lancaster House Agreement that they had not initially agreed with.

It took seven years for the nationalist ZANU PF government to remove the provision of 20 reserved white seats from the constitution and almost 20 years to make the constitutional changes with regard to acquisition of settler owned farms.[174] For Roman Catholics this new deal offered at Lancaster House, although still viewed as unfair by Africans, was acceptable. Hence for Africans, like the criticism the Roman Catholics had rightfully pointed out with regard to the Internal Settlement, they were being offered "half a loaf" instead of a "whole loaf"; but perhaps the Roman Catholics now found the "half a loaf" acceptable since assured of the involvement of ZANU in the democratic political process they were confident that the "half a loaf" would ultimately end in the hands of ZANU, as already shown, whose leadership was largely composed of their spiritual offspring.[175]

Once the all-party conference was agreed, it was clear that Mugabe's ZANU would take over political control.[176] The Catholic clergy were confident of this outcome, as Sister McLaughlin noted, "ZANU had covered more territory in the war than ZAPU and it had also a larger army"[177] and it also portrayed itself as the political party representing the Shona, being the largest ethnic group. Coming from the minority group, with nationalist politics taking an ethnic dimension Nkomo's hopes of winning the election lay in forming a coalition or an alliance, but this ZANU refused in the 1980 elections. According to Sister McLaughlin, Mugabe declared, "These people [those that advocated for unity between ZANU and ZAPU] don't understand we must go into these elections as different parties. If we are to fight the elections as the Patriotic Front our people will choose Nkomo since he is older."[178] Against this, Todd, a supporter of Nkomo, pleaded for unity for the Patriotic Front, "First, you must strive to implement the Anglo-American plan that calls for an all-party-conference to include the guerrilla chiefs. Secondly you must make certain that the two chiefs Robert Mugabe and Joshua Nkomo stick together. A split in their ranks would be

174. Tekere, *A Life Time of Struggle*, 172.

175. McLaughlin, *Catholic Church*, 143.

176. Janice McLaughlin.

177. Ibid.

178. Ibid.

disastrous for the future of Rhodesia because then their guerrillas would start fighting each other."[179]

Sister McLaughlin felt that in the refusal to embrace Nkomo, "ZANU was smart."[180] There had been hopes in some quarters that Muzorewa, Nkomo and Smith would win substantial seats and form a coalition government of "moderates," although the term is hardly appropriate for Smith himself.[181] In the 1980 elections they stood as separate candidates. ZANU won 57 seats mostly from Shona constituents, ZAPU won the 20 seats mostly in Ndebele speaking constituents, Smith won all the 20 seats reserved for settlers in the Lancaster House Agreement and Muzorewa won only 3 seats.[182] ZANU was victorious, their sacrifices in the armed struggle rewarded.

As the nation voted ethnically, instead of religiously, Muzorewa was left in the cold. Even if they had voted religiously Muzorewa would have struggled to win since half of the Christian population by the beginning of the 1980s claimed to be of Roman Catholic faith, and by then the Roman Catholic leadership was openly behind ZANU PF.[183] When Professor AJ Chennells was asked, "Why . . . the Roman Catholic Church emerge[d] so well at the end of the war?,"[184] he attributed its success to "its international dimension."[185] Its success was further accentuated by the simple fact that the political organization which the Roman Catholics supported, ZANU PF, won the elections in 1980; but the overall success in ending colonialism in Zimbabwe is to be equally shared with those within the Protestant community.

It cannot be clearly established how much intimidation, which had started once a ceasefire had been announced, affected the results of the elections. Barbara Tredgold who supported the Internal Settlement wrote to Lord Carrington, "We were told of many instances in the villages of, particularly ZANU people, waiting to beat up those who had voted for Bishop Muzorewa. This would be intensified if the Patriotic Front were involved and although the elections might be peaceful there would be tremendous

179. Associated Papers, "Rhodesia Foes," 7 October 1978.

180. Janice McLaughlin.

181. Bhebhe, *Simon Muzenda*, 235.

182. Ibid., 237.

183. Janice McLaughlin.

184. Chennells, "Anglicans and Roman Catholics," 83.

185. Ibid.

fear everywhere."[186] Bishop Paul Burrough believed that Africans were left with little choice in the way they voted: "[T]he British government decided that peace at any price must be the answer to the dreadful war in this country. The African people of Zimbabwe reached the same conclusion, so that, in effect, the country was handed to those trying to take it by force, who made it abundantly clear that murder and destruction would continue unless this were done."[187] To Burrough the results of the election, with large numbers of Shona switching from Muzorewa to Mugabe, had to be open to question: "The Shona are pragmatists and very timid; there was no problem in switching from Muzorewa to Mugabe, within a ten month period when the signs were ominous."[188] He likened the intimidation to that of the IRA in Northern Ireland, and added, "Every one of the weapons used by ZANLA and ZIPRA were donated by Marxist countries which also trained the men that used them. The result was predictable."[189] When ZANU PF and ZAPU were instructed to bring their guerrillas into camps after a political settlement had been reached at Lancaster, ZANU PF sent about half of its guerrillas into the allocated camps and clandestinely deployed the other half of the guerrillas into rural areas[190] where they both campaigned and threatened people to vote for it in the impending elections—features that would mark ZANU PF's future election campaigns in postcolonial Zimbabwe. A school teacher in rural Zimbabwe before and during the elections of 1980 commented, "Most of us voted for ZANU then because we didn't want the war to continue. They were saying, "*mukarega kutivotera tinodzokera musango*" (if you do not vote for us we will go back to the bush and continue the war.)"[191]

Others believed ZANU won the elections simply because they were popular.[192] There were undoubtedly a range of factors behind the ZANU PF victory. On 18 April 1980 Zimbabwe was officially born under a nationalist government. David Lan highlighted the role of Mbuya Nehanda at independence day celebrations: "With Nehanda established as the mhondoro

186. Barbara Tredgold, Letter to Lord Carrington, 18 August 1979, NAZ, GEN-P/TRE.

187. The Times (London), 5 March 1980.

188. Ibid.

189. Ibid.

190. Chung, *Second Chimurenga*.

191. Name withheld, personal interview, January 6, 2007.

192. Mnangagwa, "Post-Independence Zimbabwe," 227.

who protects the whole of the new nation state, it is almost as if Zimbabwe had come to be regarded as a single spirit province."[193] Although Nehanda's portrait was present at Independence Day celebrations Lan seems to have overstated the importance of her role and ATR in the celebration and within the new political era.[194] As shown in the earlier sections of this chapter Nehanda had always been viewed as a Zezuru ancestral spirit who with Kaguvi were being imposed on all Zimbabweans by the Zezuru nationalists whose confidence to take this course now stemmed from their new found access to political influence by virtue of ethnic identity with the country's leader, Mugabe -who has Zezuru ties. The Ndebele did not evoke Nehanda since she was Shona. The Karanga the largest Shona group did not largely embrace Nehanda as she was viewed as a Zezuru ancestral spirit, nor was she embraced by the Manyika another Shona group. With these three Zimbabwean ethnicities not embracing Zezuru ancestors it is difficult to comprehend how Nehanda would have had such national prominence as attributed to her by Lan. On the Karanga's disgruntlement with some of ZANU PF's Zezuru nationalists, on their foiled attempt to make Nehanda and other Zezuru spirits national honoured figures—revealing the tensions even within ZANU PF on the matter—a Karanga former guerrilla complained, "*Vanoda kukwidziridza chembere dzavo, ko isu dzeduvo chembere dzichakwidziridzawo nani? Dzichakwanavo papi?* (they [the Zezuru] want to have their old persons/ancestors [Nehanda ancestress] honoured who will honour our ethnic ancestors? Where will our old people fit in the scheme of things?"[195] At the same Independence Day celebrations of 1980 that Lan highlighted the role of Nehanda, Robert Mugabe was sworn into office by the Roman Catholic Archbishop Patrick Chakaipa.[196] Nothing much was heard about Nehanda or ATR except from songs from ZANU's "Ideological Choir."[197] Mugabe and his ministers after the latter had been sworn into office attended a service in the Roman Catholic Cathedral a break from the colonial regimes practice of attending Anglican dedication services.[198] The *Catholic Herald* about events on this day reported, "Now the Marxist wolf had come in from the wilderness into their [Roman

193. Lan, *Guns and Rain*, 218.

194. Ibid., 217–22.

195. Name withheld, former ZANU guerrilla, personal interview, December 2006.

196. Gundani, *Authority and Leadership*, 98.

197. Lan, *Guns and Rain*, 217.

198. Gundani, *Authority and Leadership*, 98.

Catholic] fold. Was he a lamb—one of God's people like them after all."[199] No mention was made of his commitment to ATR or even digression from it. For Christians, they believed as this point Marxism and not ATR would bring about a new challenge. Speaking about Mugabe's commitment to the Roman Catholic Church 27 years later McLaughlin said, "I believe he is religious. He always attends the Church's important occasions or ceremonies and Bishop Mukonori is his confidant."[200]

In his first cabinet Mugabe, now Prime Minister, appointed the nationalist Methodist Rev. Canaan Sodindo Banana to be the country's President—a symbol of the Protestant Church's nationalist credentials and also a symbol that the Church would be a welcome part within the new political era.[201] No prominent role was given either to Nehanda or ATR in his government or within the new nation. ATR became a privatized matter for individuals but Christianity was and is still employed on various national events or gatherings by the state. Mugabe appreciating what he viewed as being the "significant" role played by Roman Catholics in ending colonialism in Zimbabwe noted, "Not that they fought with arms as we did, but they opposed racialism, and refused to be made an agent of the Government implementing racial policies . . . [they] helped to internationalise our grievances and helped to mobilize international support for us."[202]

Independence finally came through talks, and then the ballot, although the bullet had helped by exerting pressure for the need for dialogue. It must be remembered that independence, although "not an act of British charity" nor "solely a product of the armed struggle" as insisted by ZANU PF stalwarts,[203] was certainly a by-product of dialogue that was ultimately realized through the visible expression of the masses' participation at the ballot. Peter Walls a Presbyterian and the army commander of the Rhodesian forces at the dusk of colonial rule in Zimbabwe in 1979 observed, "The Rhodesian conflict would not be ended by military means and required a political settlement."[204]

In this journey to political settlement various Christians and Christian institutions, who and which, respectively, sought direction from their

199. Ibid., 99

200. Janice McLaughlin.

201. Verstraelen, *Zimbabwean Realities*, 56ff.

202. Randolph, *Dawn in Zimbabwe*, 57.

203. Mnangagwa, *Turmoil and Tenacity*, 226.

204. Peter Walls quoted in Chung, *Second Chimurenga*, 244.

various interpretations of the bible, were crucial to that process, although as part of both the problem and the solution. ATR, as noted by Mutambirwa[205] and Lan,[206] and Marxism, as noted by Chung,[207] may have played a part in the struggle to ending colonialism but the role played by Christianity was more significant. The influence of leading Christians such as Todd, Sithole, Muzorewa, and Catholic priests and nuns, all of whom freely used Christian language and claimed Christian justification for their action undoubtedly had a critical role in turning Rhodesia into Zimbabwe, and ending colonial rule. But that Christian influence was expressed in different, and often conflicting, ways.

205. Mutambirwa, "Impact of Christianity," 69.

206. Lan, *Guns & Rain*, 218.

207. Chung, *Second Chimurenga*, 174.

8

The Postcolonial Aftermath

THE DEFEAT OF COLONIALISM has been a victory for Christianity across Africa in more than one way. The real development of African Christianity came after colonialism was ended. Independence has liberated the African church from missionary control into growth, even though the future of the church looked bleak on the granting of African independence. As Independent governments took over, some churches lost their privileged links, yet Christianity in Africa grew from 75 million adherents in 1965 to 351 million in 2000. By Independence, most churches had majority African leadership. As many African countries economically waned after independence, churches became more important, as channels of aid, but the weakening of church hierarchies has also meant that they have been less strong in being able to resist dictatorship.[1] In Zimbabwe, nationalist movements, built upon the need for a single desire for national unity against the common problem of "colonialism," found significant difficulties in transitioning into democratic movements. Having looked at the struggle against colonialism, there is value in briefly outlining key aspects of the postcolonial reality in Zimbabwe.

The independent nation of Zimbabwe began on a positive note. A policy of national reconciliation and a government of national unity was declared by Robert Mugabe as soon as he took political control in 1980.[2] The white settlers were allowed to keep their economic privileges. Even those

1. Maxwell, "Post-colonial Christianity," 401–4, 417.

2. The first independence cabinet catered even for some members of the opposition.

protected by the Lancaster House Agreement of 1979 with more farms than they needed were embraced. Despite the optimism shown in the area of racial reconciliation, however, significant political tensions remained. It was just a matter of time as to when and how these tensions would either be resolved, or explode. ZANU sought to consolidate its power whereas ZAPU and the white opposition on the other hand struggled with the issues of being out of power. Grudges and mistrust were common among politicians, within and across political parties, some justified and some not.

During the second year of independence the tensions erupted. In 1982 arms caches were found in ZAPU owned and controlled properties. As a result of these discoveries ZANU accused ZAPU of planning a rebellion.[3] Top ZAPU officials who had cabinet positions were removed from office.[4] Two ZAPU leaders responsible for its military wing during the liberation struggle were arrested.[5] The government also seized ZAPU properties. These developments outraged some ZAPU ex-combatants and some soldiers within the army who used to be ZAPU militants during the liberation struggle.

In protest at the alleged maltreatment of their leaders a few soldiers deserted the army and embarked on destabilization activities in Matebeleland as they attacked government infrastructure in uncoordinated fashion. At the same time the apartheid South African government was also executing its policy of destabilization in Zimbabwe, in what was termed "Operation Drama."[6] It took advantage of the situation and trained some people to commit acts of banditry in the country posing as ZAPU dissidents.[7]

The government responded to this problem by unleashing the North Korea trained regiment known as the 5th brigade, which Mugabe codenamed "Gukurahundi."[8] Gukurahundi is a Shona, Manyika dialect, word which is used to refer to early spring rains,[9] but metaphorically it could mean a violent or ferocious attack. Reports circulated of villages being burnt

3. Munangagwa, "Post-Independence Zimbabwe," 229.

4. Joshua Nkomo, Josiah Chinamano, Joseph Msika, and Jini Ntuta were part of the ZAPU leadership holding ministerial positions who were removed from office.

5. These former commanders were Lookout Masuku and Dumiso Dabengwa.

6. Alexander et al., *Violence & Memory*, 189.

7. South Africa believed that by destabilizing Zimbabwe attention and pressure would not be thrust upon it to abandon apartheid and it also wanted to prove a point to the world that Africans were incapable of ruling themselves without white authority.

8. Mugabe, *Our War of Liberation*, 27.

9. Alexander et al., *Violence & Memory*, 191.

and of villagers being beaten indiscriminately including elderly women and children. There were claims that those that harbored dissidents or knew of their whereabouts were tortured and some killed.

Besides being seen as an excuse for decisively weakening ZAPU, a party largely supported by the Ndebele, a view also circulated among the Ndebele that the hunt for dissidents was an excuse for ethnic cleansing by ZANU. The torture of children, even babies, with threats to have their heads chopped off by Gukurahundi bayonets and some killings, were reported in most parts of Matebeleland. However, there was no evidence of child soldiers among the dissidents hence the Ndebele interpreted Gukurahundi activities as a form of ethnic cleansing. The Ndebele further believed that ZANU politicians seeking to protect their political positions, which meant also unhindered access to wealth, had been prepared to subjugate the Ndebele by force since they were viewed as their archrivals for political office. Hence ZANU with its Gukurahundi was believed to have adopted the, "shoot them before they grow" policy towards Ndebele children: "I had just turned 8. The commander came to me and asked in Shona if I knew where the dissidents were. I said 'I didn't know' and he put his bayonet on my neck and said I was lying. He was surprised that I could speak in Shona since we stayed at Bankwe a Ndebele area. After interrogating me he then just said 'shame' and they left us. But my other relatives who lived up the road including my cousin who was 14 years were not that fortunate."[10] The victim of the Gukurahundi continued, "My two aunties were left with broken ribs and my 14 year old cousin, Gilbert, could not walk for weeks. What saved us was that I had spoken to them in Shona. They moved from home to home beating up everyone in the village indiscriminately and some were tortured with burning plastic on their bodies. The question that they asked was 'Have you seen any dissidents in your area.' We said no because the majority of us had not seen any dissidents."[11] The earliest voices of protest within the Christian community emerged from a few vocal individuals within the Roman Catholic Church. In 1983 protest by the Roman Catholic Commission of Justice and Peace (CCJP) against such brutality in many parts of Matebeleland was heard. Mugabe, branding the Roman Catholic Bishops who had spoken out about the atrocities of the Ndebele "a band of

10. A Gukurahundi victim [name withheld to protect identity], personal interview, December 12, 2007.

11. Ibid.

Jeremiahs," refuted the claims.[12] Five years later in April of 1988 the government called for an amnesty.[13] After the declaration of amnesty the government claimed to have killed 342 dissidents.[14] Some scholars believe the number of dissidents was at no point higher than 400.[15] 122 dissidents took advantage of the amnesty. The CCJP contends that the number of those who were tortured and killed could be higher than 3000 although some critics believe that is a very conservative estimate.[16] Professor Verstraelen believes that more than 2000 civilians were killed just in the first six weeks of Gukurahundi's operations.[17] The reports suggested that the combined government forces, and in particular the Central Intelligence Organization (CIO) and Gukurahundi, tortured and killed many more civilians than the dissidents.[18] The full extent of the terror and damage caused by the ZANU PF government in Matebeleland remains to be comprehensively investigated. A different perspective on what happened might develop in the future under a different political administration.

The 1990s in Zimbabwe were marked by reports of sporadic incidents of individual political repression and suggestions of increased corruption among government ministers. Accounts of corruption in the highest political offices had already been highlighted in the 1988 "Willowgate Scandal" in which government ministers acquired many vehicles from Willowvale Motors at a knock-down price and resold them at exorbitant prices or offered some to their relatives at knock-down prices.[19] The church's voice in Zimbabwe, whether Roman Catholic or Protestant, condemning the corruption could not be heard.

When asked by the author why the modern Zimbabwean church is not as vocal as the one in the seventies Rev. Max Chigwida, once a member

12. Verstraelen, *Zimbabwean Realities,* 68.

13. The Catholic Commission for Justice and Peace (CCJP) published a report documenting this crisis in Matebeleland and were pivotal in the bringing together of various political leaders to resolve this crisis.

14. Ibid. 73.

15. Alexander et al., *Violence*, 189ff.

16. CCJP, *Breaking the Silence*, 241ff.

17. Vertraelen, *Zimbabwean Realities*, 68.

18. Catholic Commission for Justice and Peace, *Breaking the Silence,* 161; from eyewitness records from 1982 to 1987 government forces were identified as having killed more than 1300 civilians in. Matebeleland and some parts of Midlands provinces, compared to sixty-four people that were witnessed being killed by dissidents.

19. Nyarota, *Against the Grain,* 150ff.

of the defunct United African National Council, and now a minister of the Uniting Presbyterian Church of Southern Africa (UPCSA), declared that it was the "euphoria of independence" that mellowed if not decapitated the church's ability to provide political comment in the postcolonial period.[20] After attaining independence in 1980 the Christian community, like the rest of the African populace, were caught up in celebrating what they viewed as the greatest political achievement by Zimbabwe's African populace. They did not learn from the experience in Malawi that a nationalist party that had been brutalized during the colonial era and fought for independence had the potential to become an oppressive movement. Chigwida argued that the church seemed to have lost interest in matters it regarded as of a political nature, so that when injustice began to be reported, the church appeared to have lost that prophetic ability.[21]

Beyond this, the general silence of the church in the postcolonial era should also be understood in light of developments of political competition amongst the nationalists in the preceding decade. As a consequence of the struggle for political power that occurred in the seventies, in postcolonial Zimbabwe the Christian leaders, especially the Protestant ones, were viewed not just as men of the cloth but as potential political competitors. As a result of the support that most had offered to the UANC they were no longer viewed by ZANU as impartial social mediators, but a political threat. Hence people like Muzorewa faced incarceration and harassment in 1980 by state agents.

The Roman Catholic leadership's voice of protest has been less noticeable. Their approach to ZANU rule has perhaps been influenced by the close spiritual ties between their leaderships. Mugabe and other leaders who are Roman Catholic have remained loyal to their denomination.[22] Though a few Roman Catholics were openly critical of the regime many remained supportive of its leadership. Even those that were critical did not do it with a similar resolve to that expressed in the seventies in the struggle against the settler government or to get ZANU included at the Lancaster House talks. The two movements still seem to have close religious and ecclesiological ties; hence the voice of protest from the Roman Catholics has remained largely muted.[23]

20. Max Chigwida.

21. Ibid.

22. Bhebhe, *Simon Muzenda*, 186.

23. Holland, *Dinner with Mugabe*, 52.

The efforts of the church community have been more reserved, the most dramatic effort in recent times to create dialogue between state and church has been the publication of a discussion document in 2006 "*The Zimbabwe We Want*."[24] This ecumenical effort was drafted to challenge, in a non-threatening way, the present government about the need for a new sociopolitical vision and course in the country. Due to pressure from the government against its critics, from both within or without the church, together with the incapacity of its drafters to champion the document, it has yielded little fruit.

The bigger challenge remains, over whether, Zimbabwe's current sociopolitical challenges, the churches will be able to significantly demand for sociopolitical change, as they did in the seventies, when they contributed to ending colonialism. For many the question, "How can dictatorial African nationalist leaderships, once oppressed under colonialism, be open to following similar strategies against their own people?" will remain perplexing. What is clear is that their brutality and inhumane treatment of their citizens continues to undermine the dignity of Africans to the outside world. These leaders' interests are simply self-serving, and just like the colonialists they are not friends of Africans.

Assessment

Whether decolonization was a "dishevelled process, a creative enterprise, or a passive revolution" continues to cause debate amongst scholars.[25] The process by which colonialism was challenged in Zimbabwe demonstrates patterns of both continuity and discontinuity. The churches played a significant role, although their involvement has received less attention. Assessment of a number of key factors helps highlight the reasons behind this status quo.

Socio-Political Considerations

In Zimbabwe the church was the colonialists' guest.[26] The infant church and state in Zimbabwe were separate during the early period, but in this separation of church and state the church hardly acted as check on government

24. The Zimbabwe Catholic Bishops Conference, *Zimbabwe We Want*, October 2006.
25. OU Kalu, "African Christianity," 199.
26. Zvobgo, *A History of Christian Missions*, 2.

policies or activities. White interests were closely associated with those of the church, and vice versa.

The impact of the racial attitudes and exploitative policies of Cecil John Rhodes' British South Africa Company (BSAC) for more than 30 years (1890–1923) had an enduring effect on Zimbabwe's sociopolitical terrain. The number of white settlers in Zimbabwe was significantly greater compared to many British African colonies. In 1960 the African population in Zimbabwe was around 4,800, 000 with a white population of about 230 000.[27] Being then one of the strongest economic and political constituency in sub-Saharan Africa it was unlikely that settlers would hand over power easily and quietly.

Government policies in Zimbabwe's colonial history were determined by the will of a minority settler group that was prepared and willing to adopt at times even brutal forms of repression to perpetuate their reign. Their attitudes towards Africans were largely shaped by racial ideas of superiority of the 19th century. This increased racial tensions which later deteriorated and degenerated into the armed conflict that was experienced from 1966 to 1980.

The settlers in Zimbabwe had received a considerable amount of political power in 1923 from Britain, the imperial authority, when they were allowed to form a "responsible government"—an arrangement which left Zimbabwe in a position of being a semi-independent colony. Settler colonial governments governed Zimbabwe with very limited interference or guidance from the imperial authority. A few missionaries like John White[28] and Arthur Shearly Cripps,[29] to name two of the prominent few, could be heard protesting in the early colonial period against the abuse of Africans and government policies that disadvantaged Africans. Even if they had appealed to imperial authorities there was little room for intervention since the arrangement of "responsible government" had given settlers significant power over the territory. As a result of the small numbers of Christians protesting in the early colonial period scholars such as Professor Mararike[30] and the Zimbabwean social historian Lawrence Vambe[31] could justifiably

27 Clarke, "Population and Family Planning."

28. Ranger, African Voice, 89.

29. Thomson, *Rhodesia & Its Government*, 231.

30. Professor C. Mararike, to a University of Zimbabwe Masters research student, Rev. Chirovamavi, who was interviewed by the author, Greendale, June 2004.

31. Vambe, *An Ill-fated People*, 234.

conclude that the church in general was a conservative force in Zimbabwe. However, this justification applies mainly to the early colonial period.

According to Vambe, writing in 1972, the Zimbabwean church's stand on behalf of Africans was weak: "Has the Christian Church had any positive influence in Southern Rhodesia? I think every honest African will say that the Christian Church has failed as a symbol of peace, understanding and brotherhood among men and needs to re-examine its position very seriously."[32]

Vambe's assessment stands when discussing the church's position on sociopolitical matters before the mid-sixties but the evidence suggests that a different assessment is needed of events from the mid-sixties and certainly in the 70s. The Zimbabwean church's participation in the liberation struggle for Africans in the period between c.1970 and 1980 has become clear from the evidence, as shown in the preceding chapter. In the last decade of the fight against colonialism in Zimbabwe, the endeavor of Christians to end colonialism was not just significant but it was critical.

In assessing the merits of the claim that the church was a conservative force throughout the colonial period, a key issue is the part of Zimbabwe's colonial period which is being referred to. Later developments within the church, as chapters six and seven show, challenge the assertion that the church was consistently a conservative force restricting political progress. Chapter seven demonstrates that the African Protestant leadership and some liberal Christians, just as the Roman Catholic leadership–though all these groups ascribed to different philosophies and at times divergent strategies–at vital points provided the moral and personal drive to sustain the anti-colonial struggle.

Christianity in the 1970s in Zimbabwe sought to restore the African to a respectable place of equality, sociopolitical independence and even supremacy over the African's colonial master. Muzorewa on behalf of the ANC called all Africans to join in the struggle against colonialism, "an arduous journey to Zimbabwe in a Christian and non-violent manner,"[33] although Muzorewa did not consistently ascribe to this position. He also advocated for the use of violence in the nationalist struggle as he deemed it to be a "just war."[34] The Christian Council of Rhodesia (CCR) also proclaimed, "The Church has been called by God to be a community in which race, like

32. Ibid.

33. Muzorewa, "Under the Banner of Unity," 10 March 1972, NAZ, GEN-P/MUZ.

34. Muzorewa, *Rise and Walk*, 140.

all other human distinctions, loses all divisive significance. We should not stand silent when injustice is being done."[35] Such Christian voices were an open stimulus for sociopolitical transformation particularly in this era of Zimbabwean colonial history rather than a conservative force.

Education

In the early colonial period, as well as across the later colonial era in Zimbabwe, the church played an indirect but significant role, in challenging colonialism through the provision of education, a claim strongly asserted by Zimbabwe's veteran nationalist, Ndabaningi Sithole.[36] The role and form of education, or lack of it, has stood out as one of the significant factors shaping sociopolitical events in Zimbabwe. In chapter five of *African Nationalism* Sithole argued that, the efforts of missionaries in educating Africans influenced the rise of African nationalism.[37] Generally across Africa, Sundkler and Steed agree: "Independent Africa was discovered in the schoolroom."[38] However, this line of argument is challenged by Mutambirwa who asserts that Christianity, or "The Bible had no influence on African nationalism."[39] Contrary to Sithole he believed that the education offered by missionary schools was not consciously structured to promote African advancement. Sithole's claim about African nationalism could be considered questionable in relation to Zimbabwean early colonial history.

Although Mutambirwa was correct in observing that missionary education offered in Zimbabwe was not consciously tailor-made for African advancement, the evidence suggests that this form of education indirectly promoted, rather than hindered Africans' efforts for sociopolitical advancement, especially if compared to South Africa's *Bantu Education*, which directly hindered African advancement.

Though mission school education in Zimbabwe generally did not directly contribute to the advancement of African political aspirations, it did help those Africans who had access to its education to develop their intellectual abilities and opportunities to further that education. Education enhancement opportunities were offered through church scholarships and

35. Hallencreutz, "A Council in Crossfire," 68.

36. Sithole, *African Nationalism*, 51–64.

37. Ibid.

38. Sundkler and Steed, *A History of the Church*, 609.

39. Mutambirwa, "The Impact of Christianity," 69.

other philanthropic church channels such as individual missionaries. It was largely through these partly church educated and/or supported individuals who furthered their education that nationalism would be introduced and take root in Zimbabwe. Ndabaningi Sithole, and other leading Zimbabweans, such as Joshua Nkomo and Robert Mugabe were some of the people who benefitted from mission education.

The different views of Sithole and Mutambirwa concerning the influence or lack of influence of Christianity in the overall African struggle against colonialism raises the question of whether indirect influences can be considered strategic. Mutambirwa argued that a direct correlation between African nationalism (representing African sociopolitical aspirations) and political transformation brought by mission education was absent.[40] Whereas Sithole, observing the indirect influences of that education or the impact of education that had been acquired through church channels (mission schools or Christian philanthropists), argued that Christianity played a significant part in advancing Africans' sociopolitical aspirations and the eventual rise of African nationalism.[41] The complexity of relationship between Christian education and colonial dominance needs to be recognized, as Ward notes: "Although education was significantly in the hands of missions, by the end of the colonial period, mission schools were reliant on state aid to maintain their work. In British Africa funding was open to all denominations, in return for state inspection and government-imposed curricula, and even Catholics eventually adopted a policy of co-operation. Protestant high schools trained political leaders who were to lead British African colonies into Independence, and Catholic secondary education produced Kwame Nkrumah and Julius Nyerere."[42] Kalu notes the mixed reaction this could produce. Some mission leaders considered the African leaders who were products of mission schools as their children not yet ready for maturity. Others were supportive of their leadership role, whilst others tried to use indigenous clergy to secure for the future the influence they had sought over years.[43]

In Zimbabwe during the early colonial period, not only in education offered by church institutions, but in mission programs, the correlation was less direct, until the mid-sixties. It then begins to emerge with the church's

40. Ibid.

41. Sithole, *African Nationalism*, 51–64.

42. Ward, "Christianity," 78.

43. Kalu, "African Christianity," 199.

conscious efforts to seek sociopolitical justice and practical involvement in protesting against colonialism.

What highlighted this direct correlation from the mid-sixties was the subjugation of nationalist political activities by the hard-line government of Ian Smith. By arresting the remainder of political nationalists left free during earlier arrests under the Whitehead government, Africans were left with no legal platform for political expression. In the absence of African nationalist political protest, it was the church-educated African church leadership in Zimbabwe which donned the mantle of political protest from the mid-sixties. As more mainline denominations gradually Africanized their leadership, from this period, church protest began to rise.

Church protest was further stimulated, though in the negative, by a continued agitation caused by the legislation of more repressive policies such as the 1969 Land Tenure Act by Smith's government. This state of affairs even made some traditional Christian allies of settler governments, such as the Dutch Reformed Church, and denominations that believed in being apolitical, such as the Salvation Army, conclude that some form of change was necessary. On the other hand, external influences from other anti-colonial Christian organizations such as the World Council of Churches and the wider Christian community in independent Africa and Western Europe, provided further stimuli for protest for the Zimbabwean church. A combination of these factors accelerated the process of protest within the Zimbabwean church in the 70s which culminated in the formation of the African National Council, led by the clergy. It became at its formation and in its early years the paramount voice and movement for Africans' demands for sociopolitical justice and liberation.

Politico-Economic Considerations

Zimbabwe was viewed as the "new Australia"[44] by settlers, in other words, their source of economic advancement and permanent place of dwelling. Hence it was likely to create strong tensions if the imperial power, Britain, sought to politically disempower the settlers–in a country where economic well-being and political control were closely tied. When the possibility of losing political control occurred at the cessation of Federation in 1963, the Unilateral Declaration of Independence (UDI) that followed in 1965 was not a surprising political outcome.

44. Kane, *The World's View*, 232.

Therefore in that situation when their political hold was under threat even Anglican Christian authority, which most settlers claimed to be subject to, was challenged and disregarded. When the archbishop of Canterbury, Michael Ramsey (1904–1988), suggested and supported the possibility of the use of force on Zimbabwe after UDI over 200 settlers threatened that "they would burn their bibles and send the ashes to the Archbishop."[45] Though according to Linden and Weller "the threat did not demonstrate Christian values which the settler claimed to have been preserving in Zimbabwe"[46] on the other hand it demonstrated that their commitment to "Rhodesia" would push them to consider even more radical measures.

With Africans on the other hand willing also to adopt extreme measures to attain sociopolitical freedom, which was closely tied with political control, and settlers not willing to let go, neither side was willing to reach a compromise. The logical consequence of this scenario was what ensued, that is the degeneration of the stalemate into a violent encounter in the form of an armed struggle. From 1966, when Africans were convinced that settlers would not hand over political power, as Judith Todd put it, "The stage was set for war. The whites would not share power. It had to be taken from them."[47]

Role of Missions and Missionaries

In colonial Zimbabwe there was general suspicion that even when some missionaries meant well, Africans thought they had some hidden agenda as noted in a missionary report of 1906: "Even after the missionary has resided in their midst for years, and devoted himself day after day to the work of their regeneration, he is often looked at askance by many who are persuaded that self-interest must have brought him—as it brings other white men—to their country."[48]

Many Africans, even Christians, in Zimbabwe rarely confided in missionaries. In the 1960s, almost sixty years later, that general mistrust of most missionaries by Africans had not changed much as highlighted in Henry Mugabe's[49] response to Africans' attitudes to missionaries in an

45. Linden and Weller, *Mainstream Christianity*, 211.

46. Ibid; see also Smith, "Declaration of Independence," 18 November 1965.

47. Todd, "White Policy and Politics, 121.

48. Zambezi Mission Records (ZMR), "History of the Zambesi Mission," 156.

49. Principal of Gweru Baptist Seminary.

interview with the author, "what we thought we kept inside, we did not say what we really, really thought."[50] The work of missionaries, especially their early work, was cast in a negative light especially by African nationalists who associated Christianity with "hypocrisy and colonial attitudes."[51] Therefore relations between the Africans and the church leadership, when it was dominantly white, continued to be experienced at an artificial level. Efforts at cross-ethnic dialogue, on social-political matters, would have made the white church leadership realize the problems faced by their African converts and possibly that could have spurred some to seek social justice for or alongside Africans.

Most missionaries were quickly drawn into the settler community as a result of the rapidity with which the settler community grew. Among settlers they primarily catered for their spiritual needs, but among Africans coupled with meeting spiritual needs some were colonial policy administrators.[52] The fundamental question clergy found hard to resolve was whether they were missionaries, or whether they were chaplains to the white community. Instead of identifying with the locals or offering a positive alternative in racial relations, most missionaries identified socially with settlers, a most natural social development since they also shared a similar culture. Unfortunately most failed to extricate themselves from identifying with settlers when racial divisions developed to be antagonistic. Their impartiality on sociopolitical matters was affected. For some that sought to genuinely bridge gaps between Africans and settlers, their good intentions from the outset, justifiably or not, were put in question by most Africans. Because of clerical celibacy, Catholic priests had a greater capacity to separate themselves from the settler community.

The non-liberal missionaries and church leadership's attitude to racial relations was one of the major factors that militated against Christians under their stewardship from being proactive against colonialism and identifying with those, within and without the church, that sought to fight against colonial injustice. A.R. Booth, secretary of the Commission of the Churches on International Affairs, observed about the state of affairs on church and state in central Africa in the 1950s and 1960s, "The churches of central Africa signally failed their ecumenical responsibility to hold

50. Henry J. Mugabe.

51. Boobbyer, "Moral Re-Armament," 232.

52. Brand, "African Nationalists," 72.

together the Christian community across lines of political bitterness."[53] This does not mean that the church was not politically engaged. It meant the conservative missionaries and white led church of the period circa 1958 to 1964 were polarized from the African church but still engaged on ethnic lines in political dialogue. This was the period in which the Zimbabwean church went through two forms of transition: in leadership—from a generally white to an African one; and protest—from being largely acquiescent into political activism.

Some missionaries viewed Zimbabwe as more than just a mission field, but as a permanent settling place after retirement. Those that settled or were considering citizenship shared a significant range of interests with settlers.[54] As a result of this, as missionaries there was a conflict of interest between those of the African community they conducted mission amongst, and their own interests.

In the early sixties although the voice of protest from the Zimbabwean churches was limited, among missionaries of a liberal political persuasion such as Dodge, Lamont and Todd their voice was beginning to be heard, closely echoing that of African nationalists. Such were the views of the Irish Carmelite, Lamont, that he was known as "the Red Bishop," and later tried and deported for opposing Ian Smith, attracting a demonstration of 100 African women at his trial.[55]

Political protest and the demand for Africans' political participation by some missionaries of a liberal persuasion was never a product of mission policy but it was a by-product of individual conviction and response to the realities that surrounded them. There was no mission board prior to the seventies that protested in favor of Africans' rights in Zimbabwe. Some liberal missionaries, like Todd, in the church and political leadership in Zimbabwe awakened to the fact that African rule was inevitable and started pushing the settler government to make policy changes that were necessary to accommodate this reality and thence doctrines of partnership and meritocracy emerged.

Across Africa, the appointment of Africans to positions of leadership had been slow. Protestants emphasized training pastors from peasant backgrounds for rural mission, which meant they were often given limited educational opportunities, different from the small number of educated

53 Booth quoted by Stuart, "Speaking for the Unvoiced," 189.

54. Brand, "African Nationalists," 73.

55. Isichei, *Christianity in Africa*, 320.

laymen and women. In 1950 there were no Anglican diocesan bishops in Africa.[56] A significant development in Zimbabwe that would emanate from this deficiency was the realization by the white liberal church leadership of the need for sending Africans for education and theological training in colleges and universities abroad with the hope of them coming back and taking over leadership roles. Though indirect, this became one of the critical contributions towards the fight against colonialism that the white liberal community would make in Zimbabwe.

The Africanization of Leadership

From the mid-1960s African Christians, like Abel Muzorewa, educated in America and funded by American Methodists—who were beneficiaries of this liberal initiative began to trickle back. This development coincided with the premiership of Ian Douglas Smith in 1964, who upon taking office escalated repression, deported missionaries who protested against colonialism and incarcerated African nationalists and made it impossible for any form of meaningful African political participation. Some of these Africans channeled their efforts through the church, where they became leading figures, and which was used as a vehicle from which they could make their protests. By this means a robust and fiercely anti-colonial Christian leadership was gradually introduced.

Those that were earmarked for Christian leadership, like Muzorewa, began to fill the major gaps, created by the incarceration of nationalist leaders and deportation of vocal missionaries. This development in Zimbabwe ensured both a gradual rise of African leadership in the church and church protest. This gradual rise of political protest from the church accelerated in the seventies as more mainline denominations awoke to Africanization in their leadership. A switch to Africanization was in itself evidence that some in the white church leadership had also awoken to the need for African political participation in the wider community.

Yet in the 1960s, the churches in Zimbabwe disagreed over strategies and methodologies of intervention. No viable strategies were formulated to challenge the oppressive settler governments. Those who called for a non-violent revolution offered no viable and tangible strategies on how to achieve such a revolution, leaving others convinced it was either empty

56. Ward, "Christianity," 81; Kalu, "African Christianity," 217.

talk, or evidence of insincerity.[57] Those white church leaders who spoke out strongly were deported or effectively silenced by the government, or controlled by senior clerics. Muzorewa wrote, "The Council (Christian Council of Rhodesia) gave us new hope. It voiced the concerns of the African people at the very time when our parties were banned and our leaders silenced in political detention . . . Mere statements, however, did not convince the doubters of the Church's stand. They wanted concrete actions, and had not long to wait."[58]

An Africanized church leadership brought a gradual rise in the voice of African protest, stimulated by confidence derived from western liberal education and their own situation as part of the oppressed group desiring equality. The African elements of the Zimbabwean church drew towards a consensus that colonialism was to be got rid of, and a nationalist course should be adopted.

Armed Struggle

The progression of the nationalist cause into an armed struggle was a major development in Zimbabwean history. Christians who believed that violent means should be used to bring about justice were slow to join the armed struggle as it commenced in the mid-sixties, but frustration with the failures of the white-led hierarchy of the churches encouraged confrontation ideologies, which appeared a more effective movement from below. The power of the impulse for nationalism as the paramount cause was noted by Ian Linden, who quoted the striking viewpoint of Mr. Munangatira, who argued for "the place of Christianity in Nationalism" but emphasized that if asked to choose between the "Church and Nationalism almost all Africans would choose the latter."[59]

What became another hindrance during this period to the church's participation in the fight against colonialism was a belief held by some Africans and most of the white leadership in the doctrine of neutrality. Desmond Tutu in *There is no Future without Forgiveness* highlighted the problem of "neutrality" in his Mouse and Elephant illustration, "If an elephant steps on the mouse's tail and the mouse asks for help. And you say,

57. Muzorewa, *Rise Up and Walk*, 59.

58. Ibid.

59. Linden, *The Catholic Church*, 231.

'I am neutral,' the mouse will not appreciate that response."[60] In Zimbabwe most Africans, liberals and nationalists identified with the mouse's position when some Christians had adopted the position of neutrality. The proponents of the position had been perceived generally by those suffering injustice as indifferent to their suffering. Although some may have cared and wanted to see the end of colonialism their silence was generally perceived as acquiescence to the unjust sociopolitical status quo.

Although some among the white church leadership, and some white Christians, would continue into the seventies subscribing to "neutrality," most African Christians and some, though few, within the white leadership had shifted positions and moved towards acceptance of the use of violence in Christian protest. Some Christians went as far as joining the nationalist armies as guerrillas.[61]

Liberation Theology and Marxism

Liberation Theology was not a significant factor in the struggle for liberation in Zimbabwe. The sociopolitical consciousness that had been created as a result of Vatican II[62] in the larger Roman Catholic circles had lost its impetus by the mid-seventies as a consequence of suspicious attitudes towards the rise in popularity of Liberation Theology especially in Latin America in the 1970s with its determination of achieving social justice for the poor. Its rise has been linked, ironically, to the calls for social reform and transformation proposed by Vatican II.[63] Bishop Kalilombe observing developments and his own experiences within Malawi in the 1970s and 1980s asserted that the Vatican was so disturbed with the development of Liberation Theology and its spread among its priestly ranks, that it was cautious about whom to send to places like Malawi and Zimbabwe where the ideas were not common at the time: "Experience has shown that official sentiment in Rome is quite suspicious of these communities[64] and of the movement of Liberation Theology that is associated with them. They are

60. Tutu, *No Future without Forgiveness*, 275.

61. Janice McLaughlin.

62 Dorr, *Option For The Poor*, 149–77.

63. Bradstock and Rowland, *Radical Christian Writings*, 335.

64. Kalilombe initiated Base Christian Communities in the diocese under his charge hoping to empower then and give them a voice in the decision making process of the Roman Catholic Church in Malawi.

accused of representing an ecclesiology that is anti-hierarchy, rebelliously "popular," and leaning towards Marxism."[65] Priests perceived as having Marxist leanings, such as Bishop Kalilombe, were transferred to places they could not exercise the same influence.[66] Kalilombe concluded, "I was a victim of this attitude by Rome."[67] In Zimbabwe the Ian Smith regime was also suspicious of any new ideas, theological or not. Some liberal missionaries and Christians, especially with constituencies of larger influence, were usually labeled as communists.[68]

Smith, claiming to be Christian, viewed himself as a defender of "the Christian way of life" against communism hence any ideas associated with communism were suppressed.[69] Therefore the context was largely isolated from influences such as Liberation Theology, but this does not close the possibility of a few exceptions having been influenced by such a theology such as the case of Rev. Canaan Banana. The significant fact here is that in Zimbabwe liberation theology as experienced in Latin America was not noteworthy–a factor in influencing Christians' responses to colonialism.

The views of mainline denomination Christians in Zimbabwe, based on traditional western theologies especially in relation to their understanding of *Imago Dei* in all humans, were reflected in the ANC declaration that "all humans are created in the image of the Almighty God" equal.[70] Alongside these, western liberal influences and understandings of the dignity of humanity and human rights, and traditional African understandings as represented in the Shona proverb, "*Munhu munhu asina kuzvarwa ndiani*?"[71] (making this not solely a Christian concept as Mutambirwa rightly points out),[72] were all factors and values that shaped the moral stand and commitment of African Christian leaders to ending colonialism. This struggle in Zimbabwe was never primarily an African effort—strong white liberal influence was present.

65 Kalilombe, *Doing Theology*, 37.

66. Ibid.

67. Patrick Kalilombe, personal interview, Zomba, November 7, 2007.

68. Nyasaland Government, "Confidential Report," 26 March 1959.

69. Kalilombe, *Theology*, 37.

70. Muzorewa, "Under the Banner of Unity," 10 March 1972, NAZ, GEN-P/MUZ.

71. Shona proverb translated: Every person deserves to be accorded respect in by virtue of simply being human; Mutambirwa, "The Impact of Christianity," 76.

72. Ibid.

Others have argued the case that it was not Christianity, but other ideologies that played the key role in the struggle for African liberation. Chung has shown that Marxism had a role to play in ending colonialism in Zimbabwe. Although some within the ZANU PF leadership had made the decision to take the Marxist course in 1973, that path had almost been completely abandoned by 1976 as a result of power struggles within ZANU guerrilla factions.[73] The Tongogara faction, which won this internal struggle, abandoned the communist path in favor of waging war, as Sister McLaughlin put it, focusing on "national grievances."[74] Hence from 1976, though ZANU was still labeled as Marxist and received, some aid (which ZANU said was not adequate)[75] from Communist countries and a few members in its ranks still employed communist jargon to keep their sources from this ideological bloc content, the reality was that in Mozambique, where its guerrillas were based and had begun to fruitfully prosecute the war, Marxist-Leninism had effectively been discarded. After the ZANU guerrillas internal struggle Chung wrote, "Tongogara had warned that anyone claiming to be a Marxist-Leninist was a dissident and a bandit, and kept to his word in ensuring that all the Marxist-Leninists were kept under lock and key. Thus, Mugabe's close alliance with Tongogara from 1976 until Tongogara's death in 1979 meant that, in fact, he had to go against his initial Marxist-Leninist principles."[76] In the postcolonial era Mugabe proclaimed that his party instead of following a full Marxist-Leninist path would take a socialist one.[77] Mugabe, to Isichei, was "originally a Catholic, was theoretically a Marxist, but he was essentially a pragmatist. He later took pains to work in harmony with the Church and with white farmers."[78] Since communism had been largely confined to the guerrilla camps in Zambia by ZAPU and Mozambique and Tanzania by ZANU, and was significantly weakened in ZANU from 1976, it faded into insignificance, except as a source of meagre resources, and lost the possibility of a comeback at the collapse of Union of the Soviet Socialist Republics in 1991.

73. Mugabe, *Our War of Liberation*, 153ff.

74. Janice McLaughlin.

75. Chung, *Second Chimurenga*, 89.

76. Ibid. 183.

77. Verstraelen, *Zimbabwean Realities*, 56.

78. Isichei, *Christianity in Africa*, 320.

African Traditional Religion

David Lan gave a prominent role to African Traditional Religion in the liberation struggle. However, when most evidence is considered its significance in the larger scheme of the liberation struggle was more limited, and confined to micro-level events. In scope *Masvikiro's* (spirit mediums) significant involvement to the liberation struggle within Zimbabwe were limited to a period of about 2 years in Dande Valley when ZANU was still a small army of less than 200 poorly equipped and poorly fed soldiers. By 1973 the competing ideology had become Marxism which led to the Nhari rebellion of 1974. After that year ZANU would commit itself officially to a Marxist struggle—a commitment as shown above that would also not last more than two years. In the years between 1975 and 1979 the spirit mediums largely exercised their influence outside Zimbabwe's borders.[79] At the war frontline there were no spirit mediums. In the research conducted by the author *masvikiro* were never attributed much influence within the country, outside of Lan's research in the Dande area, from early 1970s to the end of the colonial era.

ZAPU, another guerrilla movement, did not have spirit mediums within its guerrilla camps or even within its refugee camps in Zambia. In Dande the role of spirit mediums in guiding the guerrillas would have significantly diminished after the relocation of ZANU into Tanzania, and later into the south western and western parts of Mozambique after its independence in 1975, and the abandoning of Zambia by ZANU after the "Nhari saga" of 1974.[80] The religious commitment of the Zimbabwean people of Manyika stock who lived in the areas surrounding ZANU's new bases from 1975 in the country's eastern border areas with Mozambique were different from the Dande people. Among the Manyika *Masvikiro* played a very insignificant role in the 70s. To this effect in relationship to the least Christianized subsection of the Manyika, the Hwesa people, David Maxwell writes: "[S]pirit mediums did not mobilize every section of Hwesa society . . . the movement of great numbers of women and youth and some returning labour migrants into the church from 1950s onwards, brought about the first effective challenge to the ideological hegemony of local eco-religion

79. Chung, *Second Chimurenga*, 197.

80. Ibid. 91–99.

(mhondoro cults). These Christian youth and women's movements were an alternative to the patriarchal society order."[81]

Forces such as African Traditional Religion, together with secular ideologies were all operative at personal, local and national level. Christian adherence similarly involves micro-level personal choices, as well as being reflected in wider structures with greater cultural and political dimensions. African Traditional Religions share these features. Future local studies like Lan's, but of the impact of personal Christian belief patterns on the activities of individual guerrillas and others during the independence war, would yield significant further insights, but have not been attempted in this study which focuses on Christian influences on wider political structures.

In the rest of the Shona country beside Dande, where spirit mediums are given a prominent role, a similar role is not easily recognised. Ncube and Ranger's study in keeping with the findings of this research does not accord a prominent role to African Traditional Religion in Matebeleland during the liberation struggle.[82] Lan further gives a prominent role to ATR at independence: "With Nehanda established as the Mhondoro who protects the whole of the new nation state, it is almost as if Zimbabwe had become to be regarded as a single spirit province."[83] Although spirit mediums were and are part of the Shona traditional religion MFC Bourdillon commented, "mediums have no absolute sway over the Shona people."[84]

Contrary to Lan, Nehanda did not primarily appear on the ZANU PF supporters flags at independence as a symbol of "the nation's religious commitment to African Traditional Religions"[85] or to her as a spiritual leader, but she was a potent anti-colonial symbol from an earlier revolutionary movement which was now fulfilled. However, at the same independence celebration of 1980 the two major breaks from tradition were the inauguration of ZANU into power and the consecration services at the Roman Catholic Cathedral—a departure from colonial governments' dedication which had taken place in the Anglican Cathedral. Since the 1980 independence celebrations the church has continued to take this role in various

81. Maxwell, *Christians and Chiefs*, 134. For further reading on religious and cultural differences of the Shona as a result of Christianization and colonialism consult also chapters 2,3 and 4. For additional material on Shona religious and cultural differences, see also Bourdillon, *The Shona Peoples*.

82. Ncube and Ranger, "Religion in the Guerrilla War," 35.

83. Lan, *Guns and Rain*, 218.

84. Bourdillon, *Shona Peoples*, 264.

85. Lan, *Guns and Rain*, 218.

state public functions and the African Traditional Religions have not been offered any such responsibility. Mugabe on behalf of his government has publicly thanked the Roman Catholic Church for its contribution. Another ZANU stalwart, now deceased, Maurice Nyagumbo also acknowledged the importance of Christians who were in high political offices like Muzorewa of whom he said, "If it was not because of this man we would be still in the bush."[86]

Although this does not always necessarily correspond to the church's capacity to influence sociopolitical structures, Christianity has remained numerically the dominant religion. By the turn of the century Christians were estimated to constitute about 70% of the Zimbabwean population. Hence within it still remains an innate capacity and potency that if tapped can help to positively influence political decisions and fight sociopolitical injustice in the current context just as in the 1960s and 1970s.

Overall Assessment

Undoubtedly various factors and forces contributed to ending colonialism in Zimbabwe, and each operated with varying degrees of influence. Political liberalism played its role, as did Marxism and African Traditional Religion in different measures but compared to all these, at the strategic level, the evidence suggests that Christianity played a greater role. As to whether the most critical role in ending colonialism in Zimbabwe was played by the Bible (Christianity), the Bullet (the armed struggle), or the Ballot (democratic and diplomatic initiatives) there is no easy answer. All three factors were constantly at play influencing outcomes whether at the forefront or subserviently, but Christianity in its varied influences, impressions and expressions was certainly significant, and influential of developments of both the Bullet and the Ballot. At different points and junctures the three dominant forces were at times subservient to the other and at times all were intertwined in a complex historical out-working of sociopolitical events that defies a clean clear dissection of issues. This study has shown that Christianity, including significant voices from within Protestantism, as well as the more widely acknowledged voices from Catholicism, also played a most significant role in the colossal efforts to end colonialism in Zimbabwe.

This study in many ways demonstrates that latent within Christianity are both elements of conservatism as well as a capacity to being

86. Herbert Chikomo.

a transformative force in sociopolitical matters. The Christian ideology as a transformative force can be adopted for the causes of sociopolitical justice. In Zimbabwe it was used to fight colonial injustices but also in the same context it was used to perpetuate injustice by the Smith regime who on behalf of the settlers claimed "in humble submission to almighty God" they were "preserving Christian civilisation."[87] The answer to the question whether by nature the Christian religion is a conservative force or a transformative one in sociopolitical matters can be given in contrasting forms, resting on interpretive decisions, theological commitments and sociopolitical commitments of its adherents rather than to be inherently found in the religion itself.

More recent events have demonstrated that distinct national patterns have been established in church-state relations in Zimbabwe. In the postcolonial period churches have found it more difficult to speak out against governmental injustice; they have preferred to be apolitical. This suggests a reversion to the mindset of the early colonial era when the churches felt dependent on the colonial government for their well-being and indeed their very existence. Modern Zimbabwean churchmen will offer their own reasons for the quiescence of their churches after the 1970s but it is surely significant that this is a stance which comes almost as second nature to the churches in Zimbabwe. If Zimbabwean churches are to become a sustained and constructive influence in the political life of the nation, they need to confront the extensive historical legacy that predisposes them to a subservient or marginal role. It remains to be seen how Christianity will be interpreted and applied by its adherents in light of the various, recent, current and future sociopolitical challenges in Zimbabwe.

87. Smith, *The Great Betrayal*, 105.

Glossary

This glossary consists of African terms that have been used more than once.

Amabutho	warriors
Chembere	elderly woman
Chimurenga	liberation struggle
Gukurahundi	ferocious rain at the start of a Zimbabwean rain season
Masvikiro	spirit mediums
Mfecane	scattering or upheaval
Munhu	person
Umvukela	liberation struggle
Vafundisi	church ministers/pastors
Vakomana	boys
Vanasekuru	elderly men
Vashandi	workers

Bibliography

Acton, Judith. "Recollections of a Conversation with Ndabaningi Sithole." The Waldorf Hotel, London, February 18, 1978, NAZ, GEN-P/TOD.

African National Council. "List." Muzorewa Central Committee Members, n.d. NAZ, Acc: MS 771/1–3.

Ahlstrom, E. S. *A Religious History of the American People.* New Haven: Yale University Press, 1972.

Alderson, Cecil. "1 Sam. 10:24, 'And all the people shouted and said, "God save the Queen!"'" A sermon preached at the Salisbury Cathedral, three days after the UDI, November 14, 1965, NAZ, GEN-P/ALD.

———. Letter addressed to Anglican clergy over Father Hugh Bishop's sermon that caused offense in the Salisbury Anglican cathedral, March 3, 1966, NAZ, GEN-P/ALD.

———. "My Dear." General letter addressed to British friends who had sent Christmas cards, January 1, 1966, NAZ, GEN-P/ALD.

Alexander, J., J. McGregor, and T. Ranger. *Violence and Memory.* Oxford: Currey, 2000.

All-Africa Conference of Churches. *Drumbeats from Kampala.* London: Lutterworth, 1963.

Associated Papers. "Rhodesia Foes." New York, October 7, 1978.

Atkinson, N. D. *Teaching Rhodesians.* London: Longman, 1972.

Auret, D. *Reaching for Justice.* Gweru, Zimbabwe: Mambo, 1992.

Azikiwe, Nnamdi. "Has an African a God?" *African Morning Post* (Ghana) 1936.

Baker, C. *State of Emergency: Crisis in Central Africa, Nyasaland 1959–1960.* London: Tauris, 1997.

Banana, C. S. "Racialism Our Worst Enemy." Address at Hellenic Hall, Gwelo, August 29, 1972, NAZ, GEN-P/MUZ.

———. "The Case for a New Bible." In *Rewriting the Bible,* edited by J. Mukonyora, J. L. Cox, and F. J. Verstraelen. Harare, Zimbabwe: Mambo, 1993.

———. *The Church and the Struggle for Zimbabwe.* Upsala: Swedish Institute of Missionary Research, 1996.

———. "What Is What about the African National Council." May 1973, NAZ, GEN-P/MUZ.

———. *Politics of Repression and Resistance.* Gweru, Zimbabwe: Mambo, 1996.

Barrett, B. D., ed. *World Christian Encyclopaedia.* Oxford: Oxford University Press, 1982.

BCC and Christian Aid. "Action to Combating Racism." Interim Statement, September 30, 1970, NAZ, GEN-P/WOR.

Beach, D. N. *The Shona and Their Neighbours*. Oxford: Blackwell, 1994.

———. *The Shona and Zimbabwe, 900–1850*. London: Heinemann, 1980.

———. *Zimbabwe before 1900*. Gweru, Zimbabwe: Mambo, 1984.

———. "The Impact of Christianity on the Shona: The Protestants and the Southern Shona." In *Christianity South of Zambezi*, edited by J. A. Dachs. Gweru, Zimbabwe: Mambo, 1973.

Beaucoup de Bruit: 200 000 Dollars Qui Font (helas)." *La Vie Protestante*. September 18, 1970, NAZ, GEN-P/WOR.

Bent, A. J., ed. *Breaking Down the Walls*. Geneva: World Council of Churches, 1986.

Bhebhe, N. "The Nationalist Struggle, 1957–1962." In *Turmoil and tenacity: Zimbabwe, 1890–1990*, edited by C.S. Banana. Harare: College, 1989.

———. *Christianity and Traditional religion in Western Zimbabwe, 1859–1923*. London: Longman, 1979.

———. *Simon Vengai Muzenda*. Gweru: Mambo, 2004.

———. *The ZAPU and ZANU Guerrilla War*. Gweru: Mambo,1999.

Bhila, H. "Trade and the Early Missionaries in Southern Zambezia." In *Christianity South of the Zambezi*, edited by M. F. C. Bourdillon, 25–42. Gweru: Mambo, 1977.

Blake, R. *A History of Rhodesia*. London: Eyre Methuen, 1977.

Boobbyer, P. "Moral Re-Armament in Africa in the Era of Decolonization." In *Missions, Nationalism, and the End of Empire*, edited by B. Stanley, 232–35. Cambridge: Eerdmans, 2003.

Bourdillon, M., and P. Gundani. "Rural Christians and the Zimbabwe Liberation War: A Case Study." In *Church and State in Zimbabwe*, edited by C. F. Hallencreutz and A. M. Moyo, 151–61. Gweru: Mambo, 1988.

Bourdillon, M. F. C. *Shona Peoples: an ethnography of the contemporary Shona*. 3rd ed. Gweru: Mambo, 1987.

Bradstock, A., and C. Rowland, eds. *Radical Christian Writings*. Massachusetts: Blackwell, 2002.

Brand, C.M. "African Nationalists & Missionaries in Rhodesia." In *Christianity South of the Zambezi*, edited by M. F. C. Bourdillon. Gweru: Mambo, 1977.

British Council of Churches. *Violence in Southern Rhodesia*. London: SCM, 1970.

Brown, R., and E. Stokes, eds. *The Zambesian Past*. Manchester: Manchester University Press, 1966.

Bulhan, H. A. *Frantz Fanon & The Psychology of Oppression*. New York: Plenum, 1985.

Bull, T., ed. *Rhodesian Perspective*. London: Joseph, 1967.

Burrough, J. P. "Confidential Notes of a Meeting between the Prime Minister and Representatives of the Anglican Church in the Prime Minister's Office, Milton Building, Salisbury." May 13, 1970, NAZ, GEN-P/BUR.

Carnegie, D. *Among the Matebele*. London: Clowes, 1894.

Carson, C., ed. *The Autobiography of Martin Luther King Jr*. Stanford: Abacus, 1988.

Catholic Bishops of Nyasaland. *How to Build a Happy Nation: Joint Pastoral Letter of the Catholic Bishops of Nyasaland*. Lilongwe: White Fathers, 1961.

Catholic Commission for Justice and Peace. *Breaking the Silence Building True Peace*. Harare: CCJPZ, 1997.

Chambati, A. M. "National Unity—ANC." In *Turmoil and Tenacity*, edited by C. S. Banana, 147–54. Gweru: Mambo, 1989.

Chanaiwa, D. "Christianity Under Communist Attack." *Encounter* 3, no. 7 (1978), 92–97.

———. "The Premiership of Garfield Todd in Rhodesia: Racial Partnership Versus Colonial Interests, 1953–1958." *Journal of Southern African Studies* 1, no. 1 (1976) 83–94.

Chennells, A. J. "Anglicans and Roman Catholics Before and After Independence." *Zambezia* 16, no. 1 (1988).

———. "Rhodesian Nationalism: the Mistaken Years." In *Turmoil and Tenacity: Zimbabwe, 1890–1990*, edited by C. S. Banana, 123–39. Harare: College, 1989.

———. Review of *Here to Stay: the Story of Anglican Church in Zimbabwe*, by W. E.Arnold. *Zambezia IX*. Harare: University of Zimbabwe.

Chikomo, H. Letter addressed to the Hon. R. S. G. Todd, Houkoni Ranch, Dadaya, from Mufakose Township, Salisbury, 1 August 1962, NAZ, GEN-P/TOD.

Chinamano, J. M. Speech delivered at a ZAPU rally. Ascot, Gwelo, June 10, 1978, NAZ, GEN-P/CHI.

Christian Action. "Canon Collins on Mapolisa Reprieve." A Press Statement, 2 Amen Court, London, April 29, 1965, NAZ, GEN-P/CHR.

Christian Care. "Richard Mapolisa." Case files for legal assistance for political prisoners, February 18, 1964, NAZ, GEN-P/CHR.

Christian Council of Rhodesia. "Emergency Meeting Held at the University of Rhodesia to deliberate on the Anglo-Rhodesian Proposals in light of the impending arrival of the Pearce Commission." Salisbury, December 30, 1971, NAZ, GEN-P/WOR.

———. "Minutes from the Christian Council of Rhodesia Meeting." Gweru, July 17, 1964, NAZ, GEN-P/WOR.

———. "Minutes of an emergency meeting held at the University of Rhodesia." Salisbury, December 30, 1971, NAZ, GEN-P/WOR.

Christian Council of Southern Rhodesia. *Constitution*. NAZ, GEN-P/WOR.

Christopher, A. J. *Colonial Africa*. London: Croom Helm, 1984.

Chung, F. *Re-living the Second Chimurenga*. Stockholm: The Nordic Africa Institute, 2006.

Church Times. "South African Church Council not to Leave WCC." September 25, 1970, GEN-P/WOR.

Clark, N. L., and W. H. Worger. *The Rise and Fall of Apartheid*. London: Longman, 2004.

Clarke, D. "Population and Family Planning in the Economic Department of Rhodesia." Paper presented in the Department of Economics, University of Rhodesia, Salisbury, 1969.

Clegg, E. *Race and Politics*. Oxford: Oxford University Press, 1960.

Clements, F. *Rhodesia: The Course to Collision*. London: Pall Mall, 1969.

Clutton-Brock, Guy. "Thoughts on Zimbabwe." Unpublished article, n.d., NAZ, GEN-P/CLU.

Comaroff, J., and J. L. Comaroff. *Of Revelation and Revolution*. Vol. 2, *The Dialectics of Modernity on a South African Frontier*. Chicago: University of Chicago Press, 1991.

———. *Of Revelation and Revolution*. Vol. 1, *Christianity, Colonialism and Consciousness in South Africa*. Chicago: University of Chicago Press, 1991.

Cone, H. James. *Martin & Malcolm in America*. Maryknoll, NY: Orbis, 1991.

Council of the Evangelical Church in Germany. "World Council of Churches' Programme to Combat Racism." A Statement to Congregations, 24 September 1970, NAZ, GEN-P/WOR.

Creech-Jones, A. *African Challenge: The Fallacy of Federation*. London: Africa Bureau, 1952.

Crowder, M. *West Africa under Colonial Rule*. London: Hutchinson, 1968.

Daily Telegraph. "British Priests Told to Leave South Africa." London, September 26, 1970.

Daneel, M. L. "The Growth and Significance of Shona Independent Churches." *Christianity South of the Zambezi*, edited by M. F. C. Bourdillon. Gwelo: Mambo, 1977.

David, M. and C. D.Sutton. *Social Research: The Basics*. London: SAGE, 2004.

Davidson, B. *Africa in History*. St. Albans: Aladdin, 1974.

Day, J. *International Nationalism*. London: Routledge & Kegan Paul, 1967.

De Waal, V. *The Politics of Reconciliation: Zimbabwe's First Decade*. London: Hurst, 1990.

Deb, H. C. "Central Africa Federation." *Hansard* 513 cols. 658–801. London, March 24, 1953.

Dodge, R. Edward. *The Revolutionary Bishop*. Pasadena: Carey, 1986.

———. "Top Secret: Bishop Dodge Suggested Deportation." File addressed to the Prime Minister by J. M. Greenfield (private secretary to the minister of economic affairs), June 10, 1963, NAZ, GEN-P/DOD.

Die Welt, "United Evangelical Lutheran Church in Germany Against Race Programme." September 28, 1970, NAZ, GEN-P/WOR.

Doke, C. M. *A Comparative Study in Shona Phonetics*. Johannesburg: University of Wits Press, 1931.

Dorr, D. *Option For The Poor*. Maryknoll, NY: Orbis, 1992.

Douglas, R. G. S., ed. *Zimbabwe Epic*. Harare: National Archives of Zimbabwe, 1984.

Dumbutshena, E., et al. Letter addressed to The Secretary of State for Commonwealth Relations after the riots within the Federation by Africans, 26 July 1960, NAZ, GEN-P/TOD.

Dzvova, B. James, (Chief ZANU Representative in UK and Europe and ZANU's Publicity Secretary). Letter addressed to Mrs. P. Altman, September 26, 1978, NAZ, GEN-P/SIT.

Eldredge, E. A. "Sources of Conflict c.1800–1830." In *The Mfecane Aftermath*, edited by C. Hamilton, 123–61. Johannesburg: Witwatersrand University Press, 2001.

Etherington, Norman, ed. *Missions and Empire*. Oxford: Oxford University Press, 2005.

Executive Committee of the All-Africa Conference of Churches. A Press Statement, Lome, Togo, September 21–23, 1970, NAZ, GEN-P/WOR.GEN-P/MUZ.

Fage, J. D. *A History of Africa*. London: Unwin Hyman, 1988.

Falk, P. *The Growth of the Church in Africa*. Grand Rapids: Zondervan, 1979.

Fanon, F. "Concerning Violence." *Nationalism in Asia & Africa*, edited by E. Kedourie, 488–539. London: Cass, 1970.

———. *The Wretched of the Earth*. Translated by R. Philcox. New York: Grove, 2004.

Farrant, J. *Mashonaland Martyr: Bernard Mizeki and the Pioneer Church*. Oxford: Oxford University Press, 1966.

Fieldhouse, D. K. *Colonialism, 1870–1945: An Introduction*. London: Weidenfeld & Nicolson, 1981.

Fitts, L. *A History of Black Baptists*. Nashville: Broadman, 1985.

Franck, T. M. *Race and Nationalism*. London: Fordham University Press, 1960.

Gann, L. H. and T. H. Thomas. *The Struggle for Zimbabwe*. New York: Praeger, 1981.

Gann, L. H. *The History of Southern Rhodesia*. London: Chatto & Windus, 1965.

Gelfand, M. *African Background*. Cape Town: Juta, 1965.

———. *Growing Up in Shona Society: From Birth to Marriage*. Gweru: Mambo, 1979.

———. *The Genuine Shona*. Gwelo: Mambo, 1973.

———. *The Spiritual Beliefs of the Shona*. Gweru: Mambo, 1977.

Gifford, P., and W. M. Roger-Louis, eds. *Decolonization and African Independence, 1960–1980*. New Haven: Yale University Press, 1988.

Gordon, D. F. "Decolonization and Development in Kenya and Zimbabwe: A Comparative Analysis." *Issue: A Quarterly journal of Africanist Opinion* 11, no. 3 (1981) 36–40.

Gray, R. "Christianity." In *The Colonial Moment in Africa*, edited by A. Roberts, 140–82. Cambridge: Cambridge University Press, 1996.

———. *The Two Nations*. Oxford: Oxford University Press, 1960.

———. *White Missionaries and Black Christians*. New Haven: Yale University Press, 1990.

Gundani, P. H. *Changing Patterns of Authority and Leadership*. Harare: University of Zimbabwe, 2001.

Hallencreutz, C. F., and A. M. Moyo, eds. *Church and State in Zimbabwe*. Gweru: Mambo, 1988.

Halpern, Jack. "Polarization in Rhodesia: State, Church, and Peoples." *The World Today* (1971): 1–8.

Hammond-Tooke, W.D. *The Bantu Speaking Peoples of South Africa*. London: Routledge & Keagan Paul, 1974.

Hamutyinei, M. A., and A. B. Plagger. *Tsumo—Shumo: Shona Proverbial Lore and Wisdom*. Gweru: Mambo, 1987.

Hancock, I. *White Liberals, Moderates and Radicals in Rhodesia, 1953–1980*. London: Croom Helm, 1984.

Hansen, H. B., and M. Twaddle, eds. *Christian Missionaries and the State in the Third World*. Oxford: Curry, 2002.

Hastings, A. "African Church Studies, 1967–1999. Reflections of an Editor." Paper presented at the Colloquium of the JRA hosted by Brill, Leiden, June 1999.

———. *A History of African Christianity, 1969–1975*. Cambridge: Cambridge University Press, 1979.

———. *The Church in Africa, 1450–1950*. Oxford: Clarendon, 1994.

Heads of Denominations. "Minutes on meeting held in Salisbury." 20–21 October 1971, NAZ, GEN-P/ TOD.

———. "Press Statement." October 1969, NAZ, GEN-P/CAT.

———. "Statement." N.d., [date estimated around 1970], NAZ, GEN-P/CAT.

Hellencreutz, C. F. "A Council in Crossfire." In *Church and State in Zimbabwe*, edited by C. F. Hallencreutz, and A. M. Moyo, 51–113. Gweru: Mambo, 1988.

Hepburn, E. *Jottings*. London: Simpkin, Marshall, Hamilton, Kent, 1928.

Hodder-Williams, R. *White Farmers in Rhodesia, 1890–1965*. London: Macmillan, 1983.

Holland, H. *Dinner With Mugabe*. Johannesburg: Penguin, 2008.

Howe, S. *Anti-colonialism in British Politics: The Left and the end of Empire, 1918–1964*. Oxford: Clarendon, 1995.

Hugh, C. R. "Superior of the Community of the Resurrection: Luke 23:34, Father, Forgive them, for they know not what they do." A sermon preached at Salisbury Anglican Cathedral, Rhodesia, February 27, 1966, NAZ, GEN-P/SKE.

Hutson, H. P. W. *Rhodesia Ending An Era*. London: Springwood, 1978.

Iliffe, J. *Africans: History of a Continent*. Cambridge: Cambridge University Press, 1995.

Isichei, E. *A History of Christianity in Africa*. London: SPCK, 1995.

James, C. L. R. *Nkrumah and the Ghana Revolution*. London: Allison & Busby, 1977.

Jollie, E. T. *The Real Rhodesia*. Bulawayo: Books of Rhodesia, 1971.

———. *The Real Rhodesia*. London: Hutchinson, 1923.

Juva, M. *Kotimaa*, Helsinki. September-October 1970, NAZ, GEN-P/WOR.

Kalilombe, P. A. *Doing Theology at the Grassroots: Theological Essays from Malawi*. Gweru: Mambo, 1999.

Kalu, O. U. "African Christianity from the World Wars to Decolonisation." *The Cambridge History of Christianity, c.1914–c.2000*, edited by H. McLeod, 197–218. Cambridge: Cambridge University Press, 2006.

Kane, N. S. *The World's View*. London: Cassell, 1954.

Kedourie, E., ed. *Nationalism in Asia & Africa*. London: Cass, 1970

Kelly, D. F. *The Emergence of Liberty in the Modern World*. Phillipsburg: P. & R., 1992.

Kenyatta, J. *Facing Mount Kenya*. London: Secker & Warburg, 1961.

Keppel-Jones, A. *Rhodes and Rhodesia*. Kingston: McGill-Queen's University Press, 1983.

Khapoya, Vincent B. "Zimbabwe: A Peek at the Future—Reconstruction or Redesign?" *Issue: A Quarterly Journal of Africanist Opinion* 11, no. 3 (1981) 24–41.

Koschorke, K., F. Ludwig, and M. Delagado. *A History of Christianity in Asia, Africa, and Latin America, 1450–1990*. Grand Rapids: Eerdmans, 2007.

Kuper, H. *The Shona and Ndebele of Southern Rhodesia*. London: International African Institute, 1955.

Lamont, D. R. "Purchased People." Pastoral Instruction of the Right Reverend Donal Raymond Lamont, O. Carm. Bishop of Umtali. Gwelo: Catholic Mission, 1959, NAZ, GEN-P/CAT.

———. "In Christian Country It Is for the Church to Say What is Right or Wrong." *The Rhodesia Herald*, March 20, 1970.

———. *Speech from the Dock*. London: Kevin Mayhew, 1977.

Lan, D. *Guns and Rain: Guerrillas and Spirit Mediums in Zimbabwe*. London: Curry, 1985.

Lapsley, M. *Neutrality or Co-option?* Gweru: Mambo, 1986.

Latourette, K. S. *A History of the Expansion of Christianity*. Vol. 5. London: Eyre & Spottiwoode, 1955.

Linden, I. *The Catholic Church and the Struggle for Zimbabwe*. London: Longman, 1979, 1980.

———. *Catholics, Peasants, and Chewa Resistance in Nyasaland, 1889–1939*. London: Heinemann, 1974.

Linden, J., and J.Weller. *Mainstream Christianity*. Gweru: Mambo, 1984.

Listowel, J. *The Making of Tanganyika*. London: Catto & Windus, 1965.

Loney, M. *Rhodesia: White Racism & Imperial Response*. London: Penguin African Library, 1975.

Mackenzie, J.M. *The Partition of Africa*. London: Methuen, 1983.

Macmillan, H. *Pointing the Way*. London: Macmillan, 1972

Mahoso, P. Tafataona. "Questionnaire." Filled in by Reginald Stephen Garfield Todd, Hokonui Ranch, Dayadaya, Zimbabwe, compiled for Temple University toward fulfilment of a PhD in African History, History Department, November 1983, NAZ, GEN-P/MAH.

Mamdani, M. *Citizen and Subject: Contemporary Africa and the Legacy of Late Colonialism*. Princeton: Princeton University Press, 1996.

Maritz, F. "Church-State Relations in the Dutch Reformed Church (NGK) in Zimbabwe: A Case Study." In *Church and State in Zimbabwe*, edited by C. F. Hallencreutz and A. M. Moyo, 347–60. Gweru: Mambo, 1988.

Martey, E. *African Theology: Inculturation and Liberation*. Maryknoll, NY: Orbis, 1993.

Massaquoi, Hans J. "Desmond Tutu: South Africa's Fighting Archbishop." *Ebony* 43, no. 8 (1988) 168

Maxwell, D. "Postcolonial Christianity in Africa." In *The Cambridge History of Christianity, c.1914–c.2000*, edited by H. McLeod, 401–20. Cambridge: Cambridge University Press, 2006.

Maxwell, D. J. *Christians and Chiefs in Zimbabwe: Social History of the Hwesa People.* Edinburgh: Edinburgh University Press, 1999.

———. "Christianity and the War in Eastern Zimbabwe: The Case of Elim Mission." *Society in Zimbabwe's Liberation War*, edited by N. Bhebhe and T. Ranger, 58–89. Oxford: Curry, 1996.

Mazrui, A. A. *The African Condition.* London: Heinemann, 1980.

———. *Towards a Pax Africana.* London: Trinity, 1967.

Mbali, Z. *The Churches and Racism.* London: SCM, 1987.

McLaughlin, J. "Avila Mission: A Turning Point in Church Relations with the State and with the Liberation Forces." In *Society in Zimbabwe's Liberation War*, edited by N. Bhebhe and T. Ranger, 90–101. Oxford: Curry, 1996.

———. "The Catholic Church and Zimbabwe's War of Liberation, 1972–1980." PhD diss., University of Zimbabwe, 1994.

———. *On the Frontline: Catholic Missions in Zimbabwe's Liberation War.* Harare: Baobab, 1996.

McNiff, J. *You and Your Action Research Project.* 2nd ed. London: Routledge Falmer, 2003.

Meebelo, H. S. *Reaction to Colonialism.* Manchester: Manchester University Press, 1971.

Megahey, A. *Humphrey Gibbs: Beleaguered Governor.* London: Macmillan,1998.

Meggay, M. *Transforming Society.* Oxford: Regnum, 1994.

Meredith, M. *The Past is Another Country: UDI to Zimbabwe.* London: Deutsch, 1980.

Mindolo Ecumenical Foundation. "Southern Africa Christian Consultation on Race Relations." May 25–June 2, 1964, NAZ, GEN-P/WOR.

Mnangagwa, E. "Post-Independence Zimbabwe: 1980–1987." In *Turmoil and Tenacity*, edited by C. S. Banana, 225–41. Harare: College, 1989.

Molyneux, K. G. *African Christian Theology.* Lewiston, NY: Mellen University Press, 1993.

Morris-Jones, W. H., ed. *From Rhodesia to Zimbabwe.* London: Frank Cass 9 (1981).

Moyana, J. K. "The Political Economy of Sanctions and Implications for Future Economic policy." *Journal of Southern African Affairs* 2 (1977) 493–520.

Mudenge, S. I. G. *A Political History of Munhumutapa, c.1400–1902.* Harare: Zimbabwe, 1988.

Mugabe, R. G. *Our War of Liberation.* Gweru: Mambo, 1983.

Mungazi, D. A. *The Honoured Crusade.* Gweru: Mambo, 1991.

Murphy, P., ed. *Central Africa Part II: British Documents of the End of Empire.* London: TSO, 2005.

Murray-Brown, J. *Faith and the Flag.* London: Unwin, 1977.

———. *Kenyatta.* London: Allen & Unwin, 1972.

Mutambirwa, James A. C. "The Impact of Christianity on Nationalism in Zimbabwe: A Critique of the Sithole Thesis." *Journal of Southern African Studies* 1, no. 1 (1976) 69–82.

Mutasa, D. *Black Behind Bars: Rhodesia, 1959–1974.* Harare: Longman, 1983.

Mutswairo, S. M. *Feso.* Cape Town: Oxford University Press, 1956.

———. *Zimbabwe, Prose and Poetry,* Washington, DC: Three Continents, 1974.

Muzorerwa, Abel Tendekai. Address to the UANC, September 9, 1977, NAZ, Acc. MS771/3

———. "Memorandum." Address to J. Callaghan, Jimmy Carter, Julius Nyerere, K. D. Kaunda, Samora Machel, and Sir Seretse Khama, copies sent to leaders of the opposition USA and UK, J. Nkomo and R. Mugabe, August 1, 1978, NAZ, GEN-P/MUZ.

———. "Return to Legality." Address at an African National Council Rally. Harry Margolis Hall, Salisbury, 20 July 1972, NAZ, GEN-P/MUZ.

———. "Speech to National Affairs Association." Bulawayo, May 29, 1973, NAZ, Acc. MS 771/1–3.

———. "Under the Banner of Unity." The African National Council Manifesto, March 10, 1972, NAZ, GEN-P/MUZ.

———. Address to the UANC, 1978, NAZ, Harare Acc: MS 771/3.

———. *Rise up and Walk*. London: Evans, 1978.

National Archives of Zimbabwe (NAZ) Manuscripts.

Ncube, N., and T. Ranger. "Religion in the Guerrilla War." In *Society in Zimbabwe's Liberation War,* edited by N. Bhebhe and T. Ranger, 35–57. Oxford: Curry, 1996.

Newman, P. "Foreign and Commonwealth Office." London, letter addressed to Miss Barbara Tredgold, Chizororo Farm, Waterfalls, Rhodesia, August 3, 1978, NAZ, GEN-P/TRE.

Nicolson, R. *A Black Future*. Philadelphia: Trinity, 1990.

Niesewand, P. "Guerrilla leader resigns as envoy of Rhodesia's ANC." *The Guardian,* September 7, 1973.

Njoh, A. J. *Tradition, Culture and Development in Africa*. Aldershot, UK: Ashgate, 2006.

Nkomo, Joshua. *The Story of My Life*. London: Methuen, 1984.

Nkrumah, K. *The Autobiography of Kwame Nkrumah*. Edinburgh: Nelson, 1957.

Nyangoni, C., and G. Nyandoro, eds. *Zimbabwe Independence Movements: Selected Documents*. London: Collings, 1979.

Nyarota, G. *Against the Grain: Memoirs of a Zimbabwe Newsman*. Cape Town: Zebra, 2006.

Nyasaland Government. "Confidential Report." The Secretariat, Zomba, March, 26, 1959.

Nzombe, S. "Negotiations with the British." In *Turmoil and Tenacity,* edited by C. S. Banana, 162–96. Harare: College, 1989.

Omer-Cooper, J. "The Mfecane Survives its Critics." In *The Mfecane Aftermath,* edited by C. Hamilton, 273–94. Johannesburg: Witwatersrand University Press, 2001.

Oppenheim, A. N. *Questionnaire Design, Interviewing and Attitude Measurement*. New ed. London: Continuum, 1992.

Osborne, D. "Obituary: Julius Nyerere." *Third way* 22.9 (1999) 8–12.

Palley, C. *The Constitutional History and Law of Zimbabwe, 1888–1965*. Oxford: Clarendon, 1966.

Parfitt, T. *The Lost Ark of the Covenant*. London: HarperCollins, 2008.

Parfitt, T., and E. T. Semi. *Judaising Movements*. London: RoutledgeCurzon, 2002.

Parrinder, G. *Religion in Africa*. Middlesex: Penguin, 1969.

Phimister, I. *An Economic and Social History of Zimbabwe, 1890–1948: Capital Accumulation and Class Struggle*. London: Longman, 1988.

Prime Minister's Secretary. Confidential Notes: Meeting between the Prime Minister and Representatives of the Anglican Church, Prime Minister's Office, Milton Building, Salisbury, 13 May 1970, NAZ, GEN-P/BUR.

Private Secretary to the Prime Minister. "Bishop Dodge Suggested Deportation." *Top Secret Papers,* June 13, 1963, NAZ, GEN-P/DOD.

Randolph, R. H. *Dawn in Zimbabwe.* Gweru: Mambo, 1985.

Rand Mail, "Response of the SA Church Leaders on the WCC Grant to Liberation Movements." September 12, 1970.

Ranger, T. O. *The African Voice in Southern Rhodesia.* London: Heinemann, 1972.

———. *Revolt in Southern Rhodesia 1896–97.* London: Heinemann, 1967.

Ranger, T. O., and J. Weller, eds. *Themes in the Christian History of Central Africa.* London: Heinemann, 1975.

Rea, Fred B. "The Impact of Habit and Custom on Community Relations." In *Report of the National Convention of Southern Rhodesia,* 101–8. Salisbury: Amalgamated, 1960.

———. "The Need for a United Church in Southern Rhodesia." *International Review of Missions* 47, no. 185 (1958) 84–89.

———. "To Heads of Churches and Representatives of Church Leaders." Letter on behalf of the Rhodesia Christian Conference, Belvedere, Harare, October 31, 1969, NAZ, GEN-P/REA.

———. "To Heads of Churches and Representatives of Church Leaders." Notes and Government documents on the Land Tenure Bill to be reviewed Heads of Denominations, Belvedere, Harare, 31 October 1969, NAZ, GEN-P/REA.

Rea, W. F. "The Economics of the Zambezi Missions, 1580–1759." In *Christianity South of the Zambezi,* edited by M. F. C. Bourdillon, 13–24. Gweru: Mambo, 1977.

Retief, M. W. *William Murray of Nyasaland.* Lovedale, South Africa: Lovedale, 1958.

Reuters. "Tutu Chides Bush on Oversimplifying US Terror War." *Reuters,* March 17, 2004.

Rhodesia Christian Conference. "Government ministers' minutes: Meetings held on the 20th and 27th of October 1969." Documents dispatched to heads of churches and representatives of church leaders for review by the organisation's secretary general F. Rea, October 31, 1969, NAZ, GEN-P/REA.

Rhodesia Herald. "Politics in African Clergy." *Rhodesia Herald,* March 9, 1973.

Robertson, C. "Social Change in Contemporary Africa." In *Africa,* edited by P. M. Martin and P. O'Meara, 316–29. 3rd ed. Bloomington: Indiana University Press, 1995.

Rodney, W. *How Europe Underdeveloped Africa.* London: Bogle-L'Overture, 1972.

Roman Catholic Bishops Conference. "Rhodesia: The Moral Issue." A pamphlet expressing the Catholic Bishops concerns over Zimbabweans' social problems, November 28, 1965, NAZ, GEN-P/CAT.

Rotberg, R. I. *The Rise of Nationalism in Central Africa.* Cambridge, MA: Harvard University Press, 1966.

Samkange, S. *Origins of Rhodesia.* London: Heinemann, 1968.

Sansbury, Kenneth. "Action on Combating Racism." Interim statement, General Secretary of BCC and Alan Booth, Director of Christian Aid, September 1970, NAZ, GEN-P/WOR.

Sartre, J. *Colonialism and Neo-colonialism.* London: Routledge, 2001.

Schoffeleers, M. *In Search of Truth and Justice.* Blantyre: Kachere, 1999.

Scholz, D. B. "The Catholic Church and the Race Conflict in Rhodesia." In *Christianity South of the Zambezi,* edited by M. F. C. Bourdillon, 199–211. Gweru: Mambo, 1977.

Settlement Bishop to Knight." *Financial Mail,* July 13, 1973.

Shamuyarira, N. *Crisis in Rhodesia.* London: Deustch, 1974.

Shaw, M. *The Kingdom of God in Africa: A Short History of African Christianity.* Grand Rapids: Baker.

Shoko, T. *Karanga Indigenous Religion in Zimbabwe: Health and Well Being*. Burlington, VT: Ashgate, 2007.

Short, P. *Banda*. London: Routledge & Kegan Paul, 1974.

Sibanda, M. J. "Early Foundations of African Nationalism." In *Turmoil and Tenacity: Zimbabwe, 1890–1990*, edited by C. S. Banana, 25–49. Harare: College, 1989.

Sithole, Ndabaningi. *African Nationalism*. Oxford: Oxford University Press, 1959.

———. "Anglo American All-Party Conference." A paper presented in 1978, NAZ, GEN-P/SIT.

Skelton, Kenneth. "They Shall . . . Persecute You, Luke 21:12." A sermon preached in the Bulawayo Cathedral, April 19, 1964, NAZ, GEN-P/SKE.

Slack, K. *Martin Luther King*. London: SCM, 1970.

Smith, I. D. "Unilateral Declaration of Independence." *East Africa and Rhodesia Newspaper*, November 18, 1965.

———. *The Great Betrayal*. London: Blake, 1997.

Soderstrom, H. *God Gave Growth: The History of the Lutheran Church in Zimbabwe, 1903–1980*. Gweru: Mambo, 1984.

South African Council of Churches. "Statement of South African Member Churches of the World Council of Churches." Circular 88/70, September 11, 1970, NAZ, GEN-P/WOR.

Stanley, B. *The Bible and the Flag*. Leicester: InterVarsity, 1990.

———. *The World Missionary Conference, Edinburgh 1910*. Grand Rapids: Eerdmans, 2009.

Stock, R. *Africa South of Sahara*. New York: Guilford, 2004.

Stuart, J. "Speaking for the Unvoiced." In *Missions, Nationalism, and the End of Empire*, edited by B. Stanley, 183–93. Cambridge: Eerdmans, 2003.

Sugirtharajah, R. S. *The Bible and the Third World*. Cambridge: Cambridge University Press, 2001.

Sundkler, B. and C. Steed. *A History of the Church in Africa*. Cambridge: Cambridge University Press, 2000.

Swiss Der Bund. "Statement by the Swiss Evangelische Landeskirchen." September 27, 1970, NAZ, GEN-P/WOR.

Taber, C. R., ed. *The Church in Africa: Papers Presented at Symposium at Milligan College, March 31–April 3, 1977*. Pasadena, CA: Carey, 1979.

Tekere, E. *Lifetime of Struggle*. Harare: SAPES, 2007.

The Rhodesia Herald. "Church Call: Quit WCC," February 6, 16, 1973.

The Zimbabwe Catholic Bishops Conference, The Evangelical Fellowship of Zimbabwe and the Zimbabwe Council of Churches. "The Zimbabwe We Want: Towards a National Vision for Zimbabwe." October 2006.

Thompson, E. P. *The Making of the English Working Class*. Middlesex, UK: Penguin, 1980.

Thompson, L. *A History of South Africa*. New Haven: Yale University Press, 2000.

Thomson, H. C. *Rhodesia and its Government*. London: Smith, 1898.

Todd, Garfield R.S. "Challenge for Today." Speech given at Annual Congress of the National Union of South African Students, University of Witwatersrand, July 2, 1963, NAZ, GEN-P/Todd.

———. "For *Moto*." Article intended to be submitted for publication in the Catholic sponsored monthly magazine, *Moto*, May, 1968, NAZ, GEN-P/TOD.

———. "R.A.T.U. Meeting." Speech given at the Rhodesian African Trade Union meeting, September 1, 1962, NAZ, GEN-P/TOD.

———. "Southern Rhodesia African Trades Union Congress." Speech, October 20, 1962, NAZ, GEN-P/TOD.

———. "The World Council of Churches," article in his documents intended for the press, September 1970, NAZ, GEN-P/TOD.

Todd, Garfield R. S. and H. Holderness. A letter addressed to Sir Alec Douglas-Home, May 15, 1964, NAZ, GEN-P/TOD.

Todd, Garfield R. S. Letter addressed to Rev. Herbert Chikomo, general secretary of the African ministers fraternal, August 27, 1962, NAZ, MS 1082/1/14.

———. Paper presented at the QueQue Lions Club Banquet, August 29, 1964, NAZ, GEN-P/TOD.

Todd, Judith. "Chikarubi." A letter from prison to Anthony Eastwood, February 18, 1972, NAZ, GEN-P/TOD.

———. *Rhodesia*. Bristol: MacGibbin & Kee, 1966.

———. *The Right to Say No*. New York: Third, 1972.

———. "White Policy and Politics, 1890–1980." In *Turmoil and Tenacity,* edited by C. S. Banana, 116–22. Harare: College, 1989.

Todd, R. S. G. "No Sudden Death." *Sunday Mail,* December 30, 1971.

———. "World Council's Object is to Seek Equality." *Sunday Mail*, September 27, 1970.

Tredgold, Barbara. Letter addressed to Ian Douglas Smith, Prime Minister's Office, January 13, 1979, NAZ, GEN-P/TRE .

———. Letter addressed to Lord Carrington, the Foreign Secretary, Foreign and Commonwealth Office, London, from Waterfalls, Salisbury, August 18, 1979, NAZ, GEN-P/TRE.

Tutu, Desmond. *Hope and Suffering*. London: Collins, 1983.

———. *No Future Without Forgiveness*. Cape Town: Rider, 2000.

———. *Rainbow People of God*. London: Doubleday, 1994.

Tutu, Naomi. *The Words of Desmond Tutu*. London: New Market, 1989.

Vambe, L. *An Ill-Fated People*. London: Heinemann, 1972.

Van Den Heuvel, A. H. Director in the WCC's Department of Communication, 3 September 1970, NAZ, GEN-P/WOR.

Verrier, A. *The Road to Zimbabwe, 1890–1980*. London: Cape, 1986.

Verstraelen, F. J. "The Christian Bible and African Cultural and Religious realities." In *Rewriting the Bible,* edited by J. Mukonyora, J. L. Cox, and F. J. Verstraelen, 219–41. Harare: Mambo, 1993.

———. *Zimbabwean Realities and Christian Responses*. Gweru: Mambo, 1998.

Vincent, J. *The Race Race*. London: SCM, 1970.

Ward, K. "Christianity, Colonialism and Missions." In *The Cambridge History of Christianity, c. 1914–c. 2000,* edited by H. McLeod, 71–88. Cambridge: Cambridge University Press, 2006.

Warren, M., ed. *To Apply the Gospel*. Grand Rapids: Eerdmans, 1971.

Watyoka, C. D. *25 Years of Struggle*. Harare: Zimbabwe Council of Churches, 1991.

WCC Actions Regarding Zimbabwe Since Nairobi (1976). "Todd's papers, documents and articles collection," August 1978, NAZ, GEN-P/WOR.

Wilson, H.S. *African Decolonization*. London: Arnold, 1994.

Windrich, E. *The Rhodesian Problem*. London: Butler and Tanner, 1975.

Wood, J. R. T. *The Welensky Papers: A History of the Federation of Rhodesia and Nyasaland*. Durban: Graham, 1983.

World Council of Churches. "Statement of the General Secretary of the in Response to the statement of the Council of the Evangelical Church in Germany." 24 September 1970, NAZ, GEN-P/WOR.

———. *Oikoumene,* Communication Nb/34–70, NAZ, GEN-P/WOR.

Yamauchi, E. M. *Africa and the Bible*. Grand Rapids: Baker, 2004.

Zambezi Mission Records (ZMR), "History of the Zambesi Mission 1906–1909." III.34, October, 1906, NAZ, GEN-P/ZAM.

ZAPU Publicity Bureau. "Z.A.P.U.: Its Origins and Direction." Paper presented at the World Conference Against Apartheid, Racism and Colonialism in Southern Africa, 16–19 June 1977, NAZ, GEN-P/WOR.

Zvobgo, C. J. M. *A History of Missions in Zimbabwe, 1890–1939*. Gweru: Mambo, 1996.

———. "Southern Rhodesia Under Edgar Whitehead: 1958–1962." *Journal of Southern African Affairs* 2, no. 4 (1977).

Zvobgo, Edison. Letter addressed to Judy (Judith Todd), from Massachusetts, United States of America, January 21, 1973, NAZ, GEN-P/TOD.